Islam, Constitutional La
Human Rights

This book focuses on Islamic constitutionalism, and in particular on the relation between religion and the protection of individual liberties potentially clashing with shariʿa and the Islamic ethos. The analysis goes from general to particular, starting with a theoretical overview on constitutionalism, human rights and Islam, moving to the assessment of the post-Arab Spring Constitutions of Egypt and Tunisia, and concluding with a specific focus on the rights of sexual minorities and freethinkers.

Part I provides a theoretical account of the conception of constitutionalism and human rights in Islam, compared and contrasted with Western constitutionalism. A set of issues where the tension between shariʿa and human rights is accentuated is analysed against the backdrop of the main Islamic charters of rights. Part II conducts a similar assessment based on the Constitutions of Tunisia and Egypt – the two main epicentres of the Arab Spring. Part III moves to two specific rights in the same countries, from the twofold perspective of the Constitutions and international law: the freedom from interference in one's intimate life, with particular regard to homosexuality; and the freedom of holding and expressing nonconventional beliefs, deemed unacceptable from the point of view of traditional Islam. These issues have been chosen as representative of the most controversial, still considered taboo in both legal and social terms, hence at the fringes of the debate on individual freedoms. Focusing on two overlooked and underexplored issues, the work thus pushes the boundaries of the human rights discourse in Muslim contexts.

Tommaso Virgili is a Postdoctoral Research Fellow at the WZB Berlin Social Science Center, where he works on modernization movements and reform theology within Islam in response to the challenge of fundamentalism, with a focus on Europe and the MENA region. He received his Ph.D. in Comparative Public Law from Sant'Anna School of Advanced Studies in Pisa, Italy. Dr. Virgili is also a Research Associate at the Wilfried Martens Centre for European Studies and a Visiting Fellow at the European Foundation for Democracy in Brussels.

Comparative Constitutionalism in Muslim Majority States

Series Editor: Javaid Rehman

This series encourages research into all aspects of comparative constitutionalism within the Muslim-Majority States of South Asia and the Middle East. Key areas of investigation include the post 9–11 implications on constitutionalism and the consequences of the Arab Spring. The studies within the series span across all aspects of constitutionalism, including constitutional rights, constitutional practices, rule of law issues, human rights, sexual rights and minorities. While the focus of the series is upon the Muslim-Majority States within the South Asia and Middle East region, the comparative critical assessment will engage a global analysis of constitutionalism and application of constitutional rights. Amidst the many cases of failed constitutionalism, there are a number of positives: this series also aims to explore and identify key successes from within the region.

Titles in the series

Security, Rights and Law
The Israeli High Court of Justice and the Israeli Settlements in the Occupied West Bank
Rouba Al-Salem

Law and Politics of Constitutional Courts
Indonesia and the Search for Judicial Heroes
Stefanus Hendrianto

States of Emergency and the Law
The Experience of Bangladesh
M. Ehteshamul Bari

Islam, Constitutional Law and Human Rights
Sexual Minorities and Freethinkers in Egypt and Tunisia
Tommaso Virgili

Islam, Constitutional Law and Human Rights

Sexual Minorities and Freethinkers in Egypt and Tunisia

Tommaso Virgili

Routledge
Taylor & Francis Group
LONDON AND NEW YORK

First published 2022
by Routledge
2 Park Square, Milton Park, Abingdon, Oxon OX14 4RN

and by Routledge
605 Third Avenue, New York, NY 10158

Routledge is an imprint of the Taylor & Francis Group, an informa business

British Library Cataloguing-in-Publication Data
A catalogue record for this book is available from the British Library

Library of Congress Cataloging-in-Publication Data
Names: Virgili, Tommaso, author.
Title: Islam, constitutional law, and human rights : sexual minorities and freethinkers in Egypt and Tunisia / Tommaso Virgili.
Other titles: Comparative constitutionalism in Muslim majority states.
Description: Abingdon, Oxon ; New York, NY : Routledge, 2021. |
Series: Comparative constitutionalism in Muslim majority states |
Includes bibliographical references and index.
Identifiers: LCCN 2021007741 (print) | LCCN 2021007742 (ebook) |
ISBN 9780367200640 (hardback) | ISBN 9781032051260 (paperback) |
ISBN 9780429259418 (ebook)
Subjects: LCSH: Constitutional law (Islamic law) | Civil rights (Islamic law) |
Constitutional law—Egypt. | Constitutional law—Tunisia. | Civil rights—
Egypt. | Civil rights—Tunisia.
Classification: LCC KBP2460 .V57 2021 (print) | LCC KBP2460
(ebook) | DDC 340.59—dc23
LC record available at https://lccn.loc.gov/2021007741
LC ebook record available at https://lccn.loc.gov/2021007742

ISBN: 978-0-367-20064-0 (hbk)
ISBN: 978-1-032-05126-0 (pbk)
ISBN: 978-0-429-25941-8 (ebk)

DOI: 10.4324/9780429259418

Typeset in Galliard
by codeMantra

To the smallest and most persecuted minorities on this earth: the individuals.

Contents

Note on the transliteration

For the transliteration of the Arabic words, I follow the system recommended by the *International Journal of Middle Eastern Studies* (IJMES), characterized by mixed digraphic and diacritical romanization and by the italicization of Arabic terms. Exceptions to these rules are proper names and words that have become common in English, which are not italicized and do not present diacritical marks; similarly, titles do not present diacritics and follow the general referencing system as concerns capitalization and italicization.

Foreword

Brian Whitaker
Author of *Arabs without God: Atheism and Freedom of Belief in the Middle East* and *Unspeakable Love: Gay and Lesbian Life in the Middle East.*

While a growing number of countries have legalized same-sex marriage there are still many others where homosexual activity is punished by imprisonment and even, in a few places, by death. Similarly, there are countries where abandoning religion or expressing disbelief in God is regarded as a crime deserving execution, while in others it is seen as a personal choice and no concern of the authorities.

How individual countries deal with those who challenge prevailing attitudes to sex or voice heretical views of religion is a useful indicator of where their boundaries between the permitted and the forbidden lie, and where they stand in terms of personal freedom more generally.

As far as the forbidden is concerned, it is noticeable that laws against 'unnatural' sex and religious 'thought crime' are especially prevalent in Muslim-majority countries and that Islamic principles are usually cited by way of justification.

A key factor here is the relationship between religion and the state. In countries where Islam predominates, secularism – separating religion from the state – is generally seen as undesirable. Public opinion often mistakenly equates it with atheism and immorality. Governments, meanwhile, see benefits in linking the state to Islam: it's a way of acquiring legitimacy in the eyes of the faithful and can also compensate for a lack of legitimacy in other areas – for example, through the ballot box.

The result can be seen in national constitutions that say Islam is the country's official religion and require the head of state to be Muslim. They also incorporate Islamic law (shariᶜa) into their legal system but differences in the way this is worded indicate differing views as to how strong the connection should be. Shariᶜa is variously described as 'the source of *all* legislation', '*the* main source' of legislation or merely '*a* main source'. That opens the door for religion to intrude on legislative processes. Man-made laws are expected to be compatible with God's law and in the event of a conflict God's law would be seen as taking precedence.

Another problem with incorporating shariᶜa into constitutions is its vagueness. The term 'Islamic law' is deceptive because shariᶜa is not codified – there is no official written text – and its laws are derived from scripture by religious scholars who may provide a variety of interpretations.

This, broadly, is the religious and constitutional background for Tommaso Virgili's case study of laws relating to homosexuality and religious dissidence in two North African countries – Egypt and Tunisia. Following the Arab Spring uprisings of 2011 which saw their presidents overthrown, both countries have adopted new constitutions. Far from resolving matters, though, the insertion of some apparently progressive references to freedom and human rights has added more uncertainty and ambiguity to the legal situation.

Acknowledgements

This book is based on a Ph.D. thesis I completed at Sant'Anna School of Advanced Studies in October 2017. As this work accompanied me throughout different stages of my life, I am indebted to the many people and institutions that made this achievement possible.

First and foremost, I wish to express my profound gratitude to my Ph.D. supervisors, Prof. Giuseppe Martinico and Dr. Valentina Colombo – true examples to me. Their enthusiasm and generosity in sharing their knowledge, their constant guidance and support and, even more precious, their true friendship constitute the backbone of this endeavour. They are invaluable gifts I shall never forget.

I am grateful to the academic institutions and foundations that believed in me and provided me with the intellectual and material support to achieve this result: my *alma mater*, Sant'Anna School of Advanced Studies – a gymnasium for academic, but above all personal, growth, which indelibly marked the course of my life; the American University of Paris and Cairo, where the journey of this book began, thanks to the generous 'Future Vision Global Grant' of the Rotary Foundation; the M.G. Slosberg Foundation and the Association for the Study of the Middle East and Africa (ASMEA), whose scholarships allowed me to conduct field research in Egypt and Tunisia.

My gratitude goes also to my current employer, the WZB Berlin Social Science Center, and in particular to Prof. Ruud Koopmans, director of the Migration, Integration, Transnationalization Research Unit, for believing in this project and supporting its completion.

The views conveyed in this book are just mine, of course, as all the people and institutions mentioned above have allowed me to pursue what I consider the most important treasure in academic research (and, in fact, in life): the freedom of independent thought and expression.

I also wish to thank the participants in this study, who gave up their time to share their knowledge, personal stories and lived experiences – academics, lawyers, activists, and victims of human rights abuses: they are the protagonists of this book, and some of them are genuine heroes to me.

Man shall not live by science alone: nothing would be possible in my life without the love, trust, and unconditional support of my dearest ones. I don't see this as the right place to unveil inner feelings, but I trust that those who truly matter will recognize themselves in these words and know they have a special place in my mind and in my heart. *Grazie.*

Tommaso Virgili
9 February 2021

Introduction

Background: what this book is about

> To my siblings — I tried to find redemption and failed, forgive me. To my friends — the experience was harsh and I am too weak to resist it, forgive me. To the world — you were cruel to a great extent, but I forgive.[1]

With this final message, handwritten on a piece of paper, Egyptian lesbian activist Sarah Hegazi left this world. She took her own life, unable to escape the trauma of three months of torture in an Egyptian prison followed by forced exile. Her high crime: raising a rainbow flag during a public concert in support of the LGBT community.

Hegazi's tragically absurd story is far from being unique. It's the daily nightmare of thousands of men and women across the Middle East whose only crime is that of being different – foreign bodies whom their home countries and societies want to purge because of what they think, what they do or what they are.

This was not their expectation when they bravely took to the streets to get rid of decades-long dictatorships during the epochal phenomenon hurriedly dubbed, with naïve optimism, the 'Arab Spring'. Certainly, the Arab uprisings were a tornado that swept away the Middle East as we knew it, portending dreams of freedom, democracy, good governance and prosperity for all. Yet, the awakening from the dream to reality has been, in many cases, rude. Even in those countries where the old regimes fell, and an apparent transition to democracy was accomplished, vulnerable minorities and non-conformist individuals soon found out that spring flowers weren't going to blossom for them. In fact, the legitimate enthusiasm for the idea of 'democracy' and the emphasis on free and fair elections as the essence thereof tend too easily to obscure Albert Camus' wise adage: 'Democracy is not the law of the majority, but the protection of the minority'.[2]

This is where constitutions enter into play. Their crucial mission is, or should be, to temper the majoritarian rule by ensuring the observance of those checks

1 Berger, 'She Raised the Pride Flag in Egypt. The Price Was Torture, Exile and Her Life.'
2 'Democracy'.

and balances and individual freedoms that distinguish a true democracy from a tyranny of the majority. Constitutions are more than a collection of norms: they represent the soul of a country, and contribute to shaping its future course. The importance of constitution-making was very clear in the mind of the men and women called on to forge the post-Spring countries after the fall of the old regimes: hence, the constituent phase represented a battleground of distant, sometimes opposite, worldviews, mirroring a broader societal strife. The definition of the role of Islam in the constitutions, and the articulation of individual freedoms potentially clashing with Islamic rules and ethics, were and continue to be major components of this struggle.

In this book I will try to understand why, and to assess how the constitutional reference to Islam, in its laws or its principles, affects the enjoyment of individual liberties, especially for the most vulnerable minorities. After a theoretical overview on constitutionalism, human rights and Islam, I will direct my focus to the constitutions of the two countries that have been arguably the main protagonists of the Arab Spring, namely Egypt and Tunisia, analysing the most sensitive constitutional provisions related to human rights and Islam and the way they interrelate with each other. Finally, I will focus specifically on two of the most vulnerable and less protected categories, namely LGBT people and freethinkers, in the hope that the new constitutions will make the Spring come for them too.

Why Egypt and Tunisia?

Mohammed Bouazizi, a twenty-six-year-old street vendor from Sidi Bouzid, Tunisia, certainly was not thinking about constitutional theories or international geopolitics when he set himself on fire on 17 December 2010. He was rather conveying, with an extreme act of desperation, the frustration and lack of hope of a powerless, humble worker humiliated and left without a livelihood by the police of the authoritarian regime ruling his country. And yet, the self-immolation of an obscure individual from the Tunisian periphery triggered a series of protests that rapidly extended not only to the whole nation, but to the entire region.

Tunisia and Egypt, in particular, quickly emerged as the success stories of the Arab Spring: in contrast to other countries, the largely peaceful demonstrations happening there neither degenerated into a civil war nor were violently crushed; instead, they were successful in forcing the old-time dictators to step down, and to set in motion a democratic transition.

The long-term outcomes of this transition ended up being very different for the two countries. In Egypt, President Mohammed Morsi, a member of the Muslim Brotherhood, albeit elected in democratic elections, soon took an authoritarian turn, which alienated a large section of the population.[3] Unwilling

3 See Virgili, 'The "Arab Spring" and the EU's "Democracy Promotion" in Egypt: A Missed Appointment?'

to compromise with the opposition, whether in the parliament, in the constitutional assembly or in the streets, Morsi was eventually ousted by the army, following massive demonstrations against his regime that echoed the 2011 revolution. A new roadmap was established, the Muslim Brotherhood was outlawed and its members harshly prosecuted, and a new constitution was drafted by a new Constituent Assembly. A once-again ruthlessly authoritarian government, democratic only on paper, has been in power since then. In the Tunisian case, by contrast, the Islamist and secularist camps reached an agreement to achieve a smooth transition, and Tunisia is now the sole Arab country to boast the qualification of 'free' bestowed by the prestigious think tank Freedom House.[4] Determining the causes of such different outcomes would require a longer analysis, but the strength and maturity of Tunisian civil society has surely played an important role, which will be highlighted in the present work.[5]

In the immediate post-revolutionary phase, on the other hand, Egypt and Tunisia followed similar trajectories, marked in particular by strong clashes between liberal and Islamist forces at the level of politics and societies. In both cases, a vocal anti-Islamist camp confronted a strong Islamist front, mainly constituted by the Muslim Brotherhood and Salafist groups – the latter two being on occasion allied and on occasion in open rivalry.[6] In both cases, Islamists achieved an initial supremacy and tried to reshape the institutions of the newly born democracies in Islamist interests, meeting the fierce opposition of (more or less) secularists. The constitution-making process represented a crucial part in this clash. The comparison between the final constitutional outcomes reveals a different approach towards religion and fundamental freedoms in the two countries; nevertheless, the diatribe over the interpretation of sensitive human rights issues, and their interplay with religion and public morals, has characterized both of them and is far from being over, whether in law or society.

Human rights and shariʿa: a complicated relationship

What are those areas where the relation between Islamic norms and modern constitutional principles, based on individual freedoms, are particularly contentious?

4 Reidy, 'Report Designates Tunisia First "free" Arab Country in Decades'.

5 Compared to Egypt, Tunisia has a tradition of civil institutions, relatively free from constraints coming from the army or the religious establishment, a history of *laïcité* inherited by the independence's father, Habib Bourguiba, and a better economic and social situation; all of this has brought about a strong civil society. Most of these features are lacking in the Egyptian case, and this may contribute to explain its largely uncompleted transition to democracy. Other factors arguably played a role: one is the different strength and centrality of the army, much stronger and historically a protagonist of political life in Egypt. Furthermore, it was most probably for fear of meeting the same destiny as the Egyptian Muslim Brotherhood, after the demonstrations which followed the assassinations of two prominent secularists, that Ennahdha agreed to reach a compromise with the opposition.

6 Defining it explicitly as 'secular' would fit for some groups, but would be misleading in other cases.

This is the first question I need to address in order to sharpen the scope of my investigation and focus on what really matters.

The renowned Islamic scholar and human rights defender Abdullahi Ahmed An-Naᶜim is one among many who identifies three main respects in which shariᶜa is radically incompatible with modern constitutionalism: (1) freedom of religion and apostasy; (2) women's rights and equality with men; and (3) the status of non-Muslims.[7]

This friction between Islam and human rights descends from the legal discriminations provided by shariᶜa. Three grounds for discrimination emerge from the scriptures: Muslims vs. non-Muslims; men vs. women; and freemen vs. slaves.[8] While slavery has been revoked throughout the Muslim world, at least from a formal point of view,[9] the first two inequities are still in place to various degrees in most Muslim-majority states, and come along with other provisions severely curtailing fundamental rights, especially in the domains of sexual rights and freedom of conscience. In addition, one must take into account the problematic aspect of Qurᵓanic criminal penalties, which notoriously include flogging, amputation of limbs and stoning to death. Hence, the major issues related to Islamic documents to be theoretically put under the test of international human rights law are the following:

1) Equality between men and women;
2) Equality between Muslims and non-Muslims;
3) Freedom of religion including apostasy from Islam;
4) Freedom of expression in relation to heterodoxy and blasphemy;
5) Sexual freedom including homosexuality;
6) Prohibition of torture and inhuman and degrading punishments, with reference to Islamic penalties.

After providing a general appraisal of these issues based on contemporary Islamic charters of rights, I will use the same categories as the basis for an assessment of the Egyptian and Tunisian Constitutions.

Sexual minorities and freethinkers: the pariahs of the human rights debate

In order to shift focus from the abstract constitutional provisions to concrete life experiences, I will concentrate on two burning issues: the freedom from interference in one's sexual orientation and connected choices; and the freedom

7 This is the subject of An-Naᶜim's well-known book, *Toward an Islamic Reformation*.
8 Lewis, *The Political Language of Islam*, 64. Mayer, *Islam and Human Rights*, 85.
9 The situation of workers in the Gulf has been often denounced by human rights organizations as a *de facto* condition of slavery. One may even find in American academia bizarre and disturbing attempts to justify Islamic slavery from a moral point of view. See Ross, 'Islamic Georgetown Prof Offers Tortured Defense of Slavery and Non-Consensual Sex under Islam'.

to hold and express unconventional religious beliefs deemed unacceptable in the Islamic tradition.[10]

The reason why I have chosen these topics becomes particularly evident when we consider the words of Egyptian minister of religious endowment Mohamed Mokhtar Gomaa: '[W]e must confront atheism, nihilism, homosexuality, and moral depravity the same way we confront extremism and terrorism'.[11]

Homosexuality, atheism and offense to religion arguably represent the most controversial subjects in today's Islamic societies. As such, they are often radically excluded from the debate on individual freedoms. Indeed, while other issues, albeit sensitive, are at least acknowledged as part of the human rights discourse, homosexuality, apostasy and blasphemy still represent engrained taboos, both at the social and legal levels. For instance, not even hard-core Islamists would deny that the concept of 'women's rights' exists; their attempt would be to challenge the content of such a notion, rather than its existence. By contrast, homosexuality, atheism and 'blasphemy' (widely understood) are not accepted as part of the human rights discourse, but rather viewed as abuses of freedom.

Remarkably, this not only occurs in the framework of politics or religion – which pursue their own agendas – but even at the level of scholarship. For instance, Mashood Baderin – one of the most reputed scholars of human rights and Islam – has stated that homosexuality is 'generally seen to be strongly against the moral fabric and sensibilities of Islamic society and is prohibited morally and legally under Islamic law'.[12] This implies that, in the author's view, it does not pertain to the realm of human rights but should fall within states' 'margin of appreciation'.[13] Similarly, blasphemy is not considered by many scholars to be protected under the mantle of free speech, for it would represent an undue attack on religious sensitivity and social peace.[14] It is not by chance that, out of 110 recommendations from the Human Rights Council to Tunisia, 'the only two rejected outright concerned the decriminalization of same-sex acts and religious defamation'.[15]

The narrative does not change in the experience of atheist and homosexual individuals in the Middle East, who both often speak of the moment they decided to be open about their identities as a 'coming out'.[16] Indeed, 'the consequences of coming out as gay or an atheist can be very similar: it can lead to being ostracized by family, friends and the local community, not to mention conflict with the law'.[17]

10 As I am going to explain, those include a vast plethora of concepts.
11 'Egyptian Minister of Religious Endowment'.
12 Baderin, *International Human Rights and Islamic Law*, 117.
13 *Ibid.*
14 For instance, Modood et al., 'The Danish Cartoon Affair'.
15 Littauer, 'Tunisia Rejects UNHRC Recommendation to Decriminalise Gay Sex'.
16 An expression used by many interviewees consulted for this book.
17 Whitaker, *Arabs without God*, 15.

Hence, my intent in this book is to challenge the boundaries of the human rights discourse in Muslim contexts, focusing on two overlooked and underexplored issues from a constitutional perspective.

On 'Islam and human rights'... again? A few methodological clarifications

'Islam and human rights': how often have we heard about this dyad, especially since 9/11? Academics, activists, journalists, religious scholars, politicians and lobbyists from opposite sides have devoted considerable energy and resources to ascertain whether Islam is compatible with individual freedoms (or the other way around, depending on where they set the priority), and to provide a definitive answer, either with nuances or using a black-and-white brush.

Whatever the verdict, this operation entails a theoretical assessment of two abstract entities. In the scholarly field, for instance, Jan Michiel Otto has claimed that 'violations in Muslim countries often have little to do with sharia' and that '"it is not Sharia which is preventing the implementation of human rights", but a "lack of political will" of the governments. In contrast, Abiad argues, "the very nature of Sharia demonstrates the potential of reform in the interest of human rights"'.[18] Baderin has similarly claimed that human rights violations in the Muslim world have often occurred not because of shariᶜa, but because of its distortion.[19] He has consequently adopted an approach which 'theoretically engages international human rights practice in dialogue with Islamic jurisprudence',[20] namely the classical interpretation of Islamic sources. *Contra*, we could quote again An-Naᶜim: '[T]he inherent problems with the Shariᶜa state as the ideal to be pursued by Muslims today are more serious than the problems of realizing that "ideal". Even if that ideal were realized in practice today, it would still fall short of the standards of modern constitutionalism'.[21]

In opposition to these methods, I believe that the inner polysemy of 'Islamic law', or 'shariᶜa', impedes a final judgment on its abstract compatibility with individual liberties. To begin with, 'shariᶜa' has at least four different meanings: the abstract, divine, will of Allah; the interpretation thereof undertaken by classical scholars; the historically transferred body of interpretations developed from the beginning of Islam up to the present day; and the current reading employed in today's legislation and case law.[22] None of them is, in its turn, univocal. This is why, in my view, the best way to look at the issue of Islamic constitutionalism and individual liberties is to overcome the deductive approach focused on the

18 Otto, 'Towards Comparative Conclusions', 618.
19 Baderin, *International Human Rights and Islamic Law*, 12.
20 *Ibid.*, 5.
21 An-Na'im, *Toward an Islamic Reformation*, 86.
22 Otto, 'Introduction', 25.

theoretical rapport between abstract human rights and Islamic principles,[23] and instead adopt an inductive one[24] that examines concrete freedoms enshrined in the constitutions and laws of Muslim-majority countries in light of international human rights law.

In fact, abstract analyses may be useful to draw parallels between the Western and Islamic foundations of constitutionalism, and this might contribute to the social acceptance of human rights in the Muslim world as an endogenous, rather than exogenous and imperialistically-imposed phenomenon. However, this attempt risks becoming an exercise in futility in that it employs only certain sources and exegeses of Islamic law, which are neither the sole applicable to the cases in question nor are interpreted in the same way by all Muslim actors. An emblematic example is freedom of religion: since the Qurᵓan states clearly 'Let there be no compulsion in religion',[25] how can we explain that apostasy is almost universally considered a crime, punishable by death under shariᶜa?[26] This is a typical case showing that, due to the multiplicity of sources and interpretations of Islamic law, an adamantly liberal outcome is entirely compatible with the cruellest and most archaic one, on the same subject and starting from the same religious texts. Hence, the appropriate question is not: 'Is Islamic law compatible with human rights?', and not even 'is freedom of religion as provided in Islamic law compatible with freedom of religion as provided in international human rights law?'; the most appropriate formulation would be, instead: 'is freedom of religion, as provided in legal texts that declare themselves Islamic, or at least partially refer to Islamic sources, compatible with the meaning of freedom of religion provided in international law?'.

Consequently, I shall not delve into theological debates related to classical shariᶜa and *fiqh*, namely the Islamic rules as derived and interpreted *in primis* from the Qurᵓan and the sunna of the Prophet.[27] I am not going to, in other words, concentrate on classical sources per se, but only when those are invoked in the legal texts analysed here. This means that the assessment of what a supposed 'true Islam' says or doesn't say about the issues at stake is outside the scope of this book.[28] At the same time, I will engage with religion and culture as societal

23 Otto, 'Introduction'. Baderin, *International Human Rights and Islamic Law*. An-Naʿim, *Toward an Islamic Reformation*.

24 Gouda, 'Islamic Constitutionalism and Rule of Law'. Abu-Sahlieh, *Les musulmans face aux droits de l'homme*. Mayer, *Islam and Human Rights*.

25 2:256. Unless stated otherwise, Qur'anic translations are by Ali, *The Holy Quran*.

26 Virgili, 'Apostasy from Islam under Sharia Law'; Abu-Sahlieh, *Les musulmans face aux droits de l'homme*, 106.

27 On it, see Hallaq, *Sharīʿa*, 72–78.

28 With this, I do not intend to disregard the important and erudite work of those scholars who are trying to provide an interpretation of Islam compatible with homosexuality. *Inter alia*, 'Tunisian Professor Amel Grami: Homosexuality Emerged from Our Heritage'. Olfa Youssef, in Tais, 'The Qur'an and Homosexuality'. Kugle, *Homosexuality in Islam*. As the Tunisian professor Amel Grami commented during my interview with her, the theological and the human rights approach may integrate and complement each other (interviewed by the author, Tunis, July 2016).

elements, insofar as I consider constitutions and laws 'the products of deeply embedded societal processes',[29] inevitably influenced (in the formation and interpretation) by these societal factors.

In the same vein, I will avoid making quantitative assessments on this matter. For instance, some scholars have attempted to measure the 'number' of rights or the 'score' of Islamization in the constitutions of Muslim countries.[30] In spite of the interesting idea underlying these pieces of research, I deem such analyses inadequate to provide a clear picture of the concrete effects of Islamic provisions on the enjoyment of rights. Ahmed and Gouda, for example, have established an 'Islamic Constitution Index', the score of which is simply given by the sum of Islamic clauses in each constitution.[31] Although such a score is slightly differentiated according to the relevance of the Islamic clauses, a numerical system cannot weight the concrete impact of those provisions in courts and society – and, ultimately, on people's lives. In other words, the attempt to identify the 'most Islamic' constitution using quantitative analysis based on the number of 'Islamic clauses' does not reveal much about their effect on the legal and social ground. Equally fruitless is trying to determine the compatibility of Islamic constitutionalism with individual liberties based on the number of rights enshrined in the constitution: fundamental rights are not candies in a box, where more is better.

For these reasons, I deem the qualitative methodology more appropriate in terms of analysing and evaluating this topic. The purpose of the qualitative approach, indeed, is to *describe*, as opposed to *measure*, a problem, situation or phenomenon;[32] as such, it allows more flexibility in the research process and a more articulate analysis of the meaning and effects of Islamic stipulations, characterized as they are by a complex mixture of religious, legal and social elements.

Concerning the sources utilized for the present work, I will rely on a mixture of primary and secondary ones, including literature, original case law and interviews, with a partly theoretical, partly empirical approach. On the theoretical side, I will draw on relevant literature on human rights, constitutionalism and Islam to provide the conceptual background, which will be subsequently put to the test by analysing the constitutions and case studies. On the empirical side, I will use semi-structured interviews with experts and stakeholders from academia, human rights activism and legal practice, as well as victims of human rights abuses, to provide a more accurate picture of the issues at stake.

However, this should only happen at the level of cultural and social acceptance, not at the legal one, as stressed by all scholars and activists with whom I spoke: a proposal of decriminalization based on Islam would put the legal fight on a slippery slope, by establishing Islam, rather than the Constitution and international human rights law, as the source of rights. For a proposal based on Islam, see Othman, 'Appel à l'abolition de l'homophobie en Tunisie à l'occasion de La Journée Mondiale du 17 Mai'.

29 Thornhill, 'The Sociology of Constitutions', 495.

30 Ahmed and Gouda, 'Measuring Constitutional Islamization'; Ahmed and Ginsburg, 'Constitutional Islamization and Human Rights'.

31 Ahmed and Gouda, 'Measuring Constitutional Islamization'.

32 Kumar, *Research Methodology*, 13.

A final caveat must be made as far as the basic assumptions of this work are concerned. This research could in part be described as a classical doctrinal one, or 'black-letter law' study,[33] that is, an analysis of legal rules conducted on legal texts, case law and correlated literature. However, I will not merely adopt this approach of purely theoretical knowledge but will also take a stance on the content of the law, advocating for a change thereof – as per what may be defined as 'law reform research'.[34] Indeed, I start from a well-defined philosophico-political position, namely, constitutionalism as the guarantee of inherent individual freedoms, following the classical liberal stream which has variably been framed in philosophy of law as 'neo-natural law' or 'neo-constitutionalism'.[35] I consider, in other words, contemporary constitutionalism as a means toward the implementation of a liberal democracy – a system combining the rule of law, formal democracy and human rights.[36] On this premise, I follow the *Oxford Handbook of Comparative Law* in adopting a 'universalist justice-seeking approach', which 'entail[s] comparative work on rights, often linked with literature on human rights'.[37] This is, in fact, the 'subversive function' of comparative law described by Muir-Watt: the legal phenomenon is not considered only in its positivistic dimension, but also in the concrete social effects it brings about.[38]

Regarding the conception of human rights, I assume them to be (1) individual; and (2) universal, as testified by the very etymology of the word *human*. Thus, I dismiss outright any relativistic idea of liberty as culturally, geographically or socially determined in each different context. I regard these theorizations as an intellectual *carte blanche* given to majorities to trample on minorities' rights, and a quasi-racist way to deprive certain individuals of their freedoms on the mere basis of their ethnicity or birthplace.[39]

The yardstick I am going to use in order to assess how Islamic rules affect such rights is international human rights law, as enshrined in the Universal Declaration of Human Rights and the International Covenant on Civil and Political Rights, along with the appropriate conventions on specific issues.

Book outline

This book contains eight chapters.

In Chapter I, I will make an overview on the concept of constitutionalism both in the Western and the Islamic traditions. After a brief historical synopsis of

33 Chynoweth, 'Legal Research', 29.

34 'The purpose of the latter will generally be to facilitate a future change, either in the law itself, or in the manner of its administration'. Chynoweth, 31.

35 Barberis, 'Diritto e Morale'.

36 See Chapter I.

37 Jackson, 'Comparative Constitutional Law: Methodologies', 62.

38 Muir-Watt, 'La fonction subversive du droit comparé'.

39 As epitomized in one sentence by Prof. Alice Her-Soon Tay, recognizing the existence of universal human rights means declaring that there are no subhuman human beings. Her-Soon Tay, 'I valori asiatici e il Rule of Law'.

the two, I will compare and contrast the main concepts underlying Western constitutional philosophy with the Islamic idea of just government. Profound discrepancies will emerge in relation to the key notions of liberty, legitimate power, relation between state and religion, citizenship, political rights and democracy. Overall, I will show that the religious substratum permeating the political and institutional architecture of the Islamic tradition creates an inner tension with the key tenets of constitutionalism.

In Chapter II, I will provide a theoretical assessment of the perception of individual freedoms in an Islamic mindset. As per my premises, instead of moving from a purely conceptual analysis based on abstract ideas such as 'democracy', 'human rights', 'women's rights' and so on, I will conduct my assessment on selected documents representing, we might say, the 'Islamic Bill of Rights' – the major Islamic charters of rights that, in the mind of the proponents, should outline an ethos alternative to the Western one and compliant with religious rules. In addition, I will examine the constitutional project elaborated by the University of Al-Azhar, arguably the most authoritative Islamic institution in the Sunni world. I call such analysis 'theoretical', although conducted on para-legal documents, as the inductive examination of the provisions those contain will give a general picture of the Islamic conception of individual liberties – which shows relevant points of tension with the universal human rights system.

In Chapter III, I will move into the core of my topic by addressing Islamic constitutionalism in Egypt, in particular the constitutional article, as interpreted by the Supreme Constitutional Court, defining the principles of shariᶜa as 'the main source of legislation'. The analysis shows that the Court, while adopting an overall reformist approach, has built a chaotic and dangerous system, which pays (at least at the theoretical level) a high tribute to shariᶜa and orthodox Islamic theories. Overall, this chapter will highlight the risks for the rule of law and fundamental rights intrinsic to a supremacy clause based on shariᶜa, however tempered by reformist attempts.

Chapter IV will be devoted to examining the relation between Islam and fundamental rights in the two constitutions drafted in Egypt after the Arab Spring – in 2012 and 2014. The chapter shows that the marked Islamist connotation of the 2012 Constitution, manifested in the enhanced role of orthodox shariᶜa and in the restriction of fundamental freedoms, negatively affected the rule of law, individual liberty, women's rights, freedom of conscience and equality of non-Muslim minorities. The Constitution of 2014, while solving most of these issues, still maintains the supremacy of shariᶜa, which could potentially be problematic for a full enjoyment of rights.

With Chapter V, I will move to the Tunisian case and to the analysis of the 2014 Constitution. In particular, I will focus on those provisions which have triggered a more marked clash between Islamist and secular forces within the Constituent Assembly and in the larger society. This assessment will confirm the controversy surrounding certain sensitive issues highlighted above, namely the role of Islam in a civil state, women's equality with men, freedom of conscience and religion.

The role of Islamist actors in attempting to curtail basic rights according to their interpretation of religion will emerge.

Chapters VI, VII and VIII will be devoted to the case studies.

In Chapters VI and VII, I will concentrate on two particularly problematic topics, namely homosexuality and blasphemy, respectively in Egypt and Tunisia. Drawing from case law, interviews and reports, I will show that both LGBT behaviours and the expression of atheism, blasphemy, heterodoxy or criticism against religion remain punished under vague laws – used, misused and reinvented upon the whim of judges.

Chapter VIII will examine the prosecution of gays and freethinkers against the backdrop of the freedoms guaranteed by the Constitutions of Egypt and Tunisia as well as international law. This chapter will show that the liberticidal laws targeting homosexuals and freethinkers are in contradiction with both systems of guarantees.

An interesting and quite revealing aspect that will emerge overall is that gays, atheists and freethinkers are persecuted under similar premises, as similar are the grounds for the protection of their rights, both in the constitutions and international law. Homosexuality, atheism and blasphemy are all viewed as threats to public order and collective morals, shaped by religion. At the same time, they represent different manifestations of the same indivisible individual liberty, whose protection is the very *raison d'être* of a constitution.

Overall, my main claim in this book is that a religious *Grundnorm* is incompatible with the primacy of a human-made constitution, and that the fundamentals of shariʿa law, as interpreted by contemporary state institutions, are in contrast with a full recognition of equal and inalienable individual rights embodying the constitutional mission.

I Constitutionalism and Islam

Background

In the words of Mohammad Hashim Kamali, 'Constitutional law (*uṣul al-ḥukm*) is one of the most under-developed areas of Islamic law and jurisprudence (*fiqh*)', with juristic works on the caliphate hardly touching upon issues such as fundamental rights, separation of powers, government and state sovereignty.[1]

This mostly happens because there is no preference in Islam for a certain form of government or another, as long as shariᶜa law is scrupulously observed.[2] In the words of the Muslim Brother ᶜAbd al-Qadir ᶜAwdah,

> it does not matter whether the power is conservative or progressive, nor the regime republican or monarchical: all of this does not affect by any means the principles of shariᶜa, because those do not depend on the power or the regime, but uniquely on Islam, which is eternal and immutable.[3]

As a consequence, classical Islamic thinkers did not traditionally problematize the concept of statehood in itself, but only in its relation to religion.

While the majority of the Islamic world has now adopted formal aspects of Western constitutionalism, 'the democratic philosophy is confronted with several difficulties inherent to Islam's cultural heritage, such as the sanctification of power, the lack of an established secular tradition, the confusion of earthly powers with spiritual power, and the communitarian ethic'.[4]

In this chapter, I will try to give an account of these problematic aspects, providing an overview of the main points of contact and distance between constitutionalism and Islam. As this book is not focused on classical Islamic theories, but on modern constitutions of Muslim countries, I do not claim to provide a complete account of classical theories on state and sovereignty in Islam; rather,

1 Kamali, 'Constitutionalism in Islamic Countries', 19. See also Hefny, 'Religious Authorities', 95.
2 Fiorita, *L'islam spiegato ai miei studenti*, 83. Massimo Campanini, *Islam e politica*, 26. Hefny, 'Religious Authorities', 95. Predieri, *Sharīʿa e Costituzione*, 181.
3 Campanini, *Islam e politica*, 108. Own translation from Italian.
4 M'rad, 'The Process of Institutional Transformation', 71.

DOI: 10.4324/9780429259418-1

I concentrate on the aspects that require at least a concise preliminary explanation in order to approach the following chapters in a conscious manner. In particular, after providing a brief overview of the Western concept of constitutionalism, I will focus on the pillars of good government in Islam, comparing and contrasting the two traditions and underlying philosophies.

The analysis will show that, while modern constitutionalism deals with limitation of power, institutional checks and balances, rule of law and individual rights, the focus of the Islamic government is mainly placed on the implementation of shariᶜa law.

The Western concept of 'constitution'

The Western tradition of constitutionalism is neither recent nor univocal. Indeed, it may be traced back to the Greek *polis* and the Roman republic, with a constant evolution up to the neo-constitutional wave of the post-World War II period.[5]

Within the concept of 'constitution', one may detect mainly four elements (roughly corresponding to different times, but present in various degrees still today): '1) the "constitution" as definition of the competences of the public power and of its organization; 2) the "constitution" as safeguard of the rights of the individuals against abuses carried out by the public power; 3) the "constitution" as a normative guarantee of the legitimation of the public power by the individuals subject to it; 4) the "constitution" as the foundation of the identity of the political community.'[6]

The first element refers to the constitution as the architecture of public powers, defining their scope of application and boundaries. Since the Greek *polis*, it has been based on the concept of 'isonomy', that is, the 'state of equal laws for all and responsibility of the magistrates'[7] – the embryo of the very concept of rule of law.

The second idea, more modern, views the constitution as an instrument towards the guarantee of inalienable individual rights, attained by bridling power to prevent its abuses. The first instance of this tendency is the *Magna Carta Libertatum* of 1215, establishing a set of rights for 'free men', that is, the members of the aristocracy.[8] These rights included, *inter alia*, property, personal liberty and some guarantees for women, and their violation would trigger the right to resist against the monarch.[9] This embryonic concept of individual rights, expanded with the *Bill of Rights* of 1689, found its philosophical development in the natural-law theories of John Locke.[10] The idea of natural rights, and the

5 Barberis, *Breve storia della filosofia del diritto*, 30.
6 Dellavalle, 'Constitutionalism Beyond the Constitution', 6.
7 Hayek, *The Constitution of Liberty*, 239.
8 Dellavalle, 'Constitutionalism Beyond the Constitution', 9.
9 'English Translation of Magna Carta'.
10 Moseley, 'John Locke: Political Philosophy'.

right of resistance connected to the violation thereof, will then be enshrined in the *Declaration of Independence of the United States of America*[11] and in the *Déclaration des Droits de l'Homme et du Citoyen.*[12]

The third element refers to the constitution as the normative source of legitimacy of public power – the foundation, in other words, of power itself, as originating from the constitution. This concept closed the era of the theological approach regarding legitimation as descending from God,[13] and it is therefore particularly relevant for the topics discussed in this book for it creates a substantial tension with the Islamic conception of power (*v. infra*). Citizens are central to this conception of legitimate government, and this strictly links this understanding of constitutionalism with the two examined before:

> In a society which did not pretend anymore to be the realization of a superior idea of the "good" or to be based on the natural laws of human sociability, the legitimation-chain coming "from the bottom up" became the only possible justification of the very existence of binding public laws. The clear affirmation of the epistemic centrality of the citizens' will in the construction of the society with its rules and institutions has been thus strictly associated – in the conceptual approach as well as in history – with the declaration of individual rights.[14]

Equally, a political community that has lost its transcendental references will adopt a constitution as the foundation of its very identity – which is the fourth aspect of modern constitutionalism. From this viewpoint, the concept of 'constitution' is strongly linked with that of national citizenship, construed around and defined by the constitution of the state.

In normative terms, a constitutional order may be described as a system containing 'institutionalized mechanisms of power control for the protection of the interests and liberties of the citizenry, including those who may be in the minority'.[15] Hence, constitutionalism is deeply linked to the founding elements

11 'We hold these truths to be self-evident, that all men are created equal, that they are endowed by their Creator with certain unalienable Rights, that among these are Life, Liberty and the pursuit of Happiness. — That to secure these rights, Governments are instituted among Men, deriving their just powers from the consent of the governed, — That whenever any Form of Government becomes destructive of these ends, it is the Right of the People to alter or to abolish it, and to institute new Government, laying its foundation on such principles and organizing its powers in such form, as to them shall seem most likely to effect their Safety and Happiness.' 'Declaration of Independence of the United States of America'.

12 'Art. 1er. Les hommes naissent et demeurent libres et égaux en droits. Les distinctions sociales ne peuvent être fondées que sur l'utilité commune. Art. 2. Le but de toute association politique est la conservation des droits naturels et imprescriptibles de l'Homme. Ces droits sont la liberté, la propriété, la sûreté, et la résistance à l'oppression'. 'Déclaration des Droits de l'Homme et du Citoyen'.

13 Dellavalle, 'Constitutionalism Beyond the Constitution', 11.

14 Dellavalle, 13.

15 Gordon, *Controlling the State*, 4.

of the liberal democracy, that is, the rule of law, formal democracy and human rights.[16] As to the rule of law, it contains various principles, both of procedural and substantive nature, with control mechanisms to ensure their observance:

> The main procedural standards of the rule of law, as accepted in authoritative documents and academic literature, are that (a) state policies must employ written laws – acts, ordinances, decisions – as major instruments; (b) all state actions must be subject to law; (c) the law must be clear and consistent in substance, accessible and predictable for citizens, and general in its application; and (d) the substance of the law and its effectuation must be influenced by citizen approval.
>
> As for the main substantive standards of the rule of law, there is consensus that all laws and their interpretations must be subject to (a) fundamental principles of justice; and (b) human rights and freedoms of individuals, notably civil and political rights, social and economic rights, and group rights.
>
> In order to control compliance with these procedural and substantive principles, the rule of law [...] also requires a third set of elements to be in place, namely of control mechanisms: (a) the executive arm of the state must establish internal correction mechanisms on unlawful administrative actions; (b) an independent judiciary, accessible for every citizen, must be responsible for conflict resolution through interpretation and application of the law; and (c) complementary quasi-judicial institutions, such as an ombudsman, a national human rights-institution, and various tribunals, must be in place to further ensure compliance with the rule of law.[17]

These notions have been effectively summarized as follows: '1) Citizens are free from the arbitrary use of power, 2) Citizens benefit from legal certainty, 3) All citizens are treated as equal before the law, 4) All citizens are granted accessible and effective justice, 5) All citizens can claim their rights including religious rights with a substantial degree of legal certainty'.[18] An essential part of these principles is that nobody is above the law, not even the higher state hierarchies. This is how the 'rule of law' is opposed to the 'rule of men', as per a classical definition.[19]

It must be noted that the three components of formal democracy, rule of law and individual liberties must always be present in a constitutional system: the rule of law in the absence of guarantees of fundamental rights would ensure that laws apply to everybody, but not that those laws are not discriminatory against minorities.[20] Formal democracy, on its part, 'is illiberal if either rule

16 Halmai, 'Religion and Constitutionalism', 3.
17 Otto, 'Introduction', 37.
18 Halmai, 'Religion and Constitutionalism', 3.
19 Gordon, *Controlling the State*, 5.
20 'If a nation's legislature were dominated by fundamentalist Baptists, for example, the fact that laws apply to all offenders without exception could not be relied upon to constrain them from prohibiting the celebration of the Catholic mass'. Gordon, 7.

of law or fundamental rights are missing'.[21] Even fundamental rights alone are not enough, if they are simply *octroyés* by a despotic, albeit enlightened, ruler. In other words, when one of the above elements is lacking, a written constitution is insufficient to denote a constitutional system: after all, most autocracies, from China to North Korea, Cuba and the Soviet Union, had or have a written constitution without being constitutional systems,[22] while conversely the United Kingdom remains a constitutional system despite the absence of a written constitution.[23]

This idea of a constitutional government is considerably distant from that of a just government in the Islamic tradition, which I am going to examine now.

A brief historical overview of constitutionalism in Islam

In classical Islam, a precedent often mentioned as the embryo of constitutionalism dates back directly to the Prophet: it is about the so-called Charter of Medina, drafted by Muhammad to deal with the Jewish tribes governing the town where the Muslim community relocated after fleeing Mecca.[24] In reality, that document lacks the elements of a constitution outlined above; it has rather been described as a 'municipal charter'[25] or a 'corporate organizational document',[26] insufficient to lay down a constitutional model. Furthermore, the Medina Charter was drafted by the Prophet himself, whose unique position as solely accountable before Allah makes it 'not meaningful' to speak of it in terms of constitutionalism.[27] The historical evidence of this claim is that this document has not paved the way for further elaboration in the course of Islamic history, and it has not substantially influenced the practice of constitution-making in Islamic countries.[28] To further corroborate this conclusion, the term 'constitution' was originally absent in Arabic, as *dustūr* was originally a Persian word.[29]

In sum, 'it would be an exaggeration to claim that constitutional values or constitutionalism are inherently a part of the Islamic tradition'.[30] *De facto*, the idea of constitutionalism as a set of man-made procedures limiting the power of the ruler is a relatively recent acquisition for the Islamic world,[31] as it did not take root until the cultural contacts with Europe in the 19th century.[32]

21 Halmai, 'Religion and Constitutionalism', 6.
22 Halmai, 7.
23 Gordon, *Controlling the State*, 5.
24 Grote and Röder, 'Introduction', 3.
25 Grote and Röder, 4.
26 El Fadl, 'The Centrality of Sharī'ah to Government and Constitutionalism in Islam', 48.
27 An-Na'im, *Toward an Islamic Reformation*, 76.
28 An-Na'im, 76.
29 Hefny, 'Religious Authorities', 95.
30 El Fadl, 'The Centrality of Sharī'ah', 55.
31 Wolfrum, 'Constitutionalism in Islamic Countries : A Survey from the Perspective of International Law', 78. Grote and Röder, 'Introduction', 3. Lewis, Pellat, and Schacht, 'Dustūr'.
32 The Constitutions of the Ottoman Empire, Tunisia and Egypt were drafted following the Belgian model. Grote and Röder, 'Introduction', 4.

For a brief historical account of the penetration of constitutionalism the Islamic world, we may distinguish three phases. The first wave began in the 19th century, under the European influx. The way was paved by the Ottoman 'Noble Rescript' (1839), followed by the Tunisian 'Pledge of Security' (1857), the Ottoman Basic Law (1876) and the Egyptian Basic Statute (1882).[33] In the Sunni world, the initial *raison d'être* for drafting constitutional documents was to give equal rights to non-Muslim citizens, under the pressure of European powers. While fiercely opposed by traditional ulemas,[34] liberal ideas started to take roots into local reformist circles – the most significant and successful being the Young Ottomans and the Young Turks in Turkey. The second phase started after the decolonization. While the first wave was essentially driven by liberal ideas, in this case constitutionalism was useful for rulers to reassert the centralization of state power and the identity they wished to confer to it – the majority being characterized by a 'combination of socialist, nationalist and pan-Arabist ideas';[35] from this point of view, it was still a modernizer wave of constitutionalism, often influenced by the French tradition.[36] The third phase, begun in the 1960s, was instead influenced by the resurgence of Islamism:[37] one such example, which I will address later on, is the insertion of a reference to shariᶜa into the Egyptian constitution in 1971, something unthinkable in the Nasserist period.[38]

It is evident that these waves correspond to very different conceptions of constitutionalism. Reiterating my assumptions on the more meaningful interpretation of this term, I am going to address its main components from the perspective of Islam.

'Liberty' in Islam

> O worthy visitors! When you look upon this fascinating display of human progress, do not forget that all these achievements are the work of freedom. It is under the protection of freedom that peoples and nations attain happiness. Without freedom, there can be no security; without security, no endeavour; without endeavour, no prosperity; without prosperity, no happiness.[39]

It is by means of these words – uttered by an astonished Turkish diplomat at the sight of a giant Statue of Liberty at the Parisian *Exposition Universelle* of

33 Röder, 'The Separation of Powers', 325. I exclude from this analysis the Persian experience, which would deserve a chapter on its own.
34 Röder, 325. Lewis, Pellat, and Schacht, 'Dustūr'.
35 Röder, 'The Separation of Powers', 334.
36 Le Roy, 'Constitutionalism in the Maghreb', 110.
37 Röder, 'The Separation of Powers', 334.
38 See Chapter II.
39 Lewis, *The Shaping of the Modern Middle East*, 44.

1878 – that Bernard Lewis introduces the issue of the difficult relation between freedom and Islam.[40]

The constitutional concept of freedom as a political tool to constrain power in a net of limitation guaranteeing individuals' liberty was then unknown to Islam. The term *ḥurriyya*, freedom, had nothing to do either with a philosophical idea of self-determination, or with a legal or political concept of good government: it only denoted the condition of not being a slave.[41] For this reason, the 19th-century historian al-Jabarti could only describe the European concept of liberty by saying that 'Frenchmen are not slaves'.[42] However, the Muslim 'freeman' was not autonomous vis-à-vis the state and the community:

> The individual Muslim was expected to consider subordination of his own freedom to the beliefs, morality, and customs of the group as the only proper course of behaviour. While he valued his personal freedom and was proud of it, he was not supposed to see in it a good to be defended at all costs against group demands. Politically, the individual was not expected to exercise any free choice as to how he wished to be governed. At times, he did stress his right to be considered and treated as an equal by the men in power.[43]

Even more stringent were the constraints towards God. Orthodox Islam did not and does not conceive any possible freedom outside the boundaries of shariᶜa, because no human law may overpower the divine commandments. Hence, individual rights (*ḥuqūq al-insān*) may only be exerted within the boundaries (*ḥudūd*) established by God,[44] and they are necessarily subordinated to the 'rights of God' (*ḥuqūq Allāh*).[45] Significantly, the *Oxford Dictionary of Islam* defines *ḥurriyya* as 'freedom from everything other than God and devotion to him. Since humans are the slaves of God, freedom, as Ibn al-Arabi put it, is the perfect form of slavery'.[46]

Political freedom and good government

The discovery of the political meaning of *ḥurriyya* happened in the 19th century, by virtue of the more and more intense contacts with the proud and triumphant

40 Virgili, 'Libertà e democrazia nell'Islam', 5.

41 'In Arabic usage at that time and for some time after, the word "freedom" – ḥurriyya – was in no sense a political term. It was a legal term. One was free if one was not a slave. To be liberated, or freed, meant to be manumitted, and in the Islamic world, unlike in the Western world, "slavery" and "freedom" were not until recently used as metaphors for bad and good government'. Lewis, 'Freedom and Justice'. Rosenthal and Lewis, 'Ḥurriyya'.

42 Colombo, *Basta!: Musulmani contro l'estremismo islamico*, XLVI.

43 Rosenthal and Lewis, 'Ḥurriyya'.

44 Castro, 'Diritto Musulmano', 293.

45 Esposito, 'Human Rights'.

46 Esposito, 'Hurr'.

Western liberalism. A crucial moment for this cultural contamination was the 'explorative mission' of Al-Azhar's students who were sent by the Egyptian government in Paris to examine the Western world, deemed powerful and successful in striking contrast with the decay of the Islamic world. It was during this voyage that the sheik Tahtawi came across the French obsession with 'liberty', which struck him for its deep political and philosophical implications, and which he tried to explain to his fellow Muslims in the following way: 'what they [Europeans] call freedom and what they desire is what we call justice'.[47]

This conceptual distance did not necessarily mean hostility. Some early Islamic reformers were in fact profoundly convinced of the compatibility between European-style liberalism and Islam. Among them, the Tunisian Khayr al-Din and the Egyptian Muhammad Abdu tried to challenge the traditional Islamic discourse and to make it receptive to the new liberal ideas. The former, who was the President of the Tunisian Grand Council during the constitutional period, went as far as to equate the aims of the European and the Islamic approaches to government, for their identical demand to hold the ruler accountable.[48] Unfortunately, their ideas had scarce penetration within the dominant theology.[49] Especially with the emergence of modern Islamism, mainly embodied in the movement of the Muslim Brotherhood founded by Hassan al-Banna in 1928, the Western idea of individual freedom was rejected in favour of a collective idea of independence of the *umma* under an Islamic rule: Hassan al-Banna spoke of *ḥurriyya* in terms of 'liberation from foreign powers' and of the 'edification of a free Islamic state ruled by Islamic teachings'.[50]

The distance between the Islamic and Western liberal understanding of good government derived from two very different meaning attributed to the latter: while in the Western liberal tradition 'freedom' is an inherent aspect of a 'good government', to the point that the two concepts to a certain extent overlap, in the Islamic tradition power is legitimate if it is governed by justice (*ᶜadl*), which is in turn defined as 'accordance to the law', that is, the Law of Allah, the shariᶜa.[51] This is the yardstick for evaluating the ruler's conduct, and not the respect for individual freedoms and the rule of law. The only earthly aspects of legitimate power concern some personal characteristics of the Caliph (Muslim, male, adult, and others) and his appointment, which should not derive from usurpation.[52] However, even the last requisite may be derogated, as explained below.

The gulf between the Western and the Islamic idea of good government is reflected in radically divergent conceptions regarding the relation between state and citizens: it is antagonistic in liberal constitutionalism, which views the

47 Al-Tathtawi, in Colombo, *Basta*. See also Lewis, 'Freedom and Justice'.

48 Grote and Röder, 'Introduction', 5. Colombo, *Basta*, XLVII ff.

49 Colombo, *Basta*, XLVII ff.

50 Ferjani, *Islamisme, laïcité, et droits de l'homme*, 208. Own translation from French.

51 Virgili, 'Libertà e democrazia nell'Islam', 6. Colombo, *Basta*. Lewis, 'Freedom and Justice'.

52 Virgili, 'Libertà e democrazia nell'Islam', 18. Lewis, 'Freedom and Justice'.

constitution as an instrument to bridle the menace of power; it is unitary in Islam, 'based on the concept of tahwīd (i.e., the Oneness of God) and thus provid[ing] a set of principles oriented toward an essential unity of basic interests between the individual and the state'.[53] Because of that, some Muslim scholars regard the democratic multi-party system, with the crucial checking role exerted by the opposition, as the seed of sinful societal discord (*fitna*).[54] After all, opposition has little role to play in a system where the ruler is only responsible before God.[55]

'Right of resistance'?

However far from the idea of modern constitutionalism, the Islamic model of governance is not an absolute one; it is 'a limited, as opposed to a totalitarian, form of government with powers constrained by reference to the definitive injunctions and guidelines of the Qur'ān and authenticated Sunnah'.[56] These boundaries are as strong as alien to the premise of democratic constitutionalism: 'In a democracy the people may establish any legal order or system they wish for themselves, whereas in Islam the state is bound by implementing the Sharī'ah as expression of the sovereign will of the Lawgiver, and its powers are limited to that extent'.[57] Hence, it is the observance of shariatic injunctions that shapes the limits of a legitimate government as opposed to a tyranny.

How should the *umma* react against an illegitimate government? Since the yardstick to evaluate the Islamic political system is not the degree of liberty, but the respect of shariᵉa law, the Lockean 'right of resistance' is not conceived in terms of rebellion against a ruler who does not take into due account individuals' natural rights (because the Qurᵓanic duty of obedience would prevail in that case)[58] but rather as an obligation to be fulfilled in the limited cases when the ruler deviates from the path of shariᵉa. In this sense, and only in this sense, it is possible to speak not only of a *right*, but a downright *duty* of disobedience against the un-Islamic tyrant. It is interesting, from this point of view, to make a comparison with the right of resistance as emerging from the *Magna Carta Libertatum* highlighted above, outlined in terms of reaction to the violation of established individual rights.

De facto, Islamic history tells a quite different story, marked by the connotation in terms of *fitna* of any attempt to challenge the ruler.[59] This is because two opposite principles in Islam inform the relation between the ruler and his subjects: one 'authoritarian and quietist' and the other 'radical and activist'.[60]

53 Kamali, 'Constitutionalism in Islamic Countries', 21.
54 Virgili, 'Libertà e democrazia nell'Islam', 25–31.
55 Arzt, 'Heroes or Heretics', 352.
56 Kamali, 'Constitutionalism in Islamic Countries', 22.
57 Kamali, 29.
58 'O ye who believe! Obey Allah, and obey the Messenger, and those charged with authority among you.'
59 Lewis, *The Political Language of Islam*, 95.
60 Lewis, 92.

Both of them actually derive their legitimacy from the Prophet's life and deeds: while the first principle is inspired by his role as the highest ruler, deserving obedience and respect, the second looks at his religious and political revolution against Mecca's sovereigns. Although both traditions are deep-rooted, and the radical activist one has acquired new appeal in modern times among Islamist circles driven by the idea of the Islamic revolution, the quietist principle became prevalent in the Sunni world.[61] Certainly, this happened more for political than for religious reasons; nevertheless, Islamic clerics based this duty of obedience on religious grounds, arguing that tyranny, albeit despicable, is still largely preferable to anarchy, for 'only in this way can the basic religious and legal prescription of Islam be maintained'.[62] Al-Ghazali considered tyranny an instance of legal necessity (*ḍarūra*), a subsidiary source of law which admits derogations to established norms when the alternative is worse.[63] When the influence of the West made 'revolution' a term with positive connotations, Arabic had to use another word: not *fitna* anymore, but *thawra*.[64]

It is worth noting that, for most contemporary Islamic scholars, the requisites outlined above remain unchanged. For instance, a 2014 open letter to ISIS' leader Al Baghdadi, drafted by 126 prestigious Sunni scholars, mentions the right to rebellion in these terms:

> It is impermissible to rebel against the leader who is not guilty of declared and candid disbelief (*al-kufr al-bawwah*); i.e. disbelief that he himself admits to openly and where all Muslims are in consensus regarding such a person being a non-Muslim – or by his prohibiting the establishment of prayers.[65]

A theocratic state?

'Islam is a religion that does not concern itself only with the faith of its believers but also seeks to regulate civil, social, and even political aspects of the life of society'.[66] This is the ultimate reason why the limits of power in Islam derive from the observance of shariᶜa law. Shariᶜa is, indeed, 'sacred law',[67] whose primary sources, the Qurᵓan and the sunna (i.e. the tradition of the Prophet), are considered divine.[68] Human-made sources, such as scholarly consensus and analogy, need always to find a justification in the divine primary sources.[69]

61 Lewis, 92.
62 Lewis, 100. See more *infra*.
63 Virgili, 'Libertà e democrazia nell'Islam', 17.
64 Lewis, *The Political Language of Islam*, 96.
65 'Open Letter to Dr. Ibrahim Awwad Al-Badri, Alias "Abu Bakr Al-Baghdadi", and to the Fighters and Followers of the Self-Declared "Islamic State"'.
66 Horchani, 'Islam and the Constitutional State', 199.
67 Rahnema, 'Islamic Jurisprudence and Public Policy', 105.
68 Pizzorusso, *Sistemi giuridici comparati*, 345.
69 Rahnema, 'Islamic Jurisprudence and Public Policy', 109.

From this perspective, the Islamic state is intrinsically *theocratic*. To dispel possible misunderstandings, I borrow Bernard Lewis' fundamental distinction: 'In the sense of a state ruled by the church or by priests, Islam was not and indeed could not be a theocracy';[70] however, it was in a broader sense: 'In the universal Islamic polity as conceived by Muslims, there is no Caesar but only God, who is the sole sovereign and the sole source of Law'.[71] Secularism was so alien to the Islamic concept of governance that Arabic originally lacked even the words to express the duality between 'religious' and 'secular':

> The distinction between church and state, so deeply rooted in Christendom, did not exist in Islam, and in classical Arabic, as well as in other languages which derive their intellectual and political vocabulary from classical Arabic, there were no pairs of words corresponding to spiritual and temporal, lay and ecclesiastical, religious and secular. It was not until the nineteenth and twentieth centuries, and then under the influence of Western ideas and institutions, that new words were found, first in Turkish and then in Arabic, to express the idea of secular.[72]

This is not to claim that Christianity did not concern itself with politics, or that it did not influence legislation. In fact, it did, heavily, and continues to do so to a lesser extent. However, the conceptual distinction and institutional separation between the Church and the State always existed, under the banner of the evangelical maxims 'render unto Caesar the things that are Caesar's' and 'my kingdom is not of this world'.[73] This was not the reality of the classical Islamic statehood, in which 'Church and state, political and religious authority, are the same thing'.[74]

In modern times, Muslim states have mostly acquired, to a larger or smaller extent, the formal distinction between state and religion. A reaction to the secularization process has come from Islamist movements, which aim to reaffirm the legal and political nature of Islam, even in its totalitarian connotation. The most successful embodiment of this project is the Iranian revolution, exploited by Ayatollah Ruhollah Khomeini to make Iran a theocracy in the more traditional sense, under the motto 'Islam is politics or it is nothing'.[75] On the Sunni side, a watershed was the foundation of the Muslim Brotherhood (MB) in 1928; while al-Banna's movement has never advocated a state run by the clergy on the Iranian model, *de facto* there are noteworthy similarities between Khomeini's constitutional model and the 'civil state with Islamic reference' the MB espouses: both share the idea that the state must be based on Islam and enforce a body of legislation that conforms to Islamic law and principles, with religious authorities

70 Lewis, *What Went Wrong?*, 114.
71 Lewis, *The Crisis of Islam*, 7.
72 Lewis, *The Political Language of Islam*, 3.
73 Predieri, *Sharī'a e Costituzione*, 157.
74 Predieri, 165. Own translation from Italian.
75 Lewis, *The Crisis of Islam*, 8.

to ensure this control.[76] In *Towards the Light*, al-Banna listed the 'principal goals of reform founded on the spirit of genuine Islam', among which we find: a call to end the multiparty system; the imposition of sharīʿa in all branches of legislation; a widespread, omnipresent control on private and public morality, including through a system of strict censorship, harsh punishment for transgressors (such as flogging of fornicators), monitoring of officials' private behavior and 'depuration' of Western mores in private homes.[77] Khomeini and al-Banna's follower Sayyid Qutb advanced very similar arguments: both contrasted the inherent governmental and political nature of Islam with the mainly spiritual mission of Christianity,[78] and specified that Islam is a totalitarian dimension that embraces every aspect of human life.[79] This is why Sunni Islamists, while rejecting the notion of a formally 'theocratic state' in which the clergy is in control,

> do not exclude any matter of the affairs of the state, which should not be presented to scholars in order to make a judgment thereon whether is permissible or forbidden. Hence the 'civil state with Islamic reference', which they advocate, should not resolve any matter without approval of scholars. In other words, while they reject a 'clergy state' by name as it suggests undesirable connotations, yet they actually seek to realize the core of such a 'religious state', thereby contradicting the constitutional notion.[80]

To summarize this ambiguity surrounding the civil or religious nature of the state, Kamali argues that 'Islamic governance may be characterized as civilian (*madaniyyah*), which is, however, neither theocratic nor totally secular but has

76 El-Daghili, 'Al-Dawlah al-Madanīyah', 194. V. also *infra*, in the chapters on Egypt and Tunisia.

77 al-Banna, 'Towards the Light'.

78 'In the Western Christian world, the individual enters the church and listens to preaching and prayers; [...] But in leaving the church, he realizes that daily life is regulated and informed by different laws; he finds a society founded on the principles of these laws, which have nothing to do with the spirit of Christianity. [...] "Christianity is nothing but an invitation to spiritual purification, it does not involve legislation for the present life but leaves this to Caesar". The consequence, in the Christian world, is that Christianity has been relegated on one realm and life on the other'. Qutb, 'L'islam e l'organizzazione della città', 36. Own translation from Italian. 'Do not allow the true nature of Islam to remain hidden, or people will imagine that Islam is like Christianity (nominal, not true Christianity), a collection of injunctions pertaining to man's relation to God, and the mosque will be equated with the church'. Khomeini, *Islam and Revolution*, 29.

79 'If Islam is to act, it must govern. This religion did not arise to withdraw into hermitages and temples, nor to take refuge in hearts and consciences. It came to exercise power over life and to dispose of it freely to forge society according to the global conception that it has of life; not only through exhortation and advice, but also thanks to the legislative and administrative powers'. Qutb, 'L'islam e l'organizzazione della città', 35. Own translation from Italian. 'There is not a single topic in human life for which Islam has not provided instruction and established a norm'. Khomeini, *Islam and Revolution*, 30.

80 Hefny, 'Religious Authorities', 96.

characteristics of its own'.[81] This aspect maintains considerable relevance in contemporary constitutional debates, as I am going to show in the next chapters.

More 'Muslims' than 'citizens'

In the traditional Islamic state, the strongly religious framework is reflected by the absence of the idea of 'citizenship': whilst this has always been pivotal in Western civilization from the times of the Greek *polis*, in Islam it has been obscured by the role of religion. Thereby, the idea of 'nation-state', understood in modern legal terms as a permanent population, a defined territory and a system of government, was absent in classical Islam.[82] The population (*umma*) identified with the Islamic faith, while Christians and Jews were second-class citizens under a pact of protection (*dhimma*);[83] hence, the people, 'as a source of legitimization of the Islamic character of the state, become a constitutive element of it only on condition of recognizing the sovereignty of Allah in that territory'.[84] As to the territory, in Islamic sources a *summa divisio* exists between *dār al-Islām* and *dār al-ḥarb* (the first denoting 'the land of Islam' in opposition to the infidels' world, the 'land of the war').[85] Indeed, the present-day term indicating the 'country', *dawla*, was used to denote the ruling family or dynasty, while the focus of Islamic jurisprudence was on the transnational, religious entity of the 'caliphate'.[86] Concerning the government, I have already shown that it is conceived as an instrument for implementing shariᶜa. As per the classical definition proposed by Mawdudi, the Islamic state 'is an ideological one, i.e. neither territorial, nor ethic, nor cultural: it is based on the universalism of the Islamic religion'.[87]

If, nowadays, the concept of nation-states is clearly present, and geo-strategic affairs are shaped in accordance, still Islam continues to play a role that is unknown in any other civilization of the world, from the Christian (but mostly secularized) West, to the Confucian, Buddhist, or Hindu Orient. An instance of that is the Organisation of Islamic Cooperation, whose sole common element is Islam: 'The very idea of such a grouping, based on religion, in the modern world may seem anachronistic and even absurd. It is neither anachronistic nor absurd in relation to Islam'.[88] The preeminence of a religious consciousness over the feeling of national belonging has caused, according to Lewis, a lack of civic representation,[89] which is in its turn another cause of the deficit of democracy, as I am going to show in the next section.

81 Kamali, 'Constitutionalism in Islamic Countries', 22.
82 Virgili, 'Libertà e democrazia nell'Islam', 9.
83 Sbailò, 'I Costituzionalisti europei e il califfato nero', 8.
84 Sbailò, 17. Own translation from Italian.
85 Sbailò, 8.
86 Hefny, 'Religious Authorities', 95.
87 Sbailò, 'I Costituzionalisti europei e il califfato nero', 16. Own translation from Italian.
88 Lewis, *The Crisis of Islam*, 14.
89 Lewis, 'Freedom and Justice'.

'Islamic democracy'?

A possible bridge between Islamic principles and liberal constitutionalism could be constructed by finding, within shariᶜa itself, democratic rules and/or procedures the observance of which would at once guarantee compliance with religion and a democratic system of government. Indeed, something of this kind exists in the principle of *shūrā*, which denotes the consultation of the ruler with the community. In Kamali's words, 'Islamic government is committed to the implementation of Sharī'ah. Yet in a substantial sense, it is a popular government since the Sharī'ah itself approves of people's participation in government, and therefore, their direct will'.[90] *Shūrā* finds its roots directly in the Qurᵓan and the sunna, which reports that the Prophet, upon Allah's will, used to consult with the Companions before taking a decision.[91] So imperative seems such principle in religious scriptures that neglecting it means the ruler becoming an impious tyrant. Indeed, the accusation of despotism, *istibdād*, is not merely a political one, but also something evil and sinful, and practically a call to depose the ruler.[92]

But may *shūrā* be equated to democracy?

The answer seems to be negative, both on substantive and procedural grounds. As to the former, Islamic jurists have erected rigid boundaries *ratione materiae* around consultation, following the same logic of the limitations of individual reasoning (*raᵓy*): in particular, just as *raᵓy* cannot be employed whenever the shariatic rule is clear, so *shūrā* is inadmissible in such cases, for it would be at best redundant, at worst illicit.[93] In terms of procedures, consultation does not seem in any way binding for the ruler:

> According to verse 3:159 (the first of two verses of the Qu'ran which mention the term *shura*), the Prophet is enjoined to deal gently and kindly with the believers and to consult them in public affairs, but once he is resolved, he should proceed to execute his decision in reliance on God. Although he did consult in some situations, and sometimes followed the advice given to him, it was neither seen by the founding jurists as being contemplated by this verse, nor was it the invariable practice, that the Prophet always consulted his Companions and implemented their advice.[94]

Above all, 'Whatever obligation to consult his Companions the Prophet may have had, it was an obligation to God and not to his human subjects. This makes the whole process religious and moral rather than legal and constitutional in nature'.[95] Muhammad's successors, albeit lacking his religious *auctoritas*, were not

90 Kamali, 'Constitutionalism in Islamic Countries', 29.
91 Kamali, *Freedom of Expression in Islam*, 41.
92 Lewis, 'Freedom and Justice'.
93 Kamali, *Freedom of Expression in Islam*, 43.
94 An-Na'im, *Toward an Islamic Reformation*, 79.
95 An-Na'im, 79.

bound by a different, and earthly, code of conduct: their responsibility remained towards God, with no obligation towards their subjects. The latter, therefore, could neither demand to be consulted, nor could they force the ruler to implement the will of the majority or depose him for lack of compliance – unless by accusing him of apostasy. The leading Islamic jurists, in other words, never elaborated on *shūrā* to make it something more than a guiding principle devoid of legal mechanisms to enforce its application.[96]

To sum up, the principle of consultation is far from being describable in terms of modern democracy, meant as people's participation, or representation, in the power's decisions.[97] In fact, classical Islam lacks the idea of 'representative government', that is, 'people participating not just in the choice of a ruler but in the conduct of government',[98] as well as the idea of government limited by people's will: Allah's Law is the sole limitation to the ruler's power. According to the renowned Islamist ideologue Yusuf al-Qaradawi, shariᶜa is 'a complete rule over all political authorities including the body which enacts man-made laws. They have no right to change or suspend the rules of *Shariᶜah*'.[99] This is why the Islamic ruler could theoretically only implement *siyāsa sharᶜiyya* – namely administrative regulations aimed to keep up with public needs in domains where shariᶜa says little or nothing at all. He does not, however, have the authority to challenge the orthodox *fiqh*, namely the traditional interpretation of shariᶜa from Islamic scholars.[100] Hence, *siyāsa* is not something alternative or additional to shariᶜa: first of all, acting for the public good through *siyāsa* is a shariatic obligation; secondly, it cannot contradict clear shariatic provisions.[101]

This pulls *shūrā* far apart from the liberal democratic tradition: the idea of modern 'citizenship', connecting the state's fortunes to those of its equal citizens by virtue of their participation in the government's conduct, is totally absent from the classical Islamic thought. Likewise, the thesis of the absolute need of *shūrā* for the legitimacy of power is equally unsustainable.[102]

The principle of *shūrā* goes hand in hand with that of *bayᶜa*, the oath of allegiance from the subjects to the caliph at the moment of his coronation. While the pactitional nature of the *bayᶜa* may call to mind the idea behind democratic elections, it in fact applied only to the most influential notables,[103] who were not called upon to vote for potential candidates to the position of caliph, but merely to choose a suitable one (*de facto* often giving the seal of approval to the one selected by the previous caliph). The logic, goals and effects of this

96 An-Naʿim, 79. Virgili, 'Libertà e democrazia nell'Islam', 20.

97 'In general, however, governmental authority admitted of no participation of the individual as such, who therefore did not possess any real freedom vis-a-vis it.' Rosenthal and Lewis, 'Ḥurriyya'.

98 Lewis, 'Freedom and Justice'.

99 al-Qaradawi, *State in Islam*, 47.

100 Quraishi, 'The Separation of Powers', 68.

101 Quraishi, 70.

102 Lewis, 'Freedom and Justice'. An-Naʿim, *Toward an Islamic Reformation*, 78–81.

103 Lewis, 'Freedom and Justice'.

oath are clearly very different from those informing democratic elections. The scholar of Islam Francesco Castro reports in particular the theories on the caliphate of al-Mawardi, one of the leading classical Islamic jurists dealing with the question, according to whom the caliph could be selected in two ways: the first was the choice made by the 'community', referring merely to those having the 'power to bind and loose', i.e., the elites that, because of their virtues, were better able to distinguish the presence of the necessary requirements in the aspiring caliph; the second was purely and simply the designation by the predecessor. Castro continues by noting that 'a later doctrine has recognized a third way of acquiring the Caliphate, namely the occupation of power, under the principle that tyranny is preferable to anarchy'.[104] From this follows an 'obligation of obedience and service (*nuṣra*) to the caliph, provided that he does not command acts contrary to religion'.[105] In fact, such acts would trigger, more than a right of resistance, the 'very faculty for the community to terminate the contract of imamate',[106] on the basis of a much reported tradition whereby 'there is no obedience in sin' nor 'obedience to a creature against his Creator'.[107]

This connects us to what is argued above on the 'right of resistance': *shūrā* and *bayᶜa*, as earthly requisites, are not an absolute precondition for the legitimation of power, which could be, and had to be, challenged solely on religious grounds.[108] It remains obscure which authority should determine the deviation from God's path, and using what procedures.[109]

Final considerations on the inner tension between Islam and constitutionalism

The entire issue of the legitimacy and constraints of power in Islam may be summarized in the following way: between the *umma* and the ruler stands a pact of submission, which is exclusively bound to the ruler's observance of shariᶜa. Should this clause be violated, the pact would be broken and the community would not only be entitled to rebel against the authority – become, in this very narrow sense, 'tyrannical' – but would even be required to do so.[110] As long as this does not happen, however, people are bound to the strictest obedience, since Islam compels believers to obey the authority[111] to the extent that 'an hour – or

104 Castro, 'Diritto Musulmano', 296. Own translation from Italian. See also Lewis, 'Freedom and Justice'.
105 Castro, 'Diritto Musulmano', 296. Own translation from Italian. See also Lewis, 'Freedom and Justice'.
106 Castro, 'Diritto Musulmano', 297. Own translation from Italian.
107 Lewis, *The Political Language of Islam*, 94; 152.
108 Lewis, *From Babel to Dragomans*, 306.
109 Lewis, *The Political Language of Islam*, 94.
110 Virgili, 'Libertà e democrazia nell'Islam', 23.
111 Q, 4:59.

even a moment – of anarchy is worse than a hundred years of tyranny'.[112] This is because state authority is the only constraint that can ensure the due observance of God's Law.

Some scholars have been trying to challenge this conclusion by making 'a laundry list of concepts such as shūrā, the contract of the caliphate, the idea of bay'ah, and the supremacy of Sharī'ah, and then conclude that Islam is compatible with constitutionalism'.[113] Kamali, for instance, has argued that a moderate reading of Islam regards legitimacy as stemming from the application of shariᵉa *and* people's approval.[114] However, this leaves three relevant problems on the table. First, Kamali specifies that the community is to be understood as the *umma*,[115] thus excluding non-Muslims by definition.[116] Second, the application of shariᵉa includes provisions which are incompatible with substantive requirements of constitutionalism related to individual liberties.[117] Third, no specification is made in terms of *procedures* to bind the ruler's conduct.

In fact, the Islamic traditional system of governance lacks fundamental guarantees of constitutionalism, both of a procedural and substantive nature.

As to the former, *shūrā* and *bayᵉa* are not commensurate with modern democracy, for a number of reasons. First of all, they do not necessarily involve the entire population, being traditionally the prerogative of certain elites (of Muslim faith). Secondly, they only concern the moment of the election, while omitting the system of checks and balances in the *conduct* of power that a constitution eminently provides for. Finally, they are not indispensable requisites for the legitimacy of power, as this could even be exerted by usurpation, if the alternative is 'anarchy'.

From a substantive point of view, a constitutional system has stringent requirements: 'To be a constitution at all, a proposed document must respect and protect the fundamental rights of all citizens equally and without distinction on such grounds as sex, religion, race, or political opinion'.[118] In terms of goals, 'the objective of constitutionalism must always be to uphold the rule of law, enforce effective limitations on government powers, and protect fundamental rights',[119] as said above. Furthermore, it must temper the democratic, majoritarian rule by ensuring the inviolable rights of minorities.[120] In other words, an elective system is a necessary but insufficient prerequisite of constitutionalism. As we have seen, the main pillar of the Islamic state is the strict observance of

112 Lewis, 'Freedom and Justice'.
113 El Fadl, 'The Centrality of Sharī'ah', 54.
114 Kamali, 'Constitutionalism in Islamic Countries', 30.
115 Kamali, 30.
116 Esposito, 'Ummah'.
117 See Chapter II.
118 An-Na'im, 'The Legitimacy of Constitution-Making', 30.
119 An-Na'im, 31.
120 El Fadl, 'The Centrality of Sharī'ah to Government and Constitutionalism in Islam,' 37.

shariᵉa law; consequently, fundamental rights will be protected or infringed insomuch as shariᵉa commands:[121]

> In their discourses, Muslim jurists were not articulating the idea that there is a process that guards core legal values and that this process is binding upon the government. Rather, they were arguing that the positive commandments of Sharīʿah, such as the punishment for adultery or the drinking of alcohol, ought to be respected and enforced by the government.[122]

This means, ultimately, that as long as a government implements shariᵉa, including its criminal penalties, rules of modesty, and so on, it could remain a government of unlimited powers not subject to the rule of law.[123] On this point, it has been rightfully argued that Islam bears a deeply rooted idea of a government limited *by law*, that is, the provisions of shariᵉa, but not one of a government limited by the *rule of law*, that is, by a net of procedures, checks and balances and individual liberties.[124] The very concept of 'rule of law', as a man-made corpus of rules and procedures that human beings give to themselves, is in contrast with the theorization of God as the sole holder of sovereignty, to which all creatures are equally submitted – as testified by the very etymology of the word 'Islam'.[125] According to some scholars, in striving to eliminate 'the rule of human beings over other beings' so as to subject them to Allah only, Islam is ultimately incompatible with the rule of law.[126]

For the same reason, an inner tension exists between Islam and constitutionalism, insofar as they respectively claim the undisputable superiority of two different sources: the constitution in one case, God and his word in the other. Therefore, 'a "man-made" constitution in addition to the religious authority is deemed superfluous and futile',[127] because '[w]ith the exclusive sovereignty and right to command with God, an obligation to obey manmade law would be virtually impossible to justify'.[128] This is the reason why Saudi Arabia has never drawn up a proper constitution, emphasizing that its constitution is the Qurᵓan and the sunna.[129]

In conclusion, the Islamic experience is characterized by an 'absolute identification'[130] between religion and state: the Kingdom of God *is* of this world, in a pervasive and unconditional way, and the state is nothing but an instrument

121 In the next chapter, I shall address in more details the aspect of shariᵉa law and individual rights.
122 El Fadl, 'The Centrality of Sharī'ah', 39.
123 El Fadl, 39.
124 El Fadl, 39.
125 Islam means 'submission': Wehr, 'اسلام'.
126 Arzt, 'Heroes or Heretics', 369. Halm, *L'Islam*, 6.
127 Wolfrum, 'Constitutionalism in Islamic Countries', 78.
128 El-Daghili, 'Al-Dawlah al-Madanīyah', 193.
129 Wolfrum, 'Constitutionalism in Islamic Countries', 78.
130 'Immedesimazione assoluta', Pizzorusso, *Sistemi giuridici comparati*, 346.

of shariʿa law.[131] Constitutionalism, therefore, may only denote that '"Original and Eternal Constitution", destined to constitute the foundation not of a single country, but of all humanity, in that it regulates not merely the relations among men, but man's relationship with God'.[132]

As I am going to show in the course of this book, this inner, profound tension between civil constitutionalism and transcendental Islamic principles continues to affect contemporary constitutional debates and processes deeply. Not only do most constitutions of Muslim-majority countries mention Islam and/or shariʿa,[133] but, more profoundly, the basic tenets of Islam and its law shape state legislation even as constitutions express different principles – as a mark of the supremacy religion exerts, to various degrees, over human-made law.

131 See Predieri, *Sharî'a e Costituzione*, 181.

132 Sbailò, 'I Costituzionalisti europei e il califfato nero', 21. Own translation from Italian.

133 Abiad, *Sharia, Muslim States and International Human Rights Treaty Obligations.* Stahnke and Blitt, 'The Religion-State Relationship and the Right to Freedom of Religion or Belief'.

II The Islamic conception of individual liberties

Introduction

As explained at the beginning, looking at the concrete articulation of rights in an Islamic context is, in my view, more effective than undertaking a theoretical discussion on the Islamic conception of individual liberties. Therefore, following the line traced by scholars such as Ann Elizabeth Mayer and Sami Aldeeb Abu-Sahlieh, I am going to examine four human rights documents drafted by Muslim institutions. The ones I have selected are the most relevant ones, coming from different sources and therefore providing a varied spectrum of the contemporary Islamic approaches towards fundamental rights. Although in most cases these documents are devoid of legal value,[1] they are nonetheless important in order to appraise how contemporary Islamic states and institutions conceive an 'Islamically correct' enjoyment of individual freedoms and the limits thereof.

The first group of documents consists of the three major Islamic charters on human rights. Although these have been drafted by different bodies, they all purport to represent a human rights discourse alternative to the mainstream international one (perceived as a Western 'imperialist agenda'[2]), and respectful of Islamic tradition and rules. The first is the Universal Islamic Declaration of Human Rights, drafted by a private organization linked to the Muslim Brotherhood. The second, adopted by the Organisation of the Islamic Conference,[3] is the Cairo Declaration on Human Rights in Islam. The third is the Arab Charter on Human Rights, adopted by the Arab League; albeit not being per se an *Islamic* document but an updated instance of 'Pan-Arab' nationalism, the Arab Charter may nonetheless be included within this group of conventions for three reasons: it was adopted by Muslim-majority states, it includes religious references, and it reaffirms the validity of the OIC charter.[4]

I shall then move to examine a never-enacted constitutional project, which was drafted by the Islamic University of Al-Azhar and tabled in the Egyptian

1 Except the Charter of the Arab League.
2 Baderin, *International Human Rights and Islamic Law*, 14.
3 Currently named 'Organisation of Islamic Cooperation'.
4 On the ambivalence of this document, Pacini, 'Introduzione', 18–20.

DOI: 10.4324/9780429259418-II

Parliament in 1978. In spite of remaining a dead letter, it still constitutes a cornerstone of Islamic constitutionalism due to the prestige of the drafting institution, arguably the most authoritative Islamic centre in the Sunni world. In connection with the constitutional project, I will also examine the draft penal code elaborated by Al-Azhar in the same period: this will shed light on how human rights are concretely articulated within a criminal context.

Before moving to the core of the analysis, I must preliminarily note that the Islamic charters of rights derive their authority from religion, not from reason:[5] it is the divine revelation which establishes human rights, and simultaneously the limits thereof. This religious *Grundnorm* should be borne in mind while considering the rights therein, because it gives them a very specific connotation, usually very distant from the international one in spite of occasional formal similarities.

The Universal Islamic Declaration of Human Rights

The Universal Islamic Declaration of Human Rights, proclaimed in 1981 at UNESCO, was drafted by a private body based in London, the Islamic Council of Europe.

It is important to note that this body, founded in 1973 with Saudi sponsorship,[6] is an offshoot of the Muslim Brotherhood in the West,[7] and it also has ties with the Jamaat-e-Islami, a sister organization founded in Pakistan by the radical Islamist Abu al-Aᶜla Mawdudi.[8] The Islamic Council of Europe was also in the forefront of the fight against Salman Rushdie's *Satanic Verses*.[9] This pedigree, which is not exactly encouraging, anticipates the content of the Universal Islamic Declaration of Human Rights.

Before proceeding to analyse the document, it is worth noting that the title itself reveals a well-defined mindset: the oxymoronic juxtaposition of the adjectives 'universal' and 'Islamic' follows the Muslim classical tradition, which sees in Islam, its principles and its rules a path given by God to the whole of mankind, and from which only ignorance, blindness or arrogance may divert human beings.[10] This is an old dogma of Islam: according to a classical doctrine, 'every infant has an inborn disposition to be a Muslim, but his parents make him a Jew

5 Mayer, *Islam and Human Rights*, 48.
6 Esposito, 'Islamic Council of Europe'.
7 Vidino, *The New Muslim Brotherhood in the West*, 33.
8 Vidino, 34.
9 Vidino, 120.
10 'Man possesses a double nature, his life follows two different plans. On one hand, like all other creatures, he is completely dependent on natural laws and cannot resist them. But on the other hand, man is provided with reason and intelligence [...] He can follow his own code of conduct [...] In the first case, like all other creatures, man is born and will remain Muslim, and automatically follows the injunctions of God. In the second, he has the freedom to choose, to be or not to be Muslim, and it is the way in which one exercises this freedom which divides humanity into two groups: the believers and the non-believers.' Maudoudi, *Comprendre l'Islam*, 17. Own translation from French.

or a Christian or a Zoroastrian'.[11] To quote the renowned Islamists Mawdudi and Qutb, 'Islam [...] is a universal ideology,'[12] 'the universal and eternal system for the future of humanity'.[13]

It is furthermore necessary to underline another substantial flaw of this declaration, which is by itself sufficient to cast a shadow on the whole document: the English and French translations, albeit official, contain relevant divergences from the Arabic text, most probably to make the latter more palatable for a Western audience. From this viewpoint, the most problematic element concerns the use of the term 'shariᶜa' in the Arabic version, rendered using the neutral and unproblematic terms 'law' and 'loi' in the English and French translations.[14] Only the explanatory notes at the end clarify that 'the term law denotes the *Shariᶜah*'. In fact, the term used in Arabic to mean human-made law, without religious implications, would be *qānūn*, while shariᶜa denotes *religious* law. Because of this deliberate discrepancy, the Western reader is confronted with a text that seems to follow the path of classical bills of rights but in reality does not.[15]

It is evident that the reference to shariᶜa law bears relevant consequences, potentially problematic in terms of human rights. First of all, the document radically rules out any departure from the Qurᵓan and the sunna, so that only shariᶜa can define the boundaries of human rights. Secondly, the charter, while self-proclaiming 'universal,' collocates this pretence of universalism in an exclusively Islamic dimension, thus implicitly assuming that Islamic law is the sole true guarantor of human rights for the entire humanity. This is indeed written explicitly in the foreword:

> Human rights in Islam are firmly rooted in the belief that God, and God alone, is the Law Giver and the Source of all human rights. Due to their Divine origin, no ruler, government, assembly or authority can curtail or violate in any way the human rights conferred by God, nor can they be surrendered.

The inherent submission of human beings is thereby reasserted, with the consequence of a pre-eminence of duties over rights, as stated explicitly (and quite oddly, for a declaration allegedly centred on human rights) in the preamble: '[...] by the terms of our primeval covenant with God our duties and obligations have priority over our rights.'

The religious element emerges overwhelmingly in the body of the text: in the Arabic version (but significantly not in the French or English ones), every article granting rights is built upon a Qurᵓanic verse, with the correlative limitations ending up nullifying the rights themselves.

11 Lewis, *The Political Language of Islam*, 94.
12 Maudoudi, *Comprendre l'Islam*, 163. Own translation from French.
13 Qutb, 'Il governo islamico: la giustizia sociale nell'Islam', 28. Own translation from Italian.
14 English version: Islamic Council of Europe, 'Universal Islamic Declaration of Human Rights'. Arabic version: Islamic Council of Europe, 'Al-Bayan al-ᶜAlami ᶜan Huquq al-Insan Fi al-Islam'.
15 Mayer, *Islam and Human Rights*, 77.

Let us look at the most relevant example, the right to life (Art. 1): this is called 'sacred', and protected on the grounds of Qurᵓan 5:32, whereby 'if anyone slew a person unless it be for murder or for spreading mischief [*fasād*] in the land it would be as if he slew the whole people: and if anyone saved a life it would be as if he saved the life of the whole people'. Therefore, 'no one shall be exposed to injury or death, except under the authority of the Law' – where law, as we have seen, means shariᶜa. Given this formulation, 'subjecting the right of life to shariᶜa means that this right may be "lawfully violated" every time shariᶜa law requires a person's death.'[16] Considering that he who brings *fasād*, namely vice, corruption, perversion and depravation,[17] is liable to death under shariᶜa law, which kind of guarantee could the homosexual, the adulterer or the apostate find in Article 1 of the Universal Islamic Declaration of Human Rights?

Another relevant discrepancy between the English and Arabic versions lies in the principle of equality: whereas the English version states in neutral terms that 'All persons are equal before the Law and are entitled to equal opportunities and protection of the Law'[18] (which should be a truism in a bill of rights), the Arabic version puts things under a very different light by saying that all persons are 'equal before the shariᶜa', so that 'no discrimination is admissible *in the application of shariᶜa* [emphasis added]'. This certainly reassures us on the fact that 'even if Fatima, Muhammad's daughter, were to steal, she would have her hand cut off',[19] as the hadith therein recalls, but offers fewer guarantees on the treatment certain sectors of society would suffer, given that discrimination against them is prescribed by shariᶜa itself, as explained in the introduction.[20] 'That is, people are not being guaranteed the equal protection of a neutral law but rather "equal protection" under a law that in its premodern formulations is inherently discriminatory and thereby in violation of international law.'[21] Furthermore, the bad faith of the Islamic Council on this issue bluntly emerges from the third paragraph of Article 3: whereas the English version states that 'No person shall be denied the opportunity to work or be discriminated against in any manner or exposed to greater physical risk by reason of religious belief, colour, race, origin, sex or language', the Arabic version completely omits to mention the grounds for illegitimate discrimination.

16 Anselmo, *Shariʿa e diritti umani*, 274. Own translation from Italian.

17 Wehr, 'فسد'.

18 Article 3.

19 Pacini, *L'Islam e il dibattito sui diritti dell'uomo*, 192. Own translation from Italian

20 'But if Islamic usage rejects privilege, it admits – in certain situations even imposes – inequality. Three inequalities in particular were established and regulated by law and developed through centuries of usage – the unequal status of master and slave, of man and woman, and of Muslim and non-Muslim'. Lewis, *The Political Language of Islam*, 64. 'Equality in shariᶜa is not equality between all human beings, but between *free Muslim men*, and this means that minorities do not enjoy the same rights'. Anselmo, *Shariʿa e diritti umani*, 274. Own translation from Italian. See also An-Naʿim, *Toward an Islamic Reformation*, 89–91.

21 Mayer, *Islam and Human Rights*, 91.

Similarly, equality for non-Muslims is not guaranteed. The sole reference under the chapter 'right of minorities' is the following: '[t]he Qurʾanic principle "There is no compulsion in religion" shall govern the religious rights of non-Muslim minorities.' This reaffirms the Qurʾanic ban on forced conversions, but leaves intact the system of *dhimma*, with all the discrimination against non-Muslims it entails.[22] Furthermore, while these minorities enjoy the right, *ex art.* 10.b, to be governed by their own rules in their civil and personal matters, this seems to apply only to Christians and Jews – the only religious minorities protected under shariʿa. Indeed, the Arabic version presents two Qurʾanic references, mentioning 'the People of the Gospel' (Q, 5:47) and the 'followers of the Torah' (5:43), which seems to restrict the scope of protection to the 'religions of the Book' (*ahl al-kitāb*),[23] as per the classical Islamic law on the matter.[24]

Similar observations apply in relation to freedom of religion (Article 13). While the English version reads 'Every person has the right to freedom of conscience and worship in accordance with his religious beliefs', the Arabic version adds a reference from the Qurʾanic sura *Al-Kāfirūn* ('The Infidels', with a negative connotation): 'Unto you your religion, and unto me my religion'.[25] This implies, once again, that freedom of religion is understood within the limits of Islamic shariʿa, that is, with the implicit prohibition of apostasy from Islam[26] and only for the *ahl al-kitāb*, given that Christians and Jews are the only ones to whom the right is granted, although with restrictions.

Another highly problematic provision is contained in Article 14, which states the *ḥisba* principle, that is, the right and duty of every Muslim to enjoin what is right and prevent what is wrong. The alleged 'right' to 'establish institutions and agencies meant to enjoin what is right (*ma'aroof*) and to prevent what is wrong (*munkar*)' seems to foreshadow the institution of the '*ḥisba* patrols', namely the moral police harshly controlling society's behavior in radical states (such as Iran, Saudi Arabia, Taliban's Afghanistan, ISIS ...), and reasserted by Hassan al-Banna, the Muslim Brotherhood's founder.[27]

As it concerns women, only the rights of 'married women' are mentioned in the document, in Article 20, while there is no reference at all to the rights of unmarried ones or to equality in general. Most likely, in the framework of a declaration completely hinged on the pre-modern mindset of shariʿa, a woman

22 Abu-Sahlieh, *Les musulmans face aux droits de l'homme*, 90.

23 Mayer, *Islam and Human Rights*, 141.

24 *Inter alia*, Abu-Sahlieh, *Les musulmans face aux droits de l'homme*, 88. In Chapter IV, I will show that the same happens also in the Egyptian Constitution.

25 Mayer, *Islam and Human Rights*, 178.

26 On the ban of apostasy in classical Islamic law see Abu-Sahlieh, *Les musulmans face aux droits de l'homme*, 106. Virgili, 'Apostasy from Islam under Sharia Law'.

27 On Art. 14 see Mayer, *Islam and Human Rights*, 78. and 94. On this path, Hassan al-Banna, founder of the Muslim Brotherhood, organized a group of young militants, on the model of the Nazi Youth Movement, who were trained in a steel discipline to learn and impose a strict Islamic behaviour, even by resorting to violence. Commins, 'Hasan Al-Banna (1906–1949)', 146.

free from male authority is not even envisaged, hence there is no need to focus on such a category. Whatever the rationale, it is evident that categorizing rights on the basis of marital status is outside the logic of international human rights law.[28]

Freedom of expression is yet another pseudo-right within the declaration: Article 12 states that 'every person has the right to express his thoughts and beliefs *so long as he remains within the limits prescribed by the Law* [emphasis added]'. Indeed, 'No one [...] is entitled to disseminate falsehood or to circulate reports which may outrage public decency, or to indulge in slander, innuendo or to cast defamatory aspersions on other persons.' To quote the Algerian professor Ali Merad,

> taken outside their historical context [...] and put into a human rights declaration, these doctrinal references evoke the Inquisition. What would become of tolerance in an Islamic state which reserves such treatments to those citizens having a nonconformist view of freedom of thought and expression, and thus, *a fortiori*, of non-Muslims?[29]

It is evident that such a provision would be more appropriate as the preamble of a blasphemy law than of a declaration of rights. But the Arabic version is even worse: by saying 'Everyone may think, believe and express his ideas and beliefs without interference or opposition from anyone as long as he obeys the limits [*ḥudūd*] set by the shariᶜa',[30] it seems to imply that it is not only *expression* that is subjected to Islamic law, but also inner *thoughts* and *beliefs*.

The Cairo Declaration on Human Rights in Islam

This document is an official one, although not legally binding, adopted by the Organisation of the Islamic Conference in 1990.[31] Saudi Arabia sponsored it at the 1993 Vienna World Conference on Human Rights as the document embodying the consensus of the Muslim world on human rights issues.[32]

From a structural and formal point of view, this charter is more similar to the universal ones as there are no references to the Qurᵓan. This does not mean, however, that the document is more secular: as has been observed,[33] the 25 articles at times seem to be carbon copies of Qurᵓanic verses. Nor does the content speak a different language, starting from the pre-eminence of duties over rights and the general submission of all human beings to God.[34]

28 Mayer, *Islam and Human Rights*, 108–10.
29 Merad, 'Riflessioni', 133. Own translation from Italian.
30 Mayer, *Islam and Human Rights*, 178.
31 Organisation of the Islamic Conference, 'Cairo Declaration on Human Rights in Islam'.
32 Mayer, *Islam and Human Rights*, 31.
33 Anselmo, *Shari'a e diritti umani*, 280.
34 Art. 1, section A. See Mayer, *Islam and Human Rights*, 50.

Article 1 apparently lays down a comprehensive principle of equality, 'in terms of basic human dignity and basic obligations and responsibilities, without any discrimination on the basis of race, colour, language, belief, sex, religion, political affiliation, social status or other considerations'. However, a more accurate reading immediately reveals that such equality is not in *rights* (hence a legal one), but in *dignity*. Were this not enough, even this partial equality is immediately curtailed by the clarification that '[t]he true religion is the guarantee for enhancing such dignity along the path to human integrity'. To put it in Orwell's terms, all animals are equal, but some animals are more equal than others. The natural superiority of the Muslim is inherent to his belonging to the *umma*, 'which Allah made as the best community [as written in the Qurᵓan, 3:110] and which gave humanity a universal and well-balanced civilization', to the extent that it is even vested with an out-and-out civilizing mission 'to guide all humanity which is confused because of different and conflicting beliefs and ideologies and to provide solutions for all chronic problems of this materialistic civilization'.[35]

The same rationale applies to women's equality: Article 6 grants them equality in 'dignity', but says nothing about equality in *rights*; it merely concedes that a woman 'has her own rights to enjoy as well as duties to perform', avoiding any parallelism with those enjoyed and performed by men. Rather, this article seems to be tailored to Q, 2:228, which in its first part says something very similar: 'And women shall have rights similar to the rights against them, according to what is equitable', before adding 'but men have a degree (of advantage) over them'. Article 12, on freedom of movement, may also be read as a limitation against women and be actually considered a *violation* of freedom of movement, insofar as it grants human beings[36] the right to enjoy it 'within the framework of the Shariᶜah': bearing in mind that such limits are mainly imposed on women, the provision can be read as the reaffirmation of the shariatic restrictions on women's mobility.[37] We could also mention Article 5, which, while affirming the rights of men and women to marry with 'no restrictions stemming from race, colour or nationality', omits to mention religion among the inadmissible restrictions: indeed, under shariᶜa law, a Muslim woman is not allowed to marry a non-Muslim man.[38]

While freedom of religion is not even touched upon, we may find instead a cryptic provision restricting freedom of conscience, and *de facto* reaffirming the ban on apostasy: Article 10 states indeed that 'Islam is the religion of true unspoiled nature. It is prohibited to exercise any form of pressure on man or to exploit his poverty or ignorance in order to force him to change his religion to another religion or to atheism'. This captious argument is often employed in the Islamic 'human rights' discourse to justify the prohibition of, and the harsh

35 Preamble

36 The official English translation reads 'every man', but this must be understood in generic terms as human being, like the original Arabic *insan*.

37 Mayer, *Islam and Human Rights*, 121.

38 An-Naʿim, *Toward an Islamic Reformation*, 91.

penalties against, apostasy. For instance, while an explicit mention of the right to change one's religion is present in the Universal Declaration of Human Rights (UDHR), Saudi Arabia opposed its inclusion in the International Covenant on Civil and Political Rights (ICCPR), by arguing that:

> if the individual was to enjoy real religious freedom, he had to be protected against pressure, proselytism and also against errors [*sic*] and heresies. Men could in fact be induced to change their religion not only for perfectly legitimate intellectual or moral reasons, but also through weakness or credulity.[39]

Similar arguments were advanced by Egypt.[40] According to this sophistic reasoning, apostasy from Islam is merely conceivable out of physical or psychological coercion, otherwise nobody would ever want to leave the 'religion of true unspoiled nature'. Furthermore, this declaration of Islamic supremacy, in the absence of specific guarantees for minorities, seems to reconfirm the classical shariatic discriminations against non-Muslims. This interpretation is also corroborated by Article 23b, which submits one's right to assume public offices to the provisions of shariᶜa: bearing in mind the limitations provided by Islamic law for non-Muslims in the public domain, we may clearly spot here a violation of Article 2 UDHR.

As to freedom of expression, the same considerations set out above apply here as well: it shall be enjoyed only in such manner 'as would not be contrary to the principles of the Shariᶜah',[41] while information 'may not be exploited or misused in such a way as may violate sanctities and the dignity of Prophets, undermine moral and ethical Values or disintegrate, corrupt or harm society or weaken its faith'.[42] Again, freedom of expression is linked to the *ḥisba* principle, defined as the 'right to advocate what is right, and propagate what is good, and warn against what is wrong and evil according to the norms of Islamic Shariᶜah'.[43] This would bring about dreadful limitations to free speech, insofar as

> it would enable every Muslim to go to court as a private prosecutor or 'public informant' to prevent acts deemed contrary to Islamic orthodoxy. In practical terms it would be possible to report to the court another citizen, Muslim or not, whose ideas are not in tune with certain interpretations of Islam established by the official religious authorities or consolidated by tradition[44]

as we will see in Chapter VI.

39 Baderin, *International Human Rights and Islamic Law*, 119.
40 Abu-Sahlieh, *Les musulmans face aux droits de l'homme*, 104.
41 Art. 22.
42 Art. 22.c.
43 Art. 22.b.
44 Pacini, 'Introduzione', 13. Own translation from Italian.

After all, Article 17 defines the alleged entitlement 'to live in a clean environment, away from vice and moral corruption, that would favour a healthy ethical development of his person' as a 'human right'. This article would be enough to affect the entire apparatus of the Convention, in those conservative realities where vices and moral scourges are detected almost anywhere, even in the 'impurity' of a suffered rape.[45] This is an emblematic example of how human rights provisions may be misused to actually *deprive* people of rights.

However, the crucial point lies elsewhere. Beyond the formulation of individual items, and even trying to give them a benevolent interpretation, enlightened by the general principles of international human rights law, what is virtually able to nullify the document in its entirety is the content of the final rules at articles 24 and 25. The second is an interpretation clause, sanctioning shariᶜa as the sole valid reference to shed light on each article of the declaration. The first decrees that 'All the rights and freedoms stipulated in this Declaration are subject to the Islamic Shariᶜah'. This clause, which we also find in the Al-Azhar constitutional project, is a real Trojan horse, capable of spoiling the entire declaration: if all rights must comply with shariᶜa, with all the problems outlined above, what guarantees may this declaration offer, constantly exposed as it is to manipulation, in good or bad faith, in the name of Islam?

As a final note on the Cairo Declaration and its founding body, it must be mentioned that the Organisation of the Islamic Cooperation has even established a 'separate "regional" "Islamic" human rights system',[46] by founding the 'Independent Permanent Human Rights Commission of the Organisation of Islamic Co-operation (IPHRC)'. This body was created with three main goals: '(1) promoting "an alternative discourse on women's rights, centred on the family" and "in opposition to [the established] women's sexual and reproductive rights"; (2) opposition to "a narrow 'Western' conception of sexuality"; and (3) advocacy for the concept of "defamation of religion"'.[47] The establishment of this body has been read as an attempt to build a novel 'Muslim law of nations (*siyar*)', on the path traced by the Universal Islamic Declaration of Human Rights.[48]

The Arab Charter on Human Rights

The third charter, the *Arab Charter on Human Rights*,[49] represents a slightly different case. Approved for the first time by the Council of the League of Arab States in 1994, it was then revised in 2004 to include enforcement mechanisms. It officially entered into force in 2008.[50] Although it has a geographical/ethnic

45 Amnesty International, 'Annual Report: Saudi Arabia 2010'.
46 Hamzić, 'A History in the Making', 116.
47 Hamzić, 117.
48 Hamzić, 117.
49 League of Arab States, 'Arab Charter on Human Rights'.
50 Rishmawi, 'The Arab Charter on Human Rights and the League of Arab States: An Update', 169.

connotation ('Arab') rather than a religious one ('Islamic'), I have included it here, following Pacini,[51] because it is a document whose ratifying states are all Islamic, and because it contains religious references and reaffirms the validity of the OIC declaration.

Formally, the Arab Charter is legally binding for the states parties, and provides a control mechanism, albeit a feeble one. This mechanism is entrusted to an 'Arab Human Rights Committee' (composed of seven independent members elected by secret ballot) to which states must periodically report 'on the measures they have taken to give effect to the rights and freedoms recognized in this Charter and on the progress made towards the enjoyment thereof'.[52] The committee, for its part, is required to consider the reports submitted by the states parties and publish its own yearly assessment, which should contain 'comments and recommendations' of unspecified nature.[53] Mechanisms for individual complaints are completely absent.

This charter exhibits a more moderate religious influence than the UIDHR and the Cairo Declaration. It states the intention to harmonize the Islamic inspiration with international principles, to which its preamble refers specifically by mentioning the Universal Declaration of 1948 and the Covenants of 1966. Yet, such references are accompanied by a parallel reference to the Cairo Declaration, as said before.

One point that is worth noting is the wider formulation of the principle of equality, 'without distinction on grounds of race, colour, sex, language, religious belief, opinion, thought, national or social origin, wealth, birth or physical or mental disability',[54] this time with no shariatic limitations.

Religious references are present only in the preamble, where God is mentioned as the source of human dignity, and the Arab homeland as 'the cradle of religions and civilizations'. The preamble also states the intent to further 'the eternal principles of fraternity, equality and tolerance among human beings consecrated by the noble Islamic religion and the other divinely-revealed religions'.[55]

The word *sharīʿa* is only mentioned once in the text, although in a very sensitive place, namely Art. 3.3, on equality between men and women. This states that they are 'equal in respect of human dignity, rights and obligations *within the framework of the positive discrimination established in favour of women by the Islamic Shariah, other divine laws* and by applicable laws and legal instruments'.[56]

Other controversial provisions are contained in Article 7, which allows the death penalty even for those under the age of 18, and in Article 2, which equates

51 Pacini, 'Introduzione', 19.
52 Art. 48.1.
53 Art. 48.6.
54 Art. 3.1.
55 Preamble.
56 Emphasis added.

Zionism with racism and defines it as 'an impediment to human dignity and a major barrier to the exercise of the fundamental rights of peoples'.

As regards freedom of expression (Art. 32), there is no direct reference to religiously based restrictions. Yet, among the lawful limitations to its enjoyment, we find not only the classical 'rights or reputation of others or the protection of national security, public order and public health or morals', but also an ambiguous reference to 'conformity with the fundamental values of society':[57] the latter may easily result in severe restrictions on speech deemed blasphemous, or on any other kind of heterodox thought, as I will elaborate later addressing a similar clause in the 2012 Egyptian Constitution.

A provision notably in conflict with international human rights law, *in primis* with article 18 of the Covenant on Civil and Political Rights, is Article 30. This, while guaranteeing freedom of thought, conscience and religion, states that no restriction may be imposed on their exercise 'except as provided by law'. This clause is problematic, insofar as it does not refer to freedom to *manifest* opinions (Art. 32) and creeds (as stated by the following paragraph in the same Art. 30), but to that inner, incoercible, dimension which Art. 4 ICCPR shields against any possible restriction in any circumstances whatsoever.[58] It must be stressed that article 43 decrees that:

> Nothing in this Charter may be construed or interpreted as impairing the rights and freedoms protected by the domestic laws of the States parties or those set forth in the international and regional human rights instruments which the states parties have adopted or ratified, including the rights of women, the rights of the child and the rights of persons belonging to minorities.

Since Article 30 adopts the same formulation used in the Arabic version of the UIDHR, this wording seems to be a deliberate choice, rather than a mere oversight.

In general terms, Mayer notes that the 1994 charter, albeit more secular in character than the other documents, nonetheless reduced the scope of rights by reflecting elements of the medieval Islamic tradition.[59] As to the 2004 version, the High Commissioner for Human Rights has criticized the text for being incompatible with international standards on, *inter alia*, women's rights, non-citizens' rights, death penalty of minors and the equation of Zionism with

57 Present indeed also in the 2012 Egyptian constitution, see Chapter IV.

58 'Article 18 distinguishes the freedom of thought, conscience, religion or belief from the freedom to manifest religion or belief. It does not permit any limitations whatsoever on the freedom of thought and conscience or on the freedom to have or adopt a religion or belief of one's choice. These freedoms are protected unconditionally, as is the right of everyone to hold opinions without interference in article 19.1. In accordance with articles 18.2 and 17, no one can be compelled to reveal his thoughts or adherence to a religion or belief'. U.N. Human Rights Committee, 'General Comment 22'.

59 Mayer, 'The Respective Roles of Human Rights', 80.

racism.[60] The International Commission of Jurists (ICJ) has advanced similar criticisms.[61] It has further added that:

> Any reference to cultural, religious or civilization-based specificities should be interpreted and understood as a specific effort by a region to reinforce the principle of the universality, indivisibility and complementarity of human rights and should in no case be considered as a means of eclipsing or even denying the universality of such standards or as a justification for their violation. As regards the recourse to notions such as the shariᶜa or the reference to Islamic law to which the Arab Charter refers, notably in the preamble, such recourse to notions of uncertain legal import and which are susceptible to varied or even contradictory interpretations should be limited as much as possible.[62]

In the same vein, the ICJ has stressed that '[i]n the case of normative conflicts between the Declaration on Human Rights in Islam and the provisions of the International Bill of Human Rights, the latter should prevail'.[63]

The Al-Azhar Constitutional Project

The Al-Azhar constitutional project of 1979[64] is relevant to my hypothesis for two main reasons. First, it comes from what is arguably the most prestigious institution in the Sunni world,[65] an institution whose credentials make it a widely respected interpreter of the authentic Islamic doctrine. Secondly, it is 'the only modern constitution to be developed by a religious entity with minimum interference from formal institutions of the state'.[66] This means that this charter should ostensibly represent a 'pure' by-product of Islamic constitutionalism, one not polluted by vested interests and political considerations. It is not by chance that Ahmed and Gouda use the Al-Azhar project as a paradigmatic model of Islamic constitutionalism, useful to test the level of Islamization of Islamic constitutions.[67]

It must be noted that two versions of this project exist: one is longer than the other as it contains more detailed provisions on the functioning of the parliament and the government.[68] Unless indicated otherwise, I will refer by default to the shorter text, as this is the one which was circulating in Egypt in the aftermath of the 2011 uprising.[69]

60 Arbour, 'The Arab Charter on Human Rights Is Incompatible with International Standards'.
61 International Commission of Jurists, 'The Process of "Modernising" the Arab Charter on Human Rights', paras 8, 9, 10, 16.
62 International Commission of Jurists, para. 6.
63 International Commission of Jurists, para. 7.
64 See Hefny, 'Religious Authorities', 97 ff.
65 The *Encyclopedia Britannica* defines it as the 'chief centre of Islamic and Arabic learning in the world'. 'Al-Azhar University'.
66 Gouda, 'Islamic Constitutionalism and Rule of Law', 58.
67 Ahmed and Gouda, 'Measuring Constitutional Islamization', 42. Gouda, 'Islamic Constitutionalism and Rule of Law', 58.
68 Both versions are available in Abu-Sahlieh, *Projets de constitutions islamiques*, 41–54.
69 Gouda, 'Islamic Constitutionalism and Rule of Law', 66.

The constitutional project immediately states that 'Islamic *shariᶜa* is the source of all legislation'.[70] This has multiple implications, including for state powers and fundamental freedoms.

As concerns the three state powers, the parliament (called '*shūrā* council', *majlis al-shūrā*[71]) shall only approve 'legislation that is not inconsistent with the rulings of Islamic *shariᶜa*';[72] it is not specified, however, which authority should adjudicate on the respect of shariᶜa law. The executive is represented by an 'imam' whom citizens must obey as long as he does not commit 'an action that was unanimously declared forbidden under *shariᶜa*';[73] in this case, he should be placed under impeachment,[74] but, once again, the charter does not provide further specifications on the procedure. As to the judiciary, it 'shall rule justly in accordance with the rule of Islamic *shariᶜa*',[75] and 'judges will be subject only to the Islamic *shariᶜa* in their judgments'.[76] This calls into question the role of the parliament and its legislation as a whole, insofar as it seems that judges should directly refer to shariᶜa according to their own discretion.

Concerning fundamental freedoms, the subordination to Islamic law is confirmed by other articles defining the enjoyment of rights 'in accordance with the rules', or 'within the limits' of the Islamic shariᶜa. We find such references in (apparently) trivial provisions, such as those forbidding 'finery' and 'vulgarity',[77] as well as in substantial ones. The latter include freedom of expression and religion,[78] freedom of the press,[79] freedom of association,[80] women's right to work,[81] and also a final clause stating that 'rights will be practiced in accordance

70 Art. 1b. The English translation is provided by Gouda, 'The 1978 Al-Azhar's Project for an Islamic Constitution'.

71 According to Ahmed and Gouda, it is not clear whether the shura council denotes the parliament (Ahmed and Gouda, 'Measuring Constitutional Islamization', 41.). However, it is legitimate to presume so, given that the word 'majlis' is always used throughout the Arabic text to indicate the parliament. Furthermore, art. 83 seems to describe typical legislative functions: '1. [producing] Legislation that is not inconsistent with rulings of Islamic shariᶜa. 2. Approving the annual budget of the state and its final account. 3. Monitoring the actions of the executive power. 4. Holding those responsible in any ministry accountable for their actions and withdrawing the confidence from the ministry when necessary.'

72 Art. 83.1.

73 Art. 45.

74 Art. 50.

75 Art. 61.

76 Art. 65.

77 Art. 14: 'Finery is forbidden and chastity is required. The state will issue laws and decrees in order to defend public sensibilities from vulgarity in accordance with the rules of Islamic *shariᶜa*.'

78 Article 29: 'Freedom of religion and thought, the freedom to work, the freedom to express opinion directly or indirectly, the freedom to establish trade union associations and participate in them, personal freedom, and the freedom of movement and congregation are all basic and natural rights that are protected within the framework of the Islamic *shariᶜa*'.

79 Article 41: 'The founding of newspapers will be allowed and freedom of the press is guaranteed, all within the framework of Islamic *shariᶜa*'.

80 Article 42: 'Citizens have the right to form collectives and unions according to the law. Those which go against the social system or which secretly have a military character, or which go against any aspect of Islamic *shariᶜa* are not allowed'.

81 Article 38: 'Women have the right to work within the framework of Islamic *shariᶜa*'.

with the aims of *shariʿa*'.[82] It would be redundant to repeat the arguments made elsewhere in this book about the potential consequences of this kind of clause.

Equality between citizens is barely mentioned. The sole references dictate that '[j]ustice and equality are the basis of governance'[83] and that 'the people are equal before the courts'[84] – which, as said above, are Islamic courts, and must hence abide by the legal discrimination between Muslims and non-Muslims and between men and women stipulated by shariʿa.

As regards women's rights, it has been correctly noted that 'discrimination against women is found throughout the constitution'.[85] In particular, they are not allowed to run for presidency (Art. 47), they cannot be members of the judiciary (Art. 68), their duty inside the family is to 'serve' their husband and children (Art. 8), and outside the family they are allowed to work only within the limits prescribed by shariʿa (Art. 38). The abovementioned Art. 14 on 'finery' may also represent a substantial restriction on women's rights: it is the door through which a rigid dress code could be imposed on them.

Non-Muslims, for their part, are not mentioned anywhere in the text. By combining this omission with the provisions of Art. 1a and Art. 1b, respectively stating that 'Muslims form one Islamic nation', and 'Islamic *shariʿa* is the source of all legislation', it is fair to suppose, with An-Naʿim, that the classical discriminations provided within shariʿa law would entirely apply[86] – with the courts called upon to enforce them. Like women, non-Muslims are explicitly prevented from becoming head of state.[87] In the longer draft, non-Muslims are even implicitly banned from parliamentary and governmental duties, since members of parliament and ministers are required to take an oath of obedience to the sole God and to his Prophet Muhammad.[88]

In the field of criminal law, the constitutional project explicitly imposes *ḥudūd* penalties 'for the crimes of fornication, theft, banditry, drinking alcohol, and apostasy'.[89] The imam is responsible for enforcing the *ḥudūd*,[90] with no possible amnesty or pardon.[91] It is evident how this broad range of crimes – punished with stoning, amputations and death – would encroach on fundamental

82 Art. 43.

83 Art. 28.

84 Art. 62.

85 Gouda, 72.

86 'It is very interesting that a draft constitution produced in Egypt, a country with a significant non-Muslim minority, did not contain a single word about the status and rights of non-Muslim citizens. We are not even told whether these non-Muslims are citizens. The reason for this serious omission is clear enough. The document could not specify the rule of Shariʿa on non-Muslims and yet claim to be a proposal for a constitution. It is for this reason that the document referred all relevant matters to Shariʿa, in full knowledge of the status rights of non-Muslim subjects under Shariʿa.' An-Naʿim, *Toward an Islamic Reformation*, 97.

87 Art. 47.

88 Respectively, Art. 87 and 131. Abu-Sahlieh, *Les musulmans face aux droits de l'homme*, 152.

89 Art. 71.

90 Art. 56.

91 Art. 59.

freedoms, including personal liberty and freedom of religion. As to non-*ḥudūd* crimes, the Al-Azhar constitution states that 'flogging is the principal punishment'.[92] All of them can clearly be categorized as torture or cruel, inhuman and degrading punishments.[93]

The constitutional provisions on *ḥudūd* penalties must be seen in conjunction with the draft criminal code prepared by a high committee created by Al-Azhar's sheikh ᶜAbd al-Halim Mahmud,[94] and presented to the parliament under Sadat's government, before being halted by Mubarak.[95] The draft code is divided into seven parts, one for general provisions common to Qurᵓanic penalties, and six for each specific *ḥadd* crime.

In the general part, one may find a brief description of Qurᵓanic principles on the matter of criminal law.[96] Article 3 touches upon evidential procedures, without providing details but limiting itself to stating that offenses are proven 'by the testimony of two men – as it is established – and, in case of necessity, by the testimony of one man and two women, or four women'. For each *ḥadd* crime, specific Qurᵓanic rules are mentioned, in a typical mixture of legal and religious elements, both of which the judge is supposed to master (as seen above while discussing the Al-Azhar constitution). Article 4 specifies that *taᵓzīr*, or discretionary, penalties are the residual ones, applicable in all those cases where Qurᵓanic punishments are not prescribed by shariᶜa. It is pointed out that 'it is not permitted to order the suspension of punishments defined in this Code as "Qurᵓanic", nor to commute them in other punishments, nor to reduce or quash them'.[97] This is fully consistent with the nature of *ḥudūd* as limits fixed by Allah, whose satisfaction God himself is entitled to demand as his own rights, and which men are therefore merely required to slavishly enforce with no deviation.[98]

Qurᵓanic penalties in the draft code are foreseen in the following cases: theft, banditry, fornication, slanderous accusation of fornication, alcohol consumption and apostasy. It must be noted that this is an extended interpretation of *ḥudūd*

92 Art. 79.

93 'Ḥudūd and qiṣāṣ punishments, such as amputation of hands and feet or stoning, fall reasonably within the definition of torture as defined in the Convention against Torture and other Cruel, Inhuman or Degrading Treatment or Punishment. Nevertheless, of those Islamic countries that have so far ratified the Convention, only Qatar has made reservation for any "interpretation of the provisions of the Convention that is incompatible with the precepts of Islamic law and the Islamic religion." Several Western countries have objected to this reservation. Pakistan has appended a declaration to its ratification to the effect that provisions of the Convention "shall be applied to the extent that they are not repugnant to the provisions of [...] the Sharīʿah law"'. Mahmoudi, 'International Human Rights Law', 542. See also Ingelse, *United Nations Committee Against Torture*, 215.

94 Wahba, 'Progetto di codice di pene coraniche in Egitto', 37.

95 Abu-Sahlieh, 'L'apostasia nel diritto musulmano', 43. El Fegiery, *Islamic Law and Human Rights*, 176.

96 The text is available at Wahba, 'Progetto di codice di pene coraniche in Egitto'. Own translations from Italian.

97 Art. 6.

98 See Hallaq, *Sharīʿa: Theory, Practice, Transformations*, 310.

offenses, insofar as not all Islamic schools include apostasy among the *ḥudūd*.[99] The punishments reflect the Qurʾanic ones without any attempt to soften their rigor. Lashes are to be administered for alcohol consumption[100] and for fornication (namely sexual conjunction outside of wedlock) if the culprits are not also unfaithful to a legitimate marriage.[101] The flogging shall be performed:

> with a whip of medium size, with one strap, and this without any knots. The condemned is stripped of clothes which would impede strokes from causing pain to the body. Strokes must be moderate and inflicted on the entire body, but avoiding the private and delicate parts.[102]

Theft should be punished by amputation of the right hand on the first occasion and amputation of the left foot in case of recidivism.[103] For banditry, both amputations shall be performed, unless certain conditions recur justifying mere imprisonment.[104] Article 8 specifies that 'the hand's amputation shall be conducted at the base of the wrist, where the carpal joints itself with the two bones of the forearm. The foot is amputated to half the length, so that the heel remains, thanks to which one can still walk'. The death penalty awaits married fornicators (who shall be stoned),[105] as well as apostates if they are believed to be beyond repentance, or if they do not atone within a granted delay of maximum 60 days.[106]

It is worth having a deeper look at apostasy. Article 30 defines the crime as the act of a Muslim leaving Islam, whether to adopt another religion or none.[107] Article 31 goes into more details:

Apostasy consists in the following:

1) a clear confession or an act unequivocally meaning the abandonment of Islam;
2) the denial of what is recognized as a necessary element of the religion;
3) the derision, by word or deed, against a Prophet, a Messenger, an Angel or the Holy Qurʾan.

It is thereby made clear that apostasy consists not only in the explicit abandonment of Islam to embrace another religion or none, but also in blasphemy against a sacred element of Islam and even unorthodoxy, that is, the denial of some tenets of faith recognized as dogmas. Such a definition is emblematic of the broad

99 Hallaq, *Sharīʿa: Theory, Practice, Transformations*, 311.
100 Art. 23.
101 Art. 22.
102 Art. 9.
103 Art. 13.
104 Art. 16.
105 Art. 22.
106 Art. 33.
107 Art. 30.

understanding of apostasy in Islam, affecting freedom of religion, free speech, including political speech,[108] and freedom of scientific research. I will elaborate more on this point in Chapter VI.

In conclusion, a conflict between fundamental freedoms and the Al-Azhar constitutional text (further defined by Al Azhar's draft penal code) clearly emerges. The main cause is that 'the reference to shariᶜa in the constitution obliges the authorities in general and the judiciary in particular to enforce religious proscriptions at the expense of those rights. This is because shariᶜa has not evolved in harmony with international human rights principles'.[109] As An-Naᶜim comments on this text:

> In view of the various constitutional problems of Shariᶜa, it is clear that any blanket incorporation of Shariᶜa in a constitutional document is unsatisfactory. In fact, Al-Azhar proposed constitution explicitly illustrates several of the points made. Two general points should be noted. First, the main question is not whether Shariᶜa requires a specific form of government; rather, it is whether Shariᶜa does or does not apply. *If Shariᶜa is to apply, then all its features that discriminate against women and non-Muslim citizens will necessarily follow regardless of the form of government.*[110]

Moreover, from a formal point of view, the constitution does not fulfil the conditions required to be considered 'written', as this would require a complete codification of constitutional principles, as well as their supremacy over any other legislative source.[111] The Al-Azhar constitution

> fulfills neither condition, as constitutional principles are not codified and Islamic shariᶜa is the supreme law from which the constitutional principles originate. As Article 1b states that Islamic shariᶜa is the source of all legislation, there is no real reason to have a written constitution as religious scholars are authorized to interpret shariᶜa as they see fit and as the sole source of legislation.[112]

In sum, although Al-Azhar is often presented as a bulwark of moderation,[113] and one could have reasonably expected this constitutional model to represent

108 In relation to those liberal reforms which imply the abandonment of Quranic principles in favour of equality between men and women, Muslims and non-Muslims, humane penalties, etc.
109 Gouda, 'Islamic Constitutionalism and Rule of Law', 75.
110 An-Naʿim, *Toward an Islamic Reformation*, 97. Emphasis added.
111 Gouda, 'Islamic Constitutionalism and Rule of Law', 76.
112 Gouda, 76.
113 '[T]he religious entity that supervised this constitution is considered by many as the most moderate entity in the Islamic world'. Gouda, 58. 'Even outside the Muslim world, Al-Azhar is known as the voice of moderate Islam'. Ahmed and Gouda, 'Measuring Constitutional Islamization', 38.

'a moderate version of contemporary Islamic thought',[114] it is in fact a glaring instance of militant Islamism. After all, one should not forget that Al-Azhar's members were the moral instigators of the killing of two of the most relevant Muslim reformers, namely Muhammad Taha and Farag Foda, among others.[115] Against this backdrop, it should not come as a surprise that, after the 2011 revolution, even Salafists, 'adherents of one of the most puritanical strains of Islam [...] pointed out that the main model to frame the new Constitution was the Al-Azhar Constitution'.[116]

Final Remarks

In the documents analysed above, many points of contrast with the universal principles enshrined in international human rights law clearly emerge. Contrary to those who, both in the West and in the Muslim world, consider the latter an imperialistic discourse trampling on different cultures, universalism remains the only viable theoretical and practical framework for the protection of all individuals, especially those in minorities. In fact, it would be wrong to assume that the Muslim world is a mere recipient of extraneous principles imposed from abroad: universalism is exactly what *non-Western* victims and activists have always advocated for. For instance, the 1999 Casablanca Declaration, reflecting the views of Arab human rights NGOs which met at the First International Conference of the Arab Human Rights Movement, firmly reasserted the universal human rights framework:

> The declaration included a ringing affirmation of support for international human rights law and its universality, stating that '(T)he only source of reference in this respect is international human rights law and the United Nations instruments and declarations. The Conference also emphasized the universality of human rights'.[117]

The problem with the Islamic charters of rights is that, far from providing a framework against human rights violations, they reassert all the classical shariatic discriminations, showing that the latter still permeate a certain type of Islamic discourse on individual freedoms. Mayer has rightfully observed that the references to Islamic laws and principles in these documents are '"claw-back clauses" that allow the state "almost unbounded discretion" in using domestic legal standards to restrict internationally guaranteed human rights'.[118] International law, however, 'does not accept that fundamental human rights may be restricted – much less permanently curtailed – by reference to the requirements

114 Gouda, 'Islamic Constitutionalism and Rule of Law', 58.
115 Abu-Sahlieh, *Les musulmans face aux droits de l'homme*, 110–11.V. also *infra*, Chapter VI.
116 Ahmed and Gouda, 'Measuring Constitutional Islamization', 39.
117 Mayer, 'The Respective Roles of Human Rights', 81.
118 Mayer, *Islam and Human Rights*, 69.

of any particular religion. International law provides no warrant for depriving Muslims of human rights by according primacy to Islamic criteria'.[119] According to the same author, in consonance with An-Naᶜim (*v. supra*), it is the very reference to shariᶜa that undermines the safe enjoyment of individual freedoms:

> Despite the great diversity in Islamic legal doctrines, on certain points of premodern jurisprudence there is sufficient consensus to allow reasoned calculations of how the application of Islamic principles would likely affect rights. Reliance on rules of the premodern *shariᶜa* to determine the permissible scope of modern human rights could open the way to nullification of rights in areas where the *shariᶜa* traditionally called for restrictions on rights, such as the rules relegating women and non-Muslims to subordinate status or those prohibiting conversion from Islam.[120]

In other words, shariᶜa is certainly a complex concept open to many interpretations; however, denying that serious human rights violations occur exactly *because of* shariᶜa means turning a blind eye to the reality of its implementation. In the following chapters, I will examine the influence of shariᶜa and Islamic principles on individual liberties, based on constitutions and criminal provisions actually in force.

119 Mayer, 69.
120 Mayer, 69.

III What 'shari^ca' in a constitution concretely means

The case of Egypt

Introduction

The Egyptian case is a very relevant one when it comes to the relation between shariᶜa and human rights at the constitutional level. It represents a paradigmatic instance of what Hirschl defines as 'constitutional theocracy', that is, a system characterized by:

> (1) adherence to some or all core elements of modern constitutionalism, including the formal distinction between political authority and religious authority and the existence of some form of active judicial review; (2) the presence of a single religion or religious denomination that is formally endorsed by the state, akin to a 'state religion'; (3) the constitutional enshrining of the religion and its texts, directives, and interpretations as a or the main source of legislation and judicial interpretation of laws — essentially, laws may not infringe on injunctions of the state- endorsed religion; and (4) a nexus of religious bodies and tribunals that often not only carry tremendous symbolic weight but are also granted official jurisdictional status on either a regional or a substantive basis and operate in lieu of, or in uneasy tandem with, a civil court system.[1]

The main turning point in Egypt's path toward a constitutional theocracy was an amendment to Article 2 of the constitution adopted in 1980, which crowned shariᶜa as 'the main source of legislation' – a formula which has survived any subsequent constitutional revision. In this chapter, I am going to analyse the consequences of this formulation, and expose the problems wrought by such a powerful Trojan horse in a modern system of law.[2]

Historical background

The issue of shariᶜa law within the Egyptian legal framework has been a *vexata quaestio* for a long time. The first reference to Islam in an Egyptian constitution

1 Hirschl, *Constitutional Theocracy*, 3.
2 As emblematically exemplified in the Abu Zayd case, see Chapter VI.

DOI: 10.4324/9780429259418-III

dates back to the 1923 Constitution, Article 129 of which declared that 'the religion of the state is Islam and Arabic is its official language'.[3] The same statement was repeated in all the subsequent constitutions (1930, 1956, 1964), with the relevant exception of the Constitution of the United Arab Republic, in 1958, in the aftermath of the unification between Egypt and Syria.[4] Yet, such a clause was basically a cultural and stylistic one, with no implication in terms of law.

The first actual mention of shariᵉa appeared in the 1971 Constitution, whose Article 2 made 'the principles of Islamic shariᵉa [...] *a* primary source of legislation'. This clause was subsequently amended in 1980 in the form which it has maintained thenceforth, namely describing the principles of shariᵉa as '*the* primary source of legislation'.[5]

In the amendment of 1971, shariᵉa could be considered nothing more than a cosmetic concession from Sadat to Islamists and to the religious establishment, and was intended to mark the distance from Nasser's militantly socialist Pan-Arabism. Indeed, the principles of shariᵉa were only one source among others, 'thus, it seemed, a law would not be invalid if it were inconsistent with the principles of *sharīʿa*'.[6]

However, its effects started to become visible in the new frame of mind of Egyptian judges. For instance, in 1979 the Court of Cassation stated for the first time that the concept of public policy should be informed by religious principles.[7] Likewise, in an opinion of 1976, the Supreme Court[8] held that state institutions should conform to Islamic norms because of the constitutional reform: 'According to constitutional stipulation, the legislator is committed in enacting new legislation after 1971, to go back to the *sharīʿa* and shun any regulation that appears contradictory to a given Islamic principle or source'.[9]

The uncertain meaning of the 'principles of shariᵉa' as 'the main source of the legislation'

The 1980 amendment, which elevated the principles of shariᵉa to become *the* main source of legislation, represents the apex of the Islamization process and potentially marked a decisive change in the state architecture: if the Constitution enshrines shariᵉa at the apex of the hierarchy of sources, any statute contravening Islamic law becomes possibly unconstitutional because it contravenes Article 2.

One of the major flaws of the amendment (which already emerged during the drafting works), regards the vagueness of the wording 'principles of shariᵉa'. 'Art. 2 specifies "principles of Sharīʿah," but this cannot determine which of the often

3 Abdelaal, 'Religious Constitutionalism in Egypt', 36.
4 Abdelaal, 36.
5 Abdelaal, 36.
6 Lombardi, *State Law as Islamic Law*, 125.
7 Lombardi, 129.
8 Now the Supreme Constitutional Court.
9 Lombardi, *State Law as Islamic Law*, 132.

diametrically opposed views of Muslim scholars of the principles of Sharīʿah are to be used.'[10] The committee called by the People's Assembly to assess the effect of the proposed amendment made only very broad and generic comments, stating in its official report that Article 2 'means that it is imperative to review the laws which were in effect before the Constitution of 1971 and to amend these laws in such a manner as to make them conform to the principles of Islamic law'.[11] The committee refrained, however, from clarifying whether all existing laws would automatically be null and void if not compliant with the principles of shariᵉa; and, even more significantly, it did not venture into assessing the criteria for the identification of such principles. The sole guideline for the legislature was the requirement to amend the existing statutes in conformity with 'the Qur'an, the Sunna, and the opinions of learned jurists and imams'.[12]

Thereafter, the problem of definition has always afflicted any decision concerning the compatibility of legislation with shariᵉa. This has left the courts with room and flexibility for dismissing complaints based on Article 2: for instance, in a 1982 case concerning the compatibility with shariᵉa of evidential procedures within the Egyptian criminal law,[13] the Court of Cassation rejected the claim because of 'the disagreements about the proper methods of identifying and interpreting the universally applicable principles of the *sharīʿa*'.[14] It also noted that 'Article 2 did not give any guidance to the courts as to what method they should use'.[15] In other words, this meant that only the executive and the legislature could actually interpret and apply Article 2, by investing on it a concrete meaning for its application: '[i]n practice, therefore, that choice remains in the hands of ruling elites'.[16]

Several issues arise from these assumptions, the first concerning the very notion and content of 'shariᵉa': any attempt to derive unequivocal provisions from the jurisprudential corpus of Islamic law, as if it were a digest or a modern code, would be in vain. It is impossible to deal with Islamic law in the same terms as we deal with state law – be it Western or not. The Qurᵓan and the sunna are full of contradictions and the latter is also often uncertain as to its authenticity; furthermore, no interpreter – legislator or religious scholar – may rightfully claim to be the holder of the 'true Islam'.[17] This brings about legal uncertainty to a

10 An-Na'im, 'The Legitimacy of Constitution-Making', 39.
11 Lombardi, *State Law as Islamic Law*, 133.
12 Lombardi, 134.
13 In particular, two police officers, accused of brutality and convicted under the testimony of the victim, lamented that shariᵉa requires more than a witness.
14 Lombardi, *State Law as Islamic Law*, 161.
15 Lombardi, 161.
16 An-Na'im, 'The Legitimacy of Constitution-Making Processes in the Arab World,' 39.
17 'Whatever "the principal source of legislation" might mean in terms of the influence that the shariᵉa might have on legislation [...] surely it must mean that the legislation in question cannot be repugnant to the shariᵉa. Of course, the shariᵉa is not a legal code. It is a vast juristic compendia of rules derived from sacred text, spanning centuries across various schools of thought. These rules, as developed by individual jurists, are not always consistent with one another.' Hamoudi,

large extent, and consequently the overly broad role of the judges of last resort in determining the content of the religious norms, in potential violation of the principle of legality and separation of powers. In the abovementioned 1982 verdict, the Court of Cassation highlighted this point, remarking that the judiciary has the power and the obligation to enforce only the existing law, not 'legal principles that are incompatible with a precise definition of its jurisdiction',[18] and which are per se unfathomable. In other words, 'the application of the *sharīʿa* requires that it should be determined which exactly of the manifold conflicting views of the founders of the law schools [madhhabs]... must be used as a basis for judgments'.[19]

And even if a judge were able to master the content of Islamic law, this would not exhaust the problems connected with Article 2:

> [l]ogistically, it is difficult to imagine a court examining a complex piece of legislation, trying to find a source for each and every provision in it, and then making a determination as to whether or not the legislation as a whole 'principally' derives from shariᶜa or any other source. Moreover, not only is such an approach logistically difficult, it also would almost surely result in the invalidation of large amounts of vitally important legislation.[20]

Interpretation of Article 2 by the Supreme Constitutional Court: non-retroactivity

The Supreme Constitutional Court eventually attempted to bring some order into the matter in 1985, with a casuistic and unsatisfactory decision intended to find a compromise between the Islamist and secularist factions over the shaping of the state.[21]

The decision in question concerned a case of *ribā* – a financial interest that the religious University of Al-Azhar had to disburse for having failed to pay in due time for some medical supplies. The university claimed that Article 2 required the invalidation of *ribā*, sanctioned by Article 226 of the Civil Code, on the grounds that it was incompatible with shariᶜa. The case appeared before the Supreme Constitutional Court, which found itself in a very awkward position: on the one hand, had it simply dismissed the claim, it would have deprived Article 2 of any value, while at the same time engaging in an open dispute with the prestigious Islamic university; on the other hand, had it upheld the complaint, it would have ruined the Egyptian economic system. Theoretically, a third way was

'Repugnancy in the Arab World', 431. '[L]aws stemming from [shariᶜa] are not stable due to the many differences among schools of Islamic jurisprudence as to the methodology of interpretation of *qur'an* and *sunna*'. Gouda, 'Islamic Constitutionalism and Rule of Law', 59.

18 Lombardi, *State Law as Islamic Law*, 162.

19 Lombardi, 162.

20 Hamoudi, 'Repugnancy in the Arab World', 430.

21 Decision 20/1985, in Hamoudi, 432.

possible: the Court could have tried to embrace a very loose interpretation of the prohibition of *ribā*, to contextualize it, or to employ tertiary sources of Islamic law so as to argue that such prohibition would be in present times incompatible with public interest.[22] Indeed, some modernist Islamic thinkers have tried to follow this path, although with little success.[23]

However, as perhaps this may have been too difficult to justify before the highest Islamic institution, the Court followed another path, inventing the 'doctrine of the non-retroactivity of Article 2'.[24] While acknowledging that the 1980 constitutional amendment required the legislator to harmonize legislation with the principles of shariᶜa, the Court also stated that such an obligation should be regarded as a gradual process; the legal consequence, according to the justices, was that claims under Article 2 for statutes enacted before its entry into force were not justiciable, it being up to the legislature to gradually amend the existing legislation.[25] To summarize this concept in technical terms, the Court denied direct effect to Article 2 and, rather than considering it directly applicable by the judge, regarded it as an injunction directed to the legislator.[26] Indeed, the Court remarked, this was in line with the report of the Constitutional Committee, which clearly stated that the 1980 amendment was part of a process of gradual Islamization of the Egyptian legislation, to be completed only after a due delay.[27] Furthermore, the SCC justified its choice by stressing that any statement to the contrary would bring about a total destabilization of the Egyptian juridical order, with inevitable legal chaos. On the other hand, it continued, the ***political*** responsibility to harmonize the existing legislation with the principles of shariᶜa fell upon the legislature.[28]

It is by means of this legal expedient that the Court, in later cases, could avoid amending the Criminal Code on issues like sexual relations outside marriage or

22 'For example, the SCC could have maintained that under the prevailing Sunni school of thought which historically prevailed in Egypt, the Hanafi, the prohibition as against the trading of items for delay and with gain (a common form of riba as per foundational text) did not apply to money, but only items measurable by weight or volume. [...] The SCC could have instead cited authority from a second school that permitted trades of copper coins for more coins in the future because that school, the Maliki, excluded from the forbidden trades metals that were not precious. Or the SCC could have attempted a more modernist approach in the fashion developed by the drafter of the Egyptian Civil Code, Abdul Razzaq al Sanhuri, who does justify Article 226 as being consistent with shariᶜa. Any of these approaches was, from a purely doctrinal standpoint, plausible.' Hamoudi, 433.

23 Lombardi, *State Law as Islamic Law*, 165.

24 Lombardi, 167.

25 Lombardi, 167.

26 Bernard-Maugiron and Dupret, 'Les principes de la sharia', 109.

27 See the Report of the General Committee that had drafted the 1980 amendment, cit. in Moustafa, 'The Islamist Trend in Egyptian Law', 619: '[T]he change of the whole legal organization should not be contemplated without giving the lawmakers a chance and a reasonable period of time to collect all legal materials and amalgamate them into a complete system within the framework of the Qur'an, the Sunna and the opinions of learned Muslim jurists and the ᶜUlamaᵓ'.

28 Bernard-Maugiron and Dupret, 'Les principes de la sharia', 110.

alcohol trade and consumption.[29] In the latter case, the petitioner demanded that the laws allowing alcohol and gambling be struck down under both Article 2 and Article 12 of the 1971 Constitution, whereby 'The society shall be committed to safeguarding and protecting morals, promoting the genuine Egyptian traditions and abiding by the high standards of religious education, moral and national values, historical heritage of the people, scientific facts, socialist conduct and public morality within the limits of the law. The State is committed to abiding by these principles and promoting them'.[30] It would have been interesting to see what conclusion the Court would have reached based on shariᶜa law, but it simply rejected the petition on the grounds that the plaintiff did not have a direct interest in the case.[31]

Interpretation of Article 2 by the Supreme Constitutional Court: 'absolute' vs. 'relative' principles of shariᶜa

If the non-retroactivity contrivance solved the issues opened by Article 2 for the pre-1980 cases, it also opened a Pandora's box for the future. First of all, the decision was debatable from a legal point of view: theoretically, the hierarchical criterion (*lex superior derogat inferiori*) prevails over the chronological one (*lex posterior derogat priori*), which should not apply when a statute contravenes the constitution; although the Court circumvented this problem by making Article 2 a mere principle directed to the legislator (rather than an immediately applicable rule), it was arguably conscious of venturing into shifting sands, as it felt the need to accompany the legal reasoning with pragmatic concerns about 'the separation of powers and the practical impact of an over-broad Article 2 review'.[32]

But more seriously, the Court was stating that, from then on, the legislator had no choice but to apply shariᶜa, and it was bounding itself to strike down any new statute not in compliance with Islamic law. This was probably an excess of zeal, considering that the 1980 amendment was vague enough not to imply the automatic voidance of any law in conflict with shariᶜa.[33] In so doing, the Court put itself in an awkward position, both from a socio-political and a legal point of view: on the one hand, it risked being forced to interfere with any modernization process in possible conflict with classical Islamic law; on the other hand, it had necessarily to assume the role of a qadi (the Islamic traditional judge) in assessing the content of shariᶜa and verifying the legislation's compliance with

29 Bernard-Maugiron and Dupret, 110.
30 'The Constitution of the Arab Republic of Egypt, 1971'.
31 Moustafa, 'The Islamist Trend in Egyptian Law', 621.
32 Lombardi, *State Law as Islamic Law*, 168. It must also be noted that the Court has not applied the chronological criterion to any other constitutional article, i.e. it has never shrunk from making other constitutional provisions prevail over anterior laws. Bernard-Maugiron and Dupret, 'Les principes de la sharia', 116.
33 Hamoudi, 'Repugnancy in the Arab World', 435.

its requirements. Apart from any other considerations, this is an arduous task due to the nature of Islamic law, as highlighted above, and due to the specific competences of the SCC justices, who receive a modern legal education and do not follow religious curricula.

Despite this, ever since the issuing of this ruling the Court has not backed down from interpreting shariᶜa directly, without the intermediation of ᶜulamaᵓ and Islamic scholars. 'The SCC seemed to be asserting that lay Muslims, including judges who had not received a traditional religious training, could interpret Islamic law for themselves'.[34] However, this effort has not been accompanied by a clear and consistent method of interpretation of Islamic law.

The first case in which the Court had to put itself up to the test of its own theory was judgment 7/1993, concerning a divorce law approved after 1980. In this case, the petitioner challenged the constitutionality of Law 100/1985 on wives' alimony and children's custody, claiming that it violated Article 2 insofar as it granted the woman ampler rights than those classically recognized by Islamic scholars. The Court rejected the claim, stating that only a bulk of 'authentic rules' are eternal and unchangeable, while in all other cases the ruler (*walī al-amr*) should resort to *ijtihād* in order to adapt Islamic law to the needs of the time. In this interpretation effort, the Court continued, the legislator must bear in mind shariᶜa's 'general purposes', namely religion, life, reason, honour and property,[35] with the ultimate aim of maximizing justice and general welfare.[36] This is a crucial passage, worth reading in full:

> A legislative text is not permitted to contradict Islamic legal rulings that are absolutely certain in their authenticity and meaning [...]. It is these rulings alone in which *ijtihād* is not permitted. They represent the Islamic *sharīʿa*, its universal principles and established roots which are not subject to interpretation or alteration [...]; and it is inconceivable that the interpretation of them [the universally applicable principles] (sic) will change with a change of time or place. ... [It may only contravene] (sic) the rulings that are probable whether with respect to their authenticity or their meaning or both [...]. The sphere of *ijtihād* is limited to them [the probable rulings of the *sharīʿa*]... And they [...] change with the change of times and place in order to guarantee their malleability and vigor in order to face new circumstances and in order to organize the affairs of the people, with respect to their welfare from the consideration of law ... It is necessary that *ijtihād* occurs within the frame of the universal roots of the Islamic *sharīʿa* [...] building practical rulings [...] relying on the justice of the *sharīʿa*, [and] (sic) expecting the result of them [these rulings] to be a realization of the general goals of the *sharīʿa* [...], among which are the protection of religion, life, reason, honor, and property.[37]

34 Lombardi, *State Law as Islamic Law*, 177.
35 Abdelaal, 'Religious Constitutionalism in Egypt', 39.
36 Abdelaal, 39. Lombardi, *State Law as Islamic Law*, 214.
37 SCC cit. in Lombardi, *State Law as Islamic Law*, 180.

This fundamental decision implies that statutes must be subjected to a twofold constitutional review: on the first level, they must not violate the 'authentic rules of shariᶜa'; on the second level, they must be consistent with the 'general purposes' of Islamic law.[38]

Regarding the first point, the Court has so far acknowledged the existence of absolute rules only in *obiter dicta*, which did not influence the final verdict.[39] Furthermore, it has never struck down a law on the sole basis of Article 2.[40] Yet, this does not change the fact that, when there is a contrast between an absolute rule and a fundamental right, the former must prevail, [41] thus functioning as a super-constitutional *Grundnorm*. This is not merely a theoretical hypothesis: in the above-mentioned *obiter dicta*, the Court has in fact asserted the existence of absolute principles of shariᶜa in patent conflict with constitutional rights. In particular, it has affirmed the wife's duty to obey her husband, the obligation for women to dress modestly, including the ruler's authority to dictate the standards in this domain, and the right of a man to marry up to four wives.[42]

Another aspect of the Court's approach is worth noting: in distinguishing between absolute and mutable rules, the SCC has totally neglected to address the difference between 'rules' and 'principles' of Islamic law, and to examine whether the reference to the mere *principles* (*mabādiʾ*) in Article 2 bears any legal consequences'.[43] Elaborating on this important point could have been an easy way to limit the purview of shariᶜa, perhaps to the extent of considering it nothing more than a general and inoffensive source of moral and cultural guidance. However, since the SCC has not delved into this aspect, it is not clear what the exact meaning of the word *mabādiʾ* may be. Basically, 'when the SCC interpreted Article 2, it interpreted "the principles of Islamic Sharia" to mean the authentic rules of Islamic Sharia'.[44]

Furthermore, the Court has never unequivocally defined what those 'authentic rules' are. It has contented itself with providing a superficial method of identification, based on their unambiguous character after careful examination ('absolutely certain in their authenticity and meaning'). The SCC has reserved for itself the monopoly on such examinations, without accepting external interference: it never sought the opinion of religious scholars nor cited any to support its conclusions.[45] However, as highlighted above, legislators and judges in modern states are not trained in Islamic law and are not in the best position to judge over the rules of shariᶜa. Consequently, the Court somehow (unwillingly)

38 Brown, 'Debating the Islamic Shari'a in 21st-Century Egypt', 11.

39 Bernard-Maugiron, 'La place du religieux', 52.

40 Bernard-Maugiron and Dupret, 'Les principes de la sharia', 114.

41 Bernard-Maugiron and Dupret, 117.

42 Bernard-Maugiron and Dupret, 117.

43 'Does the phrase "the principles of Islamic Sharia" signify that the law must be identical with Islamic Sharia, or does the word "principles" take the Article somewhere else?' Abdelaal, 'Religious Constitutionalism in Egypt', 39.

44 Abdelaal, 43.

45 Lombardi, *State Law as Islamic Law*, 183.

paved the way for Articles 4 and 219 of the 2012 Constitution, which respectively entrusted Al-Azhar with this task and provided guidelines for interpreting Article 2.[46]

The second point addressed by the landmark judgment of 1993 concerned the 'benefits' or 'goals' of shariᶜa, which are meant to guide the *walī al-amr* in the interpretation of Islamic law when there is no absolute clarity over a certain rule. In such cases, the SCC argued, Islamic law itself requires an elastic interpretation based on reason and directed to the best implementation of human welfare in the given circumstances. This goal can be attained by bearing in mind the 'necessaries' of Islam: while per Al-Ghazali and subsequent classical jurists they include the protection of religion, life, reason, progeny and property, the SCC omits progeny and instead mentions honour, adhering to a minority position.[47] In other words, when it comes to relative rules which are uncertain in their meaning, the Court has endowed the *walī* with the duty to exert his *ijtihād*. In so doing, he cannot simply imitate classical jurists, who could have guiltily or maliciously promoted a wrong interpretation, but has to rely on his own reason.[48] These rules are indeed characterized by continuous reinterpretation, and nobody can claim to hold the sacredness (*qudsiyya*) necessary to provide the final and correct interpretation, as if he were sinless and infallible.[49] Therefore, it is only by using the compass of reason that government, legislature and judiciary can find the right path between opposite views, with no constraint from the past, as long as the interest of society is pursued.[50] Declaring that, 'under certain circumstances, Islamic law permitted rulers to promulgate laws that were inconsistent with rulings accepted by all Sunni jurists of the past'[51] was certainly a modernist position, denying the absolute authority of orthodox scholarly consensus (*ijmāᶜ*). It follows the strand of Rashid Rida's utilitarian and modernist concept of *ijtihād*, which requires an inquiry into the rationale of shariatic norms, and even into God's objectives in prescribing such rules, in order to determine the right solution in the concrete circumstances.

A practical application of these guidelines is evidenced in a 1994 case concerning the prohibition on women wearing a niqab covering their face. The Court started from the premise that, while shariᶜa rules in women's clothing are aimed at promoting modesty, there is no clear indication in the scriptures, or consensus among scholars, as to whether modesty requires complete covering or not. Based on this, the justices subsumed the rule of modesty under the general goal of human development and welfare, and they came to the conclusion that the specific goal of a law cannot conflict with the general one of promoting women's personal development. Hence, given that the integral veil makes it difficult for

46 *V. infra*.
47 Lombardi, *State Law as Islamic Law*, 191.
48 SCC cit. in Bernard-Maugiron and Dupret, 'Les principes de la sharia', 111.
49 SCC cit. in Bernard-Maugiron and Dupret, 111.
50 Bernard-Maugiron and Dupret, 112.
51 Lombardi, *State Law as Islamic Law*, 205.

women to get an education or to work and harms their self-esteem, a law prohibiting it in the public sphere is compatible with the general goals of shariʿa.[52]

The Court made this utilitarian reasoning explicit in a 1995 case: 'The holder of power [...] has a right to act so as to push away harm [...] as much as possible and also to prevent the causing of harm. ... If two harms [...] compete, it is necessary to bear the lesser of them in order to ward off the greater'.[53]

The Court's interpretative method, based on the twofold constitutional review of the absolute rules and the general goals of shariʿa – the latter hierarchically subordinated to the former, was not without inconsistencies and ambiguities. These clearly emerge from a case concerning the compliance with Article 2 of a 1985 statute allowing a first wife to seek divorce should her husband contract a second marriage without her consent. Here the SCC could not avoid acknowledging the existence of an absolutely certain rule of shariʿa, which allows and even recommends polygamy under certain circumstances; nevertheless, it did not refrain from linking even this certain rule to the general interest of all wives and society at large, thereby limiting men's privilege. It did not come to this conclusion via religious sources, but on the basis of an independent reasoning – detached from a rigorous exegesis – whereby 'polygamy, while not in itself harmful, inevitably gives rise to ancillary harms',[54] that is, material and psychological suffering between the spouses, which the husband cannot avoid perpetrating. Therefore, as the law in question did not violate the clear shariatic rule of polygamy and was at the same time intended to prevent harm, it was judged as perfectly compatible with shariʿa.[55]

A critique of the SCC's interpretation of Article 2

The method of interpretation of Article 2 employed by the Court is problematic from various points of view. Starting with a religious perspective, it is a hybrid one, mixing elements of 'neo-*ijtihād*' with others of 'neo-*taqlīd*'. 'Neo-*ijtihād*' denotes a utilitarian form of *ijtihād* that, following the path of Rashid Rida, permits a reinterpretation and a new exegesis of the classical texts, independently from the opinion of classical jurists, with the ultimate aim of maximizing human welfare. 'Neo-*taqlīd*', conversely, is the imitation of the scholarly consensus on certain rules considered frozen and immutable and hence not reinterpretable 'with a change of time or place'.[56] Beyond this external framework, however, there is no systematic method of analysis: for example, the Court does not concern itself with explaining which classical jurists it looks at, how it defines some rules as 'absolutely certain', how it solves the contradictions inside the Qurʾan, or how it assesses the authenticity of hadiths. The latter are hardly mentioned

52 Lombardi, 197.
53 Lombardi, 197.
54 Lombardi, 234.
55 Lombardi, 234. See also Bernard-Maugiron and Dupret, 'Les principes de la sharia', 112.
56 Lombardi, *State Law as Islamic Law*, 186.

in the SCC rulings, as if to suggest that only the Qurᵓan must be taken into consideration in order to ascertain the 'authentic' and 'eternal' rules of shariᶜa. While in case 7/1993 the Court even asserted explicitly that it looked exclusively at the Qurᵓan,[57] there are still a few cases where it takes hadiths into account, but it provides no explanation for doing so or for deeming them authentic.[58] Even if one considered them a subsidiary source to be used only ***ad adiuvandum*** to confirm the Qurᵓanic injunctions, a method of exegesis of the Book itself ought to be provided – which the Court has failed to do.[59]

From a more earthly perspective, the general parameter adopted by the Court is a typically utilitarian one intended to maximize welfare and minimize harm for society. In other words, 'the SCC says the government may not regulate in a way that is likely to decrease the aggregate enjoyment of justice and human welfare in society'.[60] Having said that, the problem is to determine what 'human welfare' consists of, how to interpret the five necessaries of shariᶜa, and how to detect them among the goals of each statute.

The general impression deriving from the Court's judgments on this matter is that the Court identifies the result it wants to attain and then justifies it retrospectively by resorting to shariᶜa. For instance, in the aforementioned niqab case, the Court, being unable to find some guidelines in classical Islamic law, ended up upholding the statute on the grounds that it was generically compatible with the goal of promoting (or, at least, of not harming) women's honour. The problem with concepts like 'welfare', 'honour', etc., is that they are so vague, relative and mutable that the final outcome will depend solely on the justices' will and on the result they want to pursue. As has been correctly noted,

> [p]eople can naturally disagree about how to define welfare. To evaluate 'welfare', the Court assumes that a person's welfare is to be equated with that person's enjoyment of the 'general goals' of the *sharīʿa*. The SCC, however, does not discuss in this case how it identified these goals except to say that they include the preservation of religion (*dīn*), self (*nafs*), reason (*ʿaql*), honor (*ʿirḍ*), and property (*māl*). It does not say how it arrived at these goals. Nor does it say what other general goals there might be. Finally, it does not indicate what method the Court would use to try to determine whether such goals are, in the aggregate, being promoted.[61]

Overall, it has been rightly argued that the Court resorts to an 'impressionistic', or 'pastiche',[62] method of interpretation, which is open to multiple criticisms.

57 'In searching for absolutely certain legal rulings, it says, it was looking for rulings "rooted in principles laid down in Qur'ànic *nuṣūṣ*"'. Lombardi, 213.
58 Lombardi, 185.
59 Lombardi, 216.
60 Lombardi, 196.
61 Lombardi, 217.
62 Lombardi, 247.

From the perspective of Islamic law, it arbitrarily cherry picks some rules and principles from different sources, without being able to justify its options. After all, how could justices trained in modern law justify their choices in front of traditional scholars who have devoted their whole life to the exegesis of the Scriptures?

From the perspective of constitutional law, as well, this method raises doubts on several grounds. First, the Court has failed to meaningfully justify the odd theory of 'non-retroactivity'. Secondly, as concerns the principle of legality, it has built an unpredictable system, open to any possible interpretation (and distortion), which provides neither citizens nor state institutions with clear parameters to regulate their conduct in compliance with the Constitution. Last but not least, from the viewpoint of human rights, the Court has built a perilous structure, which pays (at least at the theoretical level) a high tribute to shariᶜa and anti-modernist Islamic theories by unequivocally asserting the eternal and unchangeable superiority of rules established in the 8th century in the Arabian desert for a Bedouin society, but hardly compatible with a 21st-century state.

The theory of 'immutable rules' of shariᶜa, in particular, could turn out to be very dangerous in relation to the *ḥudūd* penalties, which are unequivocally mentioned in the Qurᵓan: '[t]hus, a judge should follow them as prescribed in the Qur'an without relying on his Ijtihād'.[63] Consequently, if the legislature is bound not merely by the 'principles' of shariᶜa, intended as cultural and moral values, but by its actual rules, it should enforce the *ḥudūd* offenses, banning alcohol, lashing fornicators and mutilating thieves. It could try to limit their purview but could never formally expunge them from the penal code. This risk became concrete with the 2012 Constitution, which allowed criminal punishment to be inflicted directly on the basis of the Constitution, even in the absence of a specific secondary law (*v. infra*). Criminal law is only one of the fields where fundamental rights are at stake: the very concept of 'civil citizenship' is at odds with a religious system that divides citizens into different categories according to their status as men or women, Muslims or non-Muslims, free or slaves. These concerns became even more solid against the backdrop of Article 219 of the 2012 Constitution – which further restricted the possibility of interpreting Article 2 in a flexible way – and of Article 4 – which placed Al-Azhar side by side with the Constitutional Court in assessing the conformity of (unspecified) parts of the legal order with shariᶜa law.

This range of issues shows that even vague references to shariᶜa are sufficient to pave the way for an Islamic state – which explains why even the Muslim Brotherhood has shifted its focus from the application of shariᶜa to a more general 'Islamic reference' (*marjiᶜiyya islāmiyya*).[64] I will return to this point later.

To summarize, one can say that the SCC's exegesis of Article 2 has proved to be arbitrary and mainly dependent on the juridical, social, or even political result

63 Abdelaal, 'Religious Constitutionalism in Egypt', 42.
64 Brown, 'Debating the Islamic Shari'a in 21st-Century Egypt', 14.

the judge wants to achieve, more than on a rigorous legal evaluation. Furthermore, the jurisprudence devised by the Court is 'more conservative that what might appear':[65] while the SCC has occasionally promoted a reformist interpretation of individual cases, it has not challenged the conservative superstructure of a model based on Hanafi hermeneutical theories,[66] which is forged upon the traditional conceptions of *taqlīd* and *ijtihād* and is therefore open to modernization only in specific cases and in the classical light of the necessaries of Islam.[67] Random reformist verdicts, in this sense, do not change the core defects of such a system, which remains ready to be exploited by a wide range of political interests, according to the forces that will be able to extend their influence on the judiciary.

Final considerations and open challenges

Article 2, in the form assumed after the amendment of 1980, has survived all political, legal and institutional turmoil witnessed by Egypt ever since, and has been incorporated into the current constitutional text without meaningful objections. This raises a relevant question: is shariᵉa, as the main source of legislation, superior to the constitution itself? As I have argued in Chapter I, the idea of a human-made source prevailing over the law of God is inconceivable in Islam; if this supremacy is enshrined in the constitution, one could argue that the very constitution makes shariᵉa a *Grundnorm* superior to any other legislative source – including the constitution itself.

> Rather than the constitution sanctioning Islam as an official religion and observance of the Islamic Sharī'ah in specific areas, some juristic interpretations of this provision imply that the Sharī'ah supersedes the positive legal order — including, potentially and by implication, the constitution. If the Sharī'ah is a principal source — or even the principal source — of legislation, then it becomes possible to argue that it forms the fundamental legal framework.[68]

However, it is the same SCC which has stated that all constitutional provisions must be read as a harmonic whole: this implies that no norm should prevail over the others, 'hence, Art. 2 shall not be used to undermine the rest of text'.[69]

65 Parolin, '(Re)Arrangement of State/Islam', 5. Moataz El Fegiery, Egyptian scholar and human rights activist, remarked that the Court did well, but not enough: it had to seek compromises to satisfy Islamists, and this brought about stagnation on certain issues, especially regarding gender equality. Interviewed by the author, Cairo, June 2013.

66 Parolin, 5.

67 'In sum, the SCC interprets the "principles of Islamic law" as a set of firm and solid traditional obligations (what Hanafis would call *furūḍ*) that allow no re-engagement with the sources, and five generic objectives that need to be pursued when re-engaging with the sources in all other cases'. Parolin, 6.

68 Sherif, 'The Relationship between the Constitution and the Sharī'ah in Egypt', 127.

69 Sherif, 130.

Article 2 of the Egyptian Constitution, in other words, represents a litmus test of the contradictions inherent in 'Islamic constitutionalism': 'Does the constitutional norm sit at the very top of the pyramid of norms, or does it draw its validity and authority from a supra-constitutional religious norm?'[70] Given the absolutism claimed by both the religious and the constitutional principles, they are mutually exclusive and irreconcilable: either God is the supreme legislator, and therefore Article 2 is merely pleonastic and even slightly 'heretical' (for asserting the 'principles' and not the 'rules' of Islamic shariᵉa, and for allowing the presence of different sources); or the man-made Constitution is the apex of the legal architecture, which means that the status conferred on shariᵉa is *octroyé* by the Constitution itself, and all the other provisions and sources of law are on the same level. *Tertium non datur.*

This aporia has no legal or even logical solution, and only ideological and political considerations will tip the scales towards one side or the other. As the foregoing analysis will show, this debate does not merely pertain to the realm of theory, but has very concrete reverberations on the constitutionality of laws that seek to improve individual rights but conflict with clear norms of shariᵉa.

70 Horchani, 'Islam and the Constitutional State', 204.

IV Islamic law in post-Arab Spring Egyptian Constitutions

Introduction

In the previous chapter, I have shown that Article 2, as amended in 1980, has proven to be a significant source of troubles for the harmony of the Egyptian legal system, serving as a powerful Trojan horse for undefined religious norms in a modern constitutional order.

The purview of Islamic law rose to yet another level in the Constitution of 2012, adopted by an Islamist-dominated assembly under the government of the Muslim Brotherhood. The analysis of such a text, subsequently repealed, is relevant to my hypothesis because it represents a case where shariʿa was not maliciously exploited by a dictatorial government to legitimize its power, but was instead intentionally pursued at the culmination of a formally, albeit not substantially,[1] democratic process. The analysis of the constitution thereby adopted will show how the homage paid to Islamic principles and rules has the potential to dramatically affect human rights and fundamental freedoms.

I will examine the Constitution of 2012 in parallel with that of 2014, approved by a more secular assembly (although with a substantial Salafist component) after the ousting of President Morsi. The 2014 Constitution offers, at least from a purely formal point of view, significant improvements as far as individual rights are concerned.

Article 2, the untouchable

First of all, it is interesting to note that nobody, even in the non-Islamist camp, dared to push for a reform of Article 2, whether in the 2012 or in the 2014

1 With the Constitutional Decree of 22 November 2012, President Morsi shielded the Constituent Assembly – whose boycotting secular members he had replaced with Islamists – from the scrutiny of the Constitutional Court, while attributing unchecked powers to himself. A few days later, pro-government protesters even prevented the justices of the Constitutional Court from accessing the premises on the day the Court was supposed to rule on the legitimacy of the Constituent Assembly. See Virgili, 'The "Arab Spring" and the EU's "Democracy Promotion" in Egypt: A Missed Appointment?', 53. The constitutional decree 'was clearly unconstitutional', and in violation of the rule of law: 'Without the rule of law, democracy has little value. Democratic elections did not give the president a mandate to elevate his own powers even to hasten the passage of the constitution'. Pillay, 'The Rule of Law', 151.

DOI: 10.4324/9780429259418-IV

constitutional assemblies. Abu-Odeh reports that non-Islamists acquiesced to the Islamist rhetoric to the point that, in the constitutional debates, '[m]any followed the practice of prefacing their positions with the perfunctory "Nobody is opposed to Art 2" in their exchanges with the Islamists'.[2] Non-Islamists also tried to avoid being declared as 'secularists' by any means, not least because of the hideous practice of *takfir*, that is, the accusation of heresy and apostasy that may lead to judicial proceedings and even endanger one's life.[3] As I will show later on, the secular retreat over Article 2 mirrors, *mutatis mutandis*, what happened in Tunisia (a more secularized country), where liberal forces in the constitutional assembly immediately gave up on the battle for an explicitly secular system on the Turkish model.

The expansion of Article 2

In the 2012 Egyptian Constitution, the global purview of Islamic law overall largely increased, in more or less subtle ways depending on the articles.

First of all, the scope of Article 2 was broadened by two specific provisions, namely Article 219 and Article 4. The former dealt with the sources and methodology used to extract workable norms from the abstract corpus of divine commandments. The latter established an authentic interpreter of shariᶜa to be consulted by the parliament in the law-making process.

How should 'principles of shariᶜa' be interpreted?

Article 219 noticeably amplified the purview of shariᶜa in the constitution. For this reason, it was subjected to harsh criticism, and eventually abolished in the 2014 constitution.[4] The aim of this norm was to limit the scope for heterodox interpretations of Article 2 by circumscribing its content and definition. It stated the following:

> The principles of Islamic Sharia include general evidence [*adillatuha al-kulliyya*], foundational rules, rules of jurisprudence, [*qawāᶜiduha al-uṣūliyya wa-l-fiqhiyya*] and credible sources accepted in Sunni doctrines [*madhāhib ahl al-sunna*] and by the larger community [*al-jamāᶜa*].[5]

It was an 'explanatory note'[6] of Article 2 through which the 'principles' of shariᶜa could no longer be interpreted as generic moral guidance,[7] nor in light

2 Abu-Odeh, 'Egypt's New Constitution', 162.
3 Abu-Odeh, 162.
4 Sabry, '22 Key Points in Egypt's New Draft Constitution'.
5 Unless stated otherwise, the translation used here is taken from 'Egypt's Constitution of 2012'.
6 Parolin, '(Re)Arrangement of State/Islam', 5.
7 Although the Supreme Constitutional Court had never interpreted them in this way, as explained above.

of modern, reformist theories of Islamic law; conversely, these principles were now to be interpreted in the light of 'all the rules of jurisprudence and credible sources that are accepted in Sunni doctrines'.[8] This meant that those 'principles' assumed a more solid form shaped by the classical Islamic jurisprudence, which was thus officially incorporated in the constitution and made directly applicable.

The first element, *adillatuha al-kulliyya*, literally means 'the whole of its proofs', or 'its holistic evidence'.[9] It refers to the general rules of deduction, the legal sources, and, by metonymy, the foundational texts of Islam. In sum, *adillatuha al-kulliyya* constitute the backbone of the *uṣūl al-fiqh*, (the methodological principles of the Islamic jurisprudence) and refer to the classical sources of law: Qurʾan, sunna, *ijmāᶜ*, *qiyās*, and tertiary sources, such as the Hanafi juristic preference (*istiḥsān*) and the Maliki public interest (*istiṣlāḥ*).[10]

The second element, *qawāᶜiduha al-uṣūliyya wa-l-fiqhiyya*, points to the 'fundamental rules', the sources of Islamic jurisprudence both within the general theory of law (*uṣūl al-fiqh*) and substantive law (*furūᶜ al-fiqh*); in other words, shariᶜa as interpreted and systematized by Islamic scholars.[11] It must be noted that traditional *fiqh* may deal with any single aspect of individual life, regulating moral behaviour, religious rituals, daily life, or even trifling details such as the length of beards.

The third element listed in Article 219 was the 'sources acknowledged by the schools of the people of Al-Sunna' (*maṣādiruhā al-muᶜtabara fi madhāhib ahl al-sunna*), that is, basically, the same as *adillatuha al-kulliyya*,[12] but with the specification of the '*Sunni schools*': this implied that different legal doctrines, such as the Shiᶜi ones or those considered 'heretical' for being outside the four orthodox Schools (like the Muᶜtazila, for instance) should not be taken into consideration.

As to the final part, *al-jamāᶜa*, 'larger community' is only one of the possible interpretations, because 'larger' is not in the text, and the whole expression '*maṣādiruhā al-muᶜtabara fi madhāhib ahl al-sunna wa-al-jamāᶜa*' could be regarded as a reference to the orthodox scholars of Islam.[13]

Article 219 represented the reversal of a proposal circulating since 2011, consisting in leaving Article 2 unchanged while anchoring its interpretation to the constant jurisprudence of the SCC, so as to avoid radical changes should Islamists get to dominate the court. What the majority-Islamist Constituent Assembly ended up doing was the exact opposite, namely depriving the SCC of the monopoly of interpretation of Article 2 in a 'desire to depart from the existing jurisprudence'[14] that they considered too innovative. As has been said,

8 Al-Ali, 'The New Egyptian Constitution'.
9 Yaacoub, '219: A Detailed Cultural Translation'.
10 Parolin, '(Re)Arrangement of State/Islam', 7.
11 Parolin, 7.
12 Parolin, 8.
13 Yaacoub, '219: A Detailed Cultural Translation'. There is indeed an old debate in Islam on who is called to form the *ijmāᶜ*: see Kamali, *Principles of Islamic Jurisprudence*, chap. 8.
14 Parolin, '(Re)Arrangement of State/Islam', 6.

'[e]ssentially this article ensures two things; it prevents any other Islamic denominations from being used as the basis for legislation, and paves the path for literal interpretations of *Sharia* law, as well as archaic forms of the law and application of punishments'.[15]

It is not difficult to see that the main target of Islamists was the SCC and its eclectic interpretation of shariʿa. According to Moataz El Fegiery, the rigidly 'traditionalist' formulation of Article 219 was a way to restrict innovations, making it harder for the SCC to keep adopting a flexible and innovative approach.[16] Indeed, Article 219 left no scope for the technique of re-engagement with the sources (neo-*ijtihād*) constantly employed until then by the SCC; conversely, '[m]ost of Article 219's technical terms come from this traditional Sunni methodology, as taught by the madhhabs',[17] namely the orthodox schools of Islam. In other words, Article 219 imposed the 'neo-traditional', or 'neo-*taqlīd*', method of interpretation discussed in the previous chapter as the norm, forcing state institutions to interpret Islamic law 'according to the methods that had traditionally been used by pre-modern jurists associated with the four Sunni "*madhhabs*"',[18] including a strict imitation of traditional jurisprudence and a more respectful approach to hadiths.[19] Some expressed a preoccupation with the authority and the decisive role that present-day clerics (such as the renowned and controversial al-Qaradawi) would also thus acquire.[20] Article 219 posed a problem not only to the SCC, but potentially even to Al-Azhar, which had on some occasions referred to minoritarian jurists, including Shiʿi ones.[21] Furthermore, Article 219 widened the Pandora's box already opened by Article 2, by including additional 'extra constitutional principles that will operate constitutionally in the same manner as the formal provisions of the constitutions'.[22]

The role of Al-Azhar

The other provision of the 2012 Constitution aimed at expanding the scope of religion was Article 4. It read: 'Al-Azhar's Council of Senior Scholars is to be consulted in matters relating to Islamic Sharia.'

The first aim of this provision was perhaps to concentrate the monopoly of interpretation of Islamic law into one body, so as to avoid what has been defined as the 'fatwa shopping'[23] that traditionally occurred in the marketplace of legal religious opinions released by Al-Azhar, the Dar al-Ifta (office of the state mufti, appointed by the President), and the judiciary. However, this choice was prob-

15 Yaacoub, '219: A Detailed Cultural Translation'.
16 Moataz El Fegiery, interview. See also Darrag, Interview with Dr. Amr Darrag.
17 Lombardi and Brown, 'Islam in Egypt's New Constitution'.
18 Lombardi and Brown.
19 Brown and Lombardi, 'Contesting Islamic Constitutionalism', 256.
20 Gasparrini, 'Il Medio Oriente visto dal Cairo'.
21 Abu-Odeh, 'Egypt's New Constitution', 173.
22 Abu-Odeh, 169.
23 Brown, 'Debating the Islamic Shari'a in 21st-Century Egypt', 14.

lematic in that it further undermined the role of the Constitutional Court as the final interpreter of Article 2 and entrusted a body that was neither elected nor otherwise accountable with *de facto* legislative power.[24]

It must be said that this was not the first occasion on which Al-Azhar was empowered with some kind of jurisdiction on state issues: in 1993, for instance, the State Council (*Majlis al-Dawla*) endowed it with the monopoly on censorship for audio and audiovisual products, even declaring its opinion to be binding on the Ministry of Culture.[25] Yet, Article 4 went a step further, expanding the purview of Al-Azhar's control in an unforeseeable way and enshrining it in the constitution, through a broad and vague provision.

Indeed, several points of Article 4 remained unclear. In procedural terms, a doubtful aspect was the mandatory or optional nature of the consultation. While for some it was clearly mandatory, [26] not everyone agreed on this point: for instance, a representative of the Muslim Brotherhood's Freedom and Justice Party (FJP), member of the Constituent Assembly, stated the contrary;[27] the wording itself was ambiguous: the verb '*yuʾkhadhu*', referring to Al-Azhar's opinion, simply means 'is taken', thus allowing both conjectures. On a further level, it was not clear whether the legislature, after consulting Al-Azhar, was bound by its conclusion, and whether a second consultation would have to happen if parliament complied and presented an amended bill. From a substantive point of view, Article 4 did not specify what was to be regarded as 'matters pertaining to Islamic law' to be submitted to Al-Azhar: as remarked on above, potentially everything – from criminal law to clothing style – pertains to a loose interpretation of 'Islamic law', in that it may be found in hadiths. In order to define this matter, a secondary procedural rule would have been necessary, adding further sources of tension in the balance of power.[28]

Interestingly, during the short life of Article 4, these doubts moved from the theoretical realm to the practical one. In January 2013, the Ministry of Finance tabled in the parliament a bill on Islamic financial instruments. The parliament consulted Al-Azhar, which made a number of remarks, linked both to the procedure of the consultation – insufficiently deferent to the institution[29] – and to the content of the law.[30] After amending the bill, the majority of deputies, linked

24 An-Na'im, 'The Legitimacy of Constitution-Making', 39.

25 Moustafa, 'The Islamist Trend in Egyptian Law', 625.

26 Al-Ali, 'The New Egyptian Constitution'.

27 'Even if somebody has to consult al-Azhar, it doesn't mean its opinion has to be taken into account. But actually its interpretation, and this was adopted by the Shūra Council in the latest law on Islamic bonds; it says we can consult with al-Azhar, but we don't have to. This is up to the legislators and the Constitutional Court to consult with Azhar *if they want to*. And things are made clear. I mean, the Azhar can step in and give its opinion, but this opinion is *by no means obligatory*. Because if it was, ours would be a theocratic state and nobody wanted that, not in the assembly, not in the larger society.' Darrag, Interview with Dr. Amr Darrag [emphasis added].

28 Abu-Odeh, 'Egypt's New Constitution', 170.

29 Brown and Lombardi, 'Contesting Islamic Constitutionalism', 258.

30 Bernard-Maugiron, 'La Constitution égyptienne de 2014 est-elle révolutionnaire?', 16.

to the Muslim Brotherhood, estimated that the parliament was not under the obligation to submit it again to Al-Azhar for a final approval. The chamber even issued a judgment of conformity of the final text to shariʿa law, thereby triggering a potential theological struggle with the Islamic university. Given the level of criticism this decision raised, the president decided to send the text back to Al-Azhar, and the law was finally adopted only upon its approval.[31]

Another controversial point concerned the addressees of Article 4: was it directed only to the parliament during the making of legislation, or also to the government as well as to the courts implementing the law?[32] It is evident how a broad interpretation would have seriously undermined the non-theocratic nature of the state. While the constitutional section regarding the independence of the judiciary seemed to shield it against a legal requirement,[33] it did not dispel the psychological pressure for a judge to consult and obey the noble Al-Azhar. In fact, in such a scenario, even the SCC, while still maintaining the power of final decision *ex art.* 175,[34] would have been bound to request Al-Azhar's review, so that 'the legitimacy of its determinations would broadly depend on its ability to outshine the opinion of the most prestigious religious institution in the Sunni world'.[35]

Having said that for the sake of theory, we must consider that in one case decided shortly before the suspension of the 2012 constitution, the SCC considered itself bound neither by Article 4 nor by Article 219: indeed, in addressing an Article-2-based challenge to a provision regarding grandparental visitation rights, the court neither asked for Al-Azhar's opinion, nor engaged with hadiths and orthodox jurisprudence, but merely referred to its previous case law on the issue.[36] However, as Bernard-Maugiron has pointed out, this may easily be explained by the fact that the SCC's composition had not changed after the adoption of the new constitution; a different attitude could be expected should justices closer to Islamist positions be appointed.[37]

The 2012 Constitution had too short a life to permit a comprehensive assessment of the institutional conflicts Articles 4 and 219 could raise. Although

31 Bernard-Maugiron, 16.

32 Al-Ali for instance seems to take for granted that 'all bodies', included the Courts, must consult Al-Azhar, leaving it in doubt only the purview and the final weight of such a consultation. Al-Ali, 'The New Egyptian Constitution'.

33 *Inter alia*, Art. 168: 'The judiciary is independent. It is vested in the courts of justice, which issue their judgments in accordance with the law. Its powers are defined by law. Interference in judicial affairs or in proceedings is a crime to which no statute of limitations may be applied.'

34 'The Supreme Constitutional Court is an independent judicial body. It is based in Cairo. It is exclusively competent to decide on the constitutionality of laws and regulations. The law defines the Court's other competencies and regulates the procedures that are to be followed before the Court'.

35 Parolin, '(Re)Arrangement of State/Islam', 9.

36 Brown and Lombardi, 'Contesting Islamic Constitutionalism', 258. Bernard-Maugiron, 'La place du religieux', 53.

37 Bernard-Maugiron, 'La place du religieux', 54.

some saw the aspect of having multiple interpreters of shariᶜa in a positive light, as it would enable pluralistic understanding of Islamic law,[38] the few cases that emerged in 2013 showed that the system outlined in the constitution of 2012 risked either depriving the parliament and the SCC of authority over the Egyptian legal system in far-reaching ways, or of creating problematic institutional paralyses.

No equivalent provision is present in the 2014 constitution currently in force.

Nulla poena sine lege ... or maybe not?

Another item of the 2012 Constitution that represented a dangerous Trojan horse of shariᶜa, despite not even mentioning Islam, was Article 76. Addressing the principle of legality (*nullum crimen et nulla poena sine praevia lege poenali*), Article 76 could potentially open the gates of *ḥudūd* penalties. It read as follows:

> Penalty is personalized. There can be no crime or penalty except by virtue of the Constitution *or* the law [*dustūrī aw qānūnī*]. No penalty can be inflicted except by virtue of a court decision. Penalties are inflicted only for acts committed after the promulgation of the relevant law. [emphasis added]

In fact, criminal laws are not laid down in constitutions, but in ordinary statutes. The phrase 'Constitution *or* law' [*dustūrī aw qānūnī*] breached the principle of legality, in that it theoretically enabled the judge to establish a punishment not statutorily provided for by merely referring to the Constitution itself: this could have paved the way for the imposition of *ḥudūd* penalties in combination with Article 2 and Article 219.[39]

The Constitution of 2014 reverted to the classical guarantee of statutory reserve in criminal law. Article 95 currently reads as follows:

> Penalties are personal. Crimes and penalties may only be based on the law, and penalties may only be inflicted by a judicial ruling. Penalties may only be inflicted for acts committed subsequent to the date on which the law enters into effect.[40]

Civil, military or theocratic state?

A pivotal issue that is of paramount importance in the ideological battleground between liberals and Islamists is the reference to the 'civil' nature of the state (*dawla madaniyya*). This concept, which is nebulous per se, originates in the definition

38 Anello, '"Plural Sharīʿah"', 86.

39 Bernard-Maugiron, 'La Constitution égyptienne de 2014 est-elle révolutionnaire?', 17. Salem, 'Why the Salafis Agreed to the Constitution'. Parolin, '(Re)Arrangement of State/Islam', 5.

40 Unless stated otherwise, I use the following translation: 'Egypt's Constitution of 2014'.

that 19th-century Egyptian students in Europe gave of Western states.[41] Secularists attach great importance to this issue, as they read 'civil' in antithesis to 'theocratic'. On their part, Islamists accommodate this concept either by adopting a narrow meaning of 'theocratic', or by reading it in opposition to the 'military' government, with no religious implication. This ambiguity explains why Salafists despise the term as a dangerous tool of a secularist agenda, but the Muslim Brotherhood developed an accommodating position.[42] I am going to delve into the matter in further detail in my examination of the Tunisian Constitution – where ***dawla madaniyya*** became a battlefield of words and interpretations.

The 2012 Constitution did not make any reference to this concept. As for the 2014 Charter, although different drafts mentioned the civil character of the state, the conjoint pressure of religious forces (Al-Azhar, Salafists, Copts) led to the removal of the specific article, which was replaced by a reference to a 'civil government' in the preamble:[43] 'We are now drafting a Constitution that completes building a modern democratic state with a civil government'.

It is not easy to ascertain whether this concept is going to have any practical effect whatsoever. At any rate, it must be mentioned that the preamble has legal force, as per Article 227.

Contempt for the sacred

The 2012 Constitution contained, for the first time in the Egyptian constitutional history, an explicit blasphemy law in Article 44: 'Insult or abuse of all religious messengers and prophets shall be prohibited'. One should read this provision against the backdrop of multiple MB political platforms (including the 2011 one of the Freedom and Justice Party) that since the 1980s have invoked this kind of prohibition to enforce the 'Islamic values and morals' and fight 'Westernization'.[44] The article also enjoyed support by Al-Azhar.[45]

Then-President Morsi even defended the prohibition of blasphemy in front of the UN General Assembly, calling it a measure against hate speech and extremism and thus disregarding the fundamental difference between the protection of ***individuals***, targeted because of their faith, and the protection of ***dogmas***.[46] In fact, Article 44 was in conflict with the guarantee of free speech, as international bodies have repeatedly noted in relation to blasphemy laws.[47] In particular, the vague wording could easily be exploited to severely restrict freedom of expression,

41 El-Daghili, 'Al-Dawlah al-Madanīyah', 190.

42 El-Daghili, 191.

43 Bernard-Maugiron, 'La Constitution égyptienne de 2014 est-elle révolutionnaire?', 17.

44 El Fegiery, *Islamic Law and Human Rights*, 106.

45 El Fegiery, 127.

46 El Fegiery, 128.

47 See for instance the remarks of the Human Rights Committee, the control body of the International Covenant on Civil and Political Rights to which Egypt is bound: '[p]rohibitions of displays of lack of respect for a religion or other belief system, including blasphemy laws, are incompatible with the Covenant, except in the specific circumstances envisaged in article 20,

given the absence of any specification on the meaning of 'insult', 'messengers' and 'prophets'. Freedom of religion and worship were jeopardized too, insofar as denying the quality of 'prophet' to someone recognized as such in Islam could easily be regarded as 'defamation'.[48] This risk was increased by the fact that the three 'religions of the Book' enjoyed a privileged status, being the only ones explicitly mentioned in the Constitution, as explained in the next section.

The 2014 text does not contain a specific provision on blasphemy, which represents a noteworthy formal improvement. It remains to be seen what concrete effects this will have on legal practice, considering that persecution against blasphemers and atheists has been going on for decades without an explicit constitutional provision and in the presence of constitutional guarantees of free speech. I will deal with this matter in Chapter VI.

Status of non-Muslim minorities

In the 2012 Constitution, different articles established in generic terms the principle of equality between citizens in rights and duties.[49] The 2014 Constitution expands on this matter, in particular by specifying the grounds for illegitimate discrimination. Article 53 states:

> Citizens are equal before the law, possess equal rights and public duties, and may not be discriminated against on the basis of religion, belief, sex, origin, race, color, language, disability, social class, political or geographical affiliation, or for any other reason.
>
> Discrimination and incitement to hate are crimes punishable by law.
>
> The state shall take all necessary measures to eliminate all forms of discrimination, and the law shall regulate the establishment of an independent commission for this purpose.

However, both the 2012 and the 2014 Constitutions give a privileged status to the 'Heavenly religions' of Christianity and Judaism – the only ones tolerated in Islam. According to Article 3 of the 2012 constitution, '[t]he principles of Christian and Jewish laws are the main source of legislation for followers of

---

paragraph 2, of the Covenant', U.N. Human Rights Committee, 'General Comment 34', para. 48. See also Bernard-Maugiron, Which Egypt in the New Constitution.

48 Al-Ali, 'The New Egyptian Constitution'.

49 Article 6: 'The political system is based on the principles of democracy and consultation, citizenship (under which all citizens are equal in rights and public duties), political and multi-party pluralism, the peaceful transfer of power, the separation and balance of powers, the rule of law, and respect for human rights and freedoms. All of the foregoing is as provided in the Constitution. It is prohibited to form a political party that discriminates between citizens, whether on the basis of gender, origin or religion'. Article 9: 'The state commits to ensuring safety, security and equal opportunity for all citizens without discrimination'. Article 33: 'All citizens are equal before the law. They have equal public rights and duties. There can be no discrimination between them in that regard'.

Christianity and Judaism in matters pertaining to personal status, religious affairs and nomination of spiritual leaders'.

During the drafting of the subsequent text, several members of the constituent committee had proposed to extend the recognition of minority rights to all non-Muslims, but in the face of fierce opposition from Salafists and Al-Azhar, who dreaded a disruption of social order, they had to drop the idea.[50] Hence, Article 3 has been reproduced word by word.

This limited recognition also impacts on freedom of worship: in fact, Article 64, after declaring freedom of belief 'absolute', specifies: '[t]he freedom of practicing religious rituals and establishing places of worship *for the followers of revealed religions* is a right organized by law [emphasis added]'.

This provision has likewise been copied from the 2012 Constitution, and it is linked to the idea that creeds other than the 'religions of the Book' represent a threat to public order.[51]

Women's rights

In the Constitution of 2012, no specific provision addressed women's equality. Significantly, the preamble merely referred to them as 'sisters of men and partners in national gains and responsibility' to be 'respected',[52] while the body of the text incidentally mentioned women only in the article addressing the family (in striking similarity with the Universal Islamic Declaration of Human Rights – equally a Muslim Brotherhood product[53]). Article 10 read:

> The family is the basis of society and is based on religion, morality and patriotism.
>
> The state and society oversee the commitment to the genuine character of the Egyptian family, its cohesion and stability, and the consolidation and protection of its moral values. The foregoing is as organised by law.
>
> The state guarantees maternal and child services free of charge, and guarantees the reconciliation between the duties of a woman toward her family and her work.
>
> The state provides special care and protection to breadwinning and divorced women as well as widows.

This is a typically conservative norm aimed at reinforcing the concept of the heterosexual family based on 'religion, morality and patriotism', with 'state and society' as (Orwellian) guarantors 'of its moral values'. Against this backdrop, it

50 Bernard-Maugiron, 'La Constitution égyptienne de 2014 est-elle révolutionnaire?', 12.

51 *V. infra*, Chapter VI.

52 'The dignity of the individual is part and parcel of the dignity of the homeland. And a country in which women are not respected has no dignity; for women are the sisters of men and partners in national gains and responsibilities'.

53 *V. supra*, Chapter II.

is no coincidence that women's rights were placed into this context: according to this mindset, women play their 'natural' role within the family, while any external activity must not infringe on these family 'duties'. This provision raised additional doubts: would the reference to the 'cohesion and stability' of the family impair women's rights to seek divorce? And how would the state 'oversee' the safeguarding of the 'moral values' in an eminently private domain? Some feared the possible establishment of a moral police, especially when reading this norm in conjunction with Article 81 (addressed in the next section).[54]

Unsatisfactory as it was, the final version of Article 10 even marked an improvement compared to earlier drafts that Islamists proposed, which spoke of 'complementarity' of women with men inside the family.[55] The obsession with women's 'complementarity', somehow reproduced in the preamble with the ambiguous expression 'sisters of men', is a recurring Islamist *topos*, and we also find it in the Tunisian case. I will elaborate more on this later.

The constitutional text of 2014 partly maintains this conservative ethos (already present, it must be said, in the 1971 Constitution): Article 11 contains a paragraph stating that 'The state commits to the protection of women against all forms of violence, and ensures women['s] empowerment to reconcile the duties of a woman toward her family and her work requirements'. At the same time, specific clauses reinforce the position of women in a significant way. First of all, women's rights are no longer placed in the context of family protection, which is still informed by traditional values,[56] but are framed autonomously. Completing the classically liberal provisions that guarantee the equality of all citizens with no discrimination (Articles 9 and 53), Article 11 identifies a wide plethora of domains where the state commits to achieving effective parity between men and women including through elements of positive discrimination:

> The state commits to achieving equality between women and men in all civil, political, economic, social, and cultural rights in accordance with the provisions of this Constitution.
>
> The state commits to taking the necessary measures to ensure appropriate representation of women in the houses of parliament, in the manner specified by law. It grants women the right to hold public posts and high management posts in the state, and to appointment in judicial bodies and entities without discrimination.

An additional clause declares that 'the state commits to the protection of women against all forms of violence', in an implicit acknowledgement of the endemic problem in Egypt.[57]

54 Bernard-Maugiron, 'La place du religieux', 62.
55 Abu-Odeh, 'Egypt's New Constitution', 168.
56 Article 10 reads as follow: 'Family is the basis of society and is based on religion, morality, and patriotism. The state protects its cohesion and stability, and the consolidation of its values.'
57 'Egypt: Epidemic of Sexual Violence'. Begum, 'How Egypt Can Turn the Tide on Sexual Assault'.

In conclusion, while the text of 2014 is still open to criticism for assigning a 'natural' role to women – as if this were to be determined by the state and society rather than by an individual choice – it also contains positive elements that considerably improve the condition of women with respect to the Constitutions of 1971 and 2012.

Individual liberties vs. society's will

The more subtly dangerous provision – from a human rights perspective – of the 2012 Constitution was enshrined in Article 81.3:

> 'Rights and freedoms are to be exercised in a way that is consistent with the components that are set out in the Chapter on the state and Society in this Constitution.'

This meant that all articles enouncing freedoms and rights were subjugated to a set of moral and social norms which could impair their enjoyment in an unforeseeable way. The ultimate goal was that rights 'be applied and interpreted in accordance with a conservative vision of society'.[58]

For example, we have seen that Article 10 contained very specific references to the 'genuine character of the Egyptian family' and to its foundations constituted by 'religion, morality and patriotism'; it further called on both 'state and society' to 'oversee' its 'genuine character', 'cohesion', 'stability' and 'moral values', while at the same time making an ambiguous statement over the role of the woman within it. What kind of repercussions could these statements, read in combination with Article 81, have on personal freedom (Art. 34[59]), especially in the domain of sexual and reproductive rights, or on equality between men and women (not even explicitly stated, but only inferrable from the general equality provision of Art. 33)?

Along the same lines, Article 11 envisaged a problematic and overbroad mission for the state to safeguard 'ethics, public morality and public order, a high level of education and of religious and patriotic values, scientific knowledge, Arab culture, and the historical and cultural heritage of the people'. This hodgepodge of ethical purposes assumed a dangerous dimension in combination with Article 81, in that it could be used as 'guidance' or even as a 'limitation' in the enjoyment of rights: freedoms would have been in this way easily compressed by laws intended to further 'ethics', 'public morality', 'public order', and so on, defined according to the moral and religious sensibilities of legislators and judges.

Furthermore, the kind of 'final rule' enshrined at Article 81 immediately recalls the structure of the Cairo Declaration on Human Rights in Islam examined in Chapter II, and especially of Article 24 ('All the rights and freedoms stipulated in this Declaration are subject to the Islamic Shariᶜah') and Article 25 ('The Islamic Shariᶜah is the only source of reference for the explanation or clarification of any of the articles of this Declaration'). Final clauses of this kind are particularly dangerous in a bill of rights, as they might void freedoms

58 Al-Ali, 'The New Egyptian Constitution'.
59 'Personal freedom is a natural right. It is safeguarded and inviolable.'

of any meaning by submitting them to an undefined ethico-legal superstructure. Indeed, in the words of El Fegiery, Article 81 represented a direct threat to human rights, in particular of women and minorities.[60] The secular members of the Constituent Assembly made the same point.[61] In the same vein, according to Bernard-Maugiron, Article 81 implied that 'all rights and freedoms must be exercised in a manner consistent with shariᶜa (Art. 2), with the genuine character of the family (Art. 10) and with ethics and public morality (Art. 11) – which would have been indeed a potentially liberticidal interpretation.'[62]

While the Freedom and Justice Party tried to play off Article 81 as merely redundant, and lacking any practical effect,[63] it is apposite to recall that, since the 1980s, the Muslim Brotherhood had conducted vigorous campaigns, inside and outside the Parliament, against 'indecency'.[64] Furthermore, although clauses referring to 'public order' or 'public decency' are often mentioned in constitutional texts, Article 81 established an inverse hierarchy: by explicitly submitting individual liberties to superior 'social interests', it gave the latter an automatic prevalence in the balancing test. This was confirmed by some disquieting declarations on the part of Amr Darrag, member of the Freedom and Justice Party and secretary-general of the Constituent Assembly:

> Based on this article, you can never pass a law in Egypt stating that a relationship between a man and a woman outside the marriage establishment is legal, ok? This is something that is basic in the society, in Islam, Christianity, and everywhere. Maybe not in most European countries right now, and maybe not in the United States: in most of those countries they already legally accept, or are considering accepting, a family formed by two men or two women even, and it is ok, but it is not acceptable in Egyptian society. So you have to have a reference to that in the Constitution.[65]

Upon the interviewer's objection that such purpose should be clearly stated, since not all Egyptians share the same ethical views and hold the same opinions, the Muslim Brotherhood representative rebutted with a disquieting assertion:

> [O]n this issue, *you can never have dissent*. I dare you to have somebody coming out in public and say something of the sort. I mean, homosexuality

60 El Fegiery, interviewed by the author.

61 Kasanwidjojo, 'Opposition to the Draft Constitution'.

62 Bernard-Maugiron, 'La Constitution égyptienne de 2014 est-elle révolutionnaire?', 17. Own translation from French.

63 'And what is wrong with that? In my opinion this is also redundant. It is redundant to say that nothing issued can contradict any part of the Constitution. Why do you have a Constitution in the first place then? You put it because you don't want anything in it or from it to contradict that text. But if you put it here, fine. It's just explaining things further. It doesn't add anything actually.' Darrag, Interview with Dr. Amr Darrag.

64 Mohammed Morsi himself during a 2005 TV show attacked ballet and belly dance as incompatible with Islamic law. El Fegiery, *Islamic Law and Human Rights*, 107.

65 Darrag, Interview with Dr. Amr Darrag.

> is considered a crime in Egypt. For Egyptians, those for whom this Constitution applies, this article is not vague. It is very clear. [...] Yes, there are people who have other opinions, but *the society does not accept them as legitimate.*[66]

These statements clearly show the dangers enshrined in Article 81, as an instrument serving a tyranny of the majority, in the framework of a constitution conceived as a vehicle for the supremacy of certain moral views over individual rights.

The 2014 Constitution adopted a different approach in terms of limitations of rights. As per Article 92, '[r]ights and freedoms of individual citizens may not be suspended or reduced. No law that regulates the exercise of rights and freedoms may restrict them in such a way as infringes upon their essence and foundation'. This formulation, recalling human rights treaties and Article 49 of the Tunisian constitution,[67] should theoretically shelter constitutional liberties against legal abuses. Such a guarantee is further reinforced by a radical new development in the history of Egyptian constitutions, namely the force of law attributed to international agreements and conventions by Article 93.[68] Although the mere 'force of law' does not bestow international treaties with supremacy over ordinary laws, which means that in case of conflict with an internal statute the later adopted will prevail, nevertheless this marks the first formal commitment of the Egyptian state to respect international treaties.[69] Finally, Chapter 4 of the Constitution is entirely devoted to the rule of law, with the explicit assertion that '[t]he rule of law is the basis of governance in the state'.[70]

Final considerations

The 2012 Egyptian Constitution, adopted by an Islamist-dominated assembly under an Islamist government, raised a number of serious concerns from a human rights perspective. These concerns were the direct outcome of the extremely ample role that the tenets and rules of Islam, in their orthodox, conservative interpretation, came to play in the text, which was subsequently revised by a new constitutional assembly after President Morsi was deposed.

The comparison between the Constitution of 2012 and that of 2014 shows several theoretical improvements from a human rights perspective. The heavily religious mark of the 2012 Constitution has given way to a more modern and

66 Darrag.
67 *V. infra*, Chapter V.
68 'The state is committed to the agreements, covenants, and international conventions of human rights that were ratified by Egypt. They have the force of law after publication in accordance with the specified circumstances'.
69 Bernard-Maugiron, 'La Constitution égyptienne de 2014 est-elle révolutionnaire?', 7. Further considerations on this article will be developed in Chapter VIII.
70 Article 94.

tendentially liberal text. Yet, what is on paper is often not what citizens experience in their daily lives, as attested by the mass human rights violations.[71] This is the unfortunate fruit of a tradition of military authoritarianism combined with an oppressive mantle of traditions and religion, which have constantly reduced a formally constitutional system to a mere simulacrum.[72]

71 Freedom House, 'Egypt'. Amnesty International, 'Egypt 2019'. Human Rights Watch, 'Egypt: Events of 2020'.

72 'It is true that Egyptian law per legal system embodied a certain version of legal liberalism, given its origin as a European transplant, but it had on the one hand picked up a great deal of illiberal residue over the years as a result of authoritarian governance and, on the other, it had not had the benefit of political liberalism as a background ideological formation to feed its interpretation precisely for the same reason. And while by virtue of being a European transplant that had historically displaced Islamic law by cornering it, making it an instance of "secular law," it had had to make do without the benefit of ideologized secularism to feed it interpretively.' Abu-Odeh, 'Egypt's New Constitution', 164.

V Compromises and ambiguities in the 2014 Tunisian Constitution

Introduction

Perhaps even more so than in Egypt, in Tunisia the constitutional transition has been affected by the clash of two different worldviews: on the one hand, Habib Bourguiba's moderately secular legacy, influenced by a local, tolerant reading of Islam;[1] on the other hand, the Islamist ideology of the Ennahdha party – belonging to the broader Muslim Brotherhood movement[2] – and Salafist circles. The clash between these two worldviews could not but affect the drafting of the Constitution, especially given the decision of the National Constituent Assembly (ANC[3]) not to use the text of 1958 as a basis but to adopt a 'blank canvas' approach.[4]

The main points of dispute in the Tunisian constitution-drafting phase confirm the hypotheses proposed in the Introduction and Chapter II and confirmed by the Egyptian case, insofar as they point to the usual suspects: the role of Islam and shariʿa law, freedom of thought and religion, freedom of expression and women's rights.

Overall, we can say that the quest for consensus and a peaceful transition – which could not be taken for granted, considering the disastrous outcomes of the Arab Spring in the other countries of the region – has come at a price: the most controversial articles of the constitution have become characterized by a marked ambiguity. This was the inevitable result of the compromise between polarized positions, which was the only way for each party to obtain a certain room for manoeuvre while securing a deal. The consensus on the constitution

1 Country leader from the Tunisian independence in 1956 until 1987, when he was removed from power by his prime minister, Zine El Abidine Ben Ali. A moderate secularist, he consistently pursued a socio-economic modernization of Tunisia that may be largely considered a main cause of the thriving middle-class civil society of the country. Its legacy, defined as 'Bourguibism', is sometimes described as a less consistent and less radical instance of Kemalism. Cook, 'Tunisia'. Murphy, 'Habib Bourguiba'.

2 Colombo, *Tunisia: A Nascent Democracy under Siege*, 37.

3 From the French acronym *Assemblée Nationale Constituante*.

4 Gaddes, 'Il processo costituente', 55.

DOI: 10.4324/9780429259418-V

has been defined as a 'necessary legal fiction',[5] but the agreement on the words came at the expense of the agreement on their meaning.[6]

Here, I am going to examine the genesis and end result of the most sensitive and controversial articles of the 2014 Constitution, all of which involved religious debates.

Article 1: the role of Islam

The first crucial issue the Constituent Assembly had to resolve concerned the role of Islam in the new charter. The assembly's members faced three main options: at the one end of the spectrum, a possibility was the establishment of an *état laïque*, a secular state with no official role for Islam, bringing to completion the reform process started by Habib Bourguiba on a Kemalist model; at the other end of the spectrum, there was the option to radically abandon Tunisia's secular heritage by establishing an Islamic state referring to shariᶜa law; the middle ground would entail a reference to Islam but not to shariᶜa.

Regarding the first option, only some independent intellectuals argued in favour of secularism, and this idea did not take root in the Assembly itself.[7] This is a manifestation of the liberal weakness that we have seen, in more extreme terms, in the Egyptian case: it is never easy to advocate strongly against Islam, as the killing of the secular leftist politicians Chokri Belaid and Mohamed Brahmi testifies.[8]

Religious parties, including Ennahdha in the first phase, sought to install shariᶜa as a main source of legislation,[9] on the Egyptian model. In March 2012, Ennahdha circulated its own constitutional proposal, Article 10 of which decreed that '[t]he Islamic shariᶜa is a main source of the legislation'. The project also provided for a 'High Shariatic Council' entrusted with the power to scrutinize draft laws in order to assess their compatibility with shariᶜa law (in line with practices already in place in Iran and Pakistan and proposed in Egypt with the 2012 Constitution).[10] Ennahdha simultaneously advanced this effort within the ANC, where it attempted to introduce a reference to shariᶜa law in the preamble and in Article 1.[11] The renowned liberal constitutional lawyer Yadh Ben Achour

5 Bras, 'Un État "civil"', 56. Own translation from French.
6 Bras, 56.
7 Yadh Ben Achour (Professor of Public Law, member of the Human Rights Committee and President of the Higher Authority for Realization of the Objectives of the Revolution, Political Reform and Democratic transition), interviewed by the author. Tunis, August 2016.
8 The two were killed by Islamists respectively in February and July 2013 for their openly secular positions. Colombo, *Tunisia: A Nascent Democracy under Siege*, 51.
9 Bousbih and Yaalaoui, 'The Interplay of Politics and Religion', 18.
10 The original text was given to me by Chawki Gaddes, Secretary General of the Tunisian Association of Constitutional Law and President of the Tunisian Privacy Commission, and was originally available on his personal website: 'Ennahdha's Constitutional Project'. See also Ben Achour, 'La force du droit'.
11 Bras, 'Un État "civil"', 58. Bousbih and Yaalaoui, 'The Interplay of Politics and Religion', 18.

reported that certain members even demanded that shariᶜa be *the* main source of legislation. Sadok Chourou, former leader of Ennahdha, went as far as to declare those opposing this proposal 'foes of Allah', to be punished as foreseen in the Qurᵓan, 5:33, that is, either with crucifixion, amputation of the hand and feet or banishment.[12]

The middle ground consisted in granting Islam an official role while avoiding the legal implications of this recognition. This role, in turn, could be enacted in two quite different ways: Islam could be enshrined as the 'religion of the state', with an institutional role, or the 'religion of Tunisia', to be interpreted in sociological and cultural terms. In spite of the similar wording, the difference is substantial: in the first case, we have legal recognition of the institutional role of Islam as a fundamental element of the state; in other words, Islam acquires a *prescriptive* value, surreptitiously opening up the possibility of introducing shariᶜa law without mentioning it;[13] in the second case, Islam is a mere *descriptive* element, referring to the cultural and historical heritage of Tunisia.[14] In the 1959 Constitution, this issue was intentionally obfuscated, with Article 1 reading:

> 'Tunisia is a free, independent and sovereign state. Its religion is Islam, its language is Arabic and its type of government is the Republic'.[15]

In the Arabic text, the possessive adjective in the clause 'its religion' (*dīnuhā*) may grammatically refer either to the state (*dawla*) or to Tunisia, intended as the 'nation' or the 'people'.[16] This formulation was Bourguiba's strategic and ingenious stratagem to appease Islamists by mentioning Islam, while at the same time leaving a profound ambiguity over its meaning and effects on the legal system.

In the spirit of compromise that informed the ANC's work, the only solution that could seemingly be adopted by consensus was to repropose Article 1 in the same form. According to Fadhel Moussa, a member of the Constituent Assembly, 'reference to Islam in this case is ambivalent, but it must be understood as the religion of the people, namely of human entities, more than as the religion of the state. The state, in fact, is a moral entity, and as such it cannot have a religion'.[17]

It goes without saying that this interpretation was not adopted by Ennahdha and other Islamist groups. In fact, they tried another constitutional blitz, namely to introduce an explicit mention of 'Islam as the religion of the state' in a new article containing a list of non-amendable provisions.[18] Such a move would have ended the consensus around Article 1 by eliminating its ambiguity. A panel of experts appointed by the president of the republic to examine the constitutional draft even found a legal incongruity between the reference to a

12 Ben Achour, 'La force du droit'.
13 Ben Achour.
14 Ben Achour, interview.
15 'The Constitution of Tunisia, 1959'.
16 Bras, 'Un État "civil"', 60.
17 Moussa, 'Dalle tre paure', 82. Own translation from Italian.
18 Bras, 'Un État "civil"', 61.

'state religion' and Article 2, which emphasizes the civil character of the state (another non-amendable provision). The panel of experts warned that the vague concept of 'state religion' paved the way for a theocratic, totalitarian system, incompatible with the civil nature of the state and detrimental to the democratic mission of the revolution.[19] The Venice Commission of the Council of Europe also criticized this article, deeming it to go 'far beyond the wording of Article 1, which states that Islam is the religion of Tunisia (= of the majority of Tunisians). This is problematic, because it is inconsistent with Articles 1 and 2 and with the guarantees of the state's impartiality and neutrality contained in Articles 14 and 15'.[20] The only way to restore consensus was ultimately to restore the ambiguity: the article listing the non-amendable provisions was deleted and replaced with a non-amendability clause at the bottom of each affected article.

Whatever the interpretation of Article 1, one should bear in mind that the Constitution begins with the words 'In the Name of God, the Merciful, the Compassionate' and ends with 'And God is the guarantor of success'. Furthermore, Article 74 enshrines a substantial privilege for Islam, stipulating that the president of the republic must be Muslim. This obviously represents a serious breach of both the freedom of conscience (Article 6) and the principle of equality of all citizens (Article 21). When this issue emerged during the drafting process, a spokesman for Ennahdha argued that 'Islam is the religion of the majority of Tunisians, and the official religion of Tunisia is Islam. It is normal for the president of the country to be Muslim'.[21] As Brian Whitaker has commented, 'there is a big difference between saying that on the balance of probabilities any Tunisian president is *likely* to be a Muslim and saying that the president *must* be a Muslim'.[22] This deliberate obfuscation of the difference between the descriptive and prescriptive implications of Islam as the majoritarian religion partly explains why, for secularists, the battle of words around Article 1 was so crucial.

Overall, the 2014 Constitution may be classified as 'not secular, but friendly to democracy'.[23] Furthermore, with the final formulation of Article 1, 'Tunisia becomes the only Arab country not to proclaim that Islam is the religion of the state'.[24] Or not to proclaim it explicitly, at least.

Article 2: The 'civil state', *dawla madaniyya*

I have already touched upon the concept of *dawla madaniyya* in the Egyptian case. In Tunisia, a more heated debate emerged over this crucial definition, due to

19 Ben Achour et al., 'Muqtarahat Hawla Mashruᶜ Al-Dustur'. Courtesy of Prof. Ben Achour. See also Ben Achour, 'La force du droit'.
20 Venice Commission, 'Opinion on the Final Draft', 8.
21 Whitaker, *Arabs without God*, 125.
22 Whitaker, 125.
23 Longo, 'L'islam nella nuova Costituzione', 109.
24 Ben Achour, 'La force du droit'. Own translation from French.

the greater strength of secular forces. The notion of the civil state appears twice in the final text of the constitution: in the preamble and in the non-amendable Article 2. While the preamble refers to the intention of 'building a republican, democratic and participatory system, in the framework of a civil state founded on the sovereignty of the people', Article 2 explicitly states: 'Tunisia is a civil state based on citizenship, the will of the people, and the supremacy of law. This article might not be amended'.[25]

For anti-Islamists, this represents the secular counterpart to Article 1. Tunisian constitutional scholar Wahid Ferchichi has joked about this duality saying that 'Tunisians pray as per article 1 and drink as per article 2'.[26] Yet, in reality, this secularist achievement has been substantially made possible by the ambiguity of the adjective 'civil', which can have as many interpretations as there are readers: 'In the Islamic constitutional lexicon, the adjective "civil" (*madaniyya*) is used to define a state governed by civilians, as opposed to a military regime (*dawla 'askariyya*) and to a theocratic one (*dawla ilahiyya*)'.[27]

Even if we take the latter interpretation, the principle may be easily accommodated within the Islamist discourse: given the ambiguity around the concept of 'theocracy', as explained in Chapter I, Islamists can accept that the state is 'civil' and not 'theocratic' (in the sense of not being governed by the clergy), because for them 'the adjective has no meaning in relation to laicity and secularism'.[28] As Ameur Larayedh, previously head of Ennahdha's political bureau, said: 'There is no such thing as a religious state in Islam. In all phases of the Islamic history, the state has always been civil'[29] – namely governed by lay rulers. The story is likely to change radically as far as 'God's sovereignty' is concerned, as demonstrated by the attempt to introduce shariʿa in the Constitution. In other words, 'civil' does not imply a separation between religion, law and politics but merely a state ruled by lay authorities, which nevertheless has to be shaped by Islamic values (and possibly rules):[30] this is the 'civil state with Islamic reference' (*dawla madaniyya bi-marjiʿiyya islāmiyya*)[31] that both Ennahdha[32] and the Egyptian Muslim Brotherhood[33] espouse. From this perspective, Islamists find Article 2 perfectly compatible with their interpretation of Article 1:

> Al-Nahdha's emphasis on democracy was also accompanied by a desire to keep established religion at the heart of the polity. [...] This allowed the

25 English translation: 'Tunisia's Constitution of 2014'.
26 Also President of the Tunisian Association Defending Individual Liberties (ADLI). Interviewed by the author, Tunis, July 2016.
27 Longo, 'L'islam nella nuova Costituzione', 112. Own translation from Italian. El-Daghili, 'Al-Dawlah al-Madanīyah', 191.
28 Longo, 'L'islam nella nuova Costituzione', 112.
29 Bras, 'Un État "civil"', 67. Own translation from French.
30 Bras, 67.
31 El-Daghili, 'Al-Dawlah al-Madanīyah', 192.
32 Longo, 'L'islam nella nuova Costituzione', 110.
33 El Fegiery, *Islamic Law and Human Rights*, 137.

> movement to speak of the state as a 'civil state' (*dawla madaniyya*) that was nonetheless the guardian and the regulator of Islam and to keep Islam – and conservative moral values – at the center of politics.[34]

Forsaking shariᶜa *de jure* does not mean renouncing it *de facto*, as long as legislation is tailored upon Islamic principles. That is why Rached Ghannouchi, co-founder and leader of Ennahdha, 'does not talk of "shariᶜa implementation" (*tatbiq al-shariᶜa*, a phrase widely used by other Islamist movements), but rather of "Islamic implementation" (*tatbiq islami*)',[35] that is, a 'policy making based on religious values'.[36] As Baudoin Dupret has rightfully noted, the party has never renounced its Islamization project,

> but as in Erdoğan's Turkey, it prefers to substitute to symbolic moves a more gradualist approach using the de facto acceptance of Sharīʿah as a source of legislation and case law. As Rashīd al- Ghannūshī put it in a press conference on March 26, 2012: 'nearly 90% of our legislation finds its origins or sources in Sharīʿah'.[37]

This conclusion is further corroborated by a leaked video that secretly filmed Ghannouchi addressing a group of Salafists and recommending that they adopt a tactical approach in pursuing shariᶜa, by building schools and universities to spread the Islamist ideology; he further mocked secularists for opposing shariᶜa while accepting the role of Islam enshrined in Article 1, and portrayed them as 'those who accepted the content but rejected the name itself'.[38]

This ideological substratum sheds light on the type of 'secularism' that Islamists imagine. As Shawqi Bu'anani stated in the Ennahdha party's weekly journal *al-Fajr*, there are two sorts of secularism: 'the first, which he accepted, separated the state and the religious institution; the second was "radical" and sought to eliminate religion from the public space and from life altogether. For Bu'anani, radical secularism could only produce dictatorship.'[39] We find a similarly narrow acceptance of secularism in Ghannouchi's statements. In a 2012 lecture on *Secularism and Relation between Religion and the State from the Perspective of the Nadha Party*, he spoke of secularism as a '*procedural* solution', evolved as such even in the West, 'and not as a philosophy or theory of existence'.[40] This concept, according to him, has always been clearly present in the Islamic polity. Indeed, if it is true that 'Islam, since its inception, has always combined religion with politics, religion and state', this is because 'Islam is not merely a religion but

34 Zeghal, 'Competing Ways of Life', 13.
35 Zeghal, 16.
36 Zeghal, 17.
37 Dupret, 'The Relationship between Constitutions', 241.
38 Gallala-Arndt, 'Tunisia after the Arab Spring: Women's Rights at Risk?', 610.
39 Zeghal, 'Competing Ways of Life', 22.
40 Abu-Sahlieh, 'Ghannouchi's Lecture'.

also carries a civilizational meaning'.[41] According to Ghannouchi, the Charter of Medina (*Saḥīfa*) sanctioned this new order by putting Muslim and Jewish tribes under one nation, so that:

> the distinction between that which is political and that which is religious is clear in the Sahifah, in that Muslims are a religious nation (ummah) and the Jews another, but the combination of the two plus other polytheists made up a nation in the political sense.[42]

Here we have, according to him, the first instance of secularism, in its acceptable meaning: the Prophet was both 'the founder of religion as well as the state',[43] but the two entities remained distinct. At this point, it is important to understand what falls within and without the boundaries of religion. Ghannouchi answered this question as follows:

> It is not the duty of religion to teach us agricultural, industrial or even governing techniques, because reason is qualified to reach these truths through the accumulation of experiences. The role of religion, however, is [...] to provide us with a system of values and principles that would guide our *thinking, behaviour*, and the *regulations* of the state to which we aspire.[44]

This extremely revealing statement shows that only the 'technical', non-personal domains are conceived as non-religious, or 'secular', while religion must guide *thinking, behaviour* and *regulations*, that is, the entire spectrum of human life, both internal and external. In other words, what Ghannouchi champions is not a *substantive* secularism that leaves individuals free to determine their own convictions and conduct and enables the state to decide on its democratic legislation without religious interference. The very nature of Islam clearly rules this out:

> Islam since its inception and throughout its history has not known this separation between state and religion in the sense of excluding religion from public life. And Muslims, to this day, have been influenced by Islam and inspired by its teachings and guidance in their civic life, with the distinction remaining clear.[45]

When it comes more specifically to state legislation, 'Throughout Islamic history, the state has always been influenced by Islam in one way or another in its practices, and its laws were legislated for in light of the Islamic values as

41 Abu-Sahlieh.
42 Abu-Sahlieh.
43 Abu-Sahlieh.
44 Abu-Sahlieh. Emphasis added.
45 Abu-Sahlieh.

understood at that particular time and place'.[46] Democracy, in this sense, is seen as a consultative process (*shūrā*)[47] whose primary goal is not to liberate the state from religion, as in the West, but rather to avoid state interference in religious matters.[48] This also explains Ennahdha's ambivalence towards the reciprocal relationship between the state and religion, manifested in its clear calls for the state to give up control over mosques and its claims that 'the state must organize (*tanzim*) religion without controlling it'.[49] Here we find a pattern already evident in the case of Egypt and more specifically reflecting similar positions to those of the Freedom and Justice Party: while Islamists have been chiefly preoccupied with ending the control of non-Islamist regimes over religious institutions and places of worship and equally with avoiding a theocratic state where imams rule the polity, at the same time they have called on the state to enact Islamic rules.

The understanding of democracy and the civil state outlined here falls within the theory presented in Chapter I: the state is regulated by shariᶜa and its rules, but there is flexibility on *procedures*, which are largely irrelevant to Islamic law, as long as its *substance* is maintained. As said, *shūrā* can inspire people to engage in the democratic act of casting their vote in the ballot box, but it is totally silent when it comes to the rule of law, the separation of powers and individual rights.

Overall, it would be difficult to interpret the Islamist reading of *dawla madaniyya* as a secular state opposed to the *dawla dīniyya*, or 'religious state'. As Rached Ghannouchi himself has stressed, Article 1 is clear and prevents Tunisia from becoming an *état laïque*.[50]

Conversely, non-Islamists read Article 2 as the guarantee of the primacy of the constitution and democratic, human-made laws over religious rules. In other words, they look at it as a guarantee that the state's governance is not religious.[51] According to Fadhel Moussa, '[t]he entire Constitution is summarized in this Article 2, which is a bulwark against those who would go looking for the foundation of our positive law outside the Constitution'.[52] This interpretation of *madaniyya*, therefore, stands in opposition not only to a theocratic state but even to one shaped by religious rules and morals, and it comes closer to the secular state. According to Gamal al-Banna, younger brother of Muslim Brotherhood founder Hassan al-Banna, '[t]he idea of a civil state with Islamic reference

46 Abu-Sahlieh.

47 Abu-Sahlieh.

48 'While the problematique in the west revolved around ways of liberating the state from religion and led to destructive wars, in our context the problem is one of liberating religion from the state and preventing it from dominating religion, and keeping the latter in the societal realm, open to all Muslims to read the Qur'an and understand it in the manner that they deem appropriate, and that there is no harm in the plurality that is combined with tolerance'. Abu-Sahlieh.

49 Zeghal, 'Competing Ways of Life', 16.

50 Haddad, 'Ghannouchi'.

51 Groppi, 'L'identità costituzionale', 32.

52 Moussa, 'Dalle tre paure', 82. Own translation from Italian.

is a fallacy. Religious and civilian outlooks differ and eventually one will always try to trump the other'.[53]

Once again, the various parties ultimately reached agreement on Article 2 in the Assemblée National Constituante because each was left with room to interpret the provision as it wanted.

Article 6, *sive 'Le pot-pourri de la constitution tunisienne'*

Article 6 is one of the most sensitive, controversial and also innovative articles in the Constitution. It is the amalgam par excellence of the various ideologies informing the constitutional process, which makes it '*le pot-pourri de la constitution tunisienne*', to quote Yadh Ben Achour.[54] It stipulates:

> The state is the guardian of religion. It guarantees freedom of conscience and belief, the free exercise of religious practices and the neutrality of mosques and places of worship from all partisan instrumentalisation.
>
> The state undertakes to disseminate the values of moderation and tolerance and the protection of the sacred, and the prohibition of all violations thereof. It undertakes equally to prohibit and fight against calls for Takfir and the incitement of violence and hatred.

At first glance, we can notice a multitude of components, each of them requiring scrupulous analysis. There are four main pillars:

1. Protection of religion and prohibition of attacks against the 'sacred';
2. Protection of freedom of conscience and belief;
3. Promotion of moderation and tolerance;
4. Prohibition of *takfir*.

The overall goal of this article is to strike a delicate balance between liberal and religious elements, by guaranteeing freedom of conscience while ensuring that it stops short of abusing 'religion' and the 'sacred'. At the same time, the kind of religion deserving protection must not be radical but based on the values of 'moderation' and 'tolerance', while any attempt to impose the former, through the odious practice of excommunication (*takfir*), is to be banned.

The formulation of Article 6, however, is problematic and ambiguous, especially as far as the safeguarding of religion is concerned. Starting from the very beginning, what does it mean to say that the state is the 'guardian of religion'? First of all, what religion are we talking about? Is Article 6 referring to all religions, as the generic reference to the 'sacred' in the same article would

53 El-Daghili, 'Al-Dawlah al-Madanīyah', 192.
54 Ben Achour, interview.

suggest,[55] or Islam,[56] as it would seem based on a reading of Article 6 in combination with Article 1 (sanctioning Islam as Tunisia's religion), and Article 146 (requiring that all articles of the Constitution be read harmonically as an indissoluble whole)? While the second interpretation would be manifestly incompatible with international standards,[57] the first would also be problematic for discriminating against non-religious philosophies and creeds.

The term 'guardian' is extremely ambiguous as well: what role does it vest in the state? 'It could mean it is a general overseer of religion, empowered only to manage its broad outlines; or it could mean it is a promoter of religion, and as such invested with the power to refashion it'.[58] The Arabic term is *rāᶜiya*, from the root *raᶜā*, which the Wehr dictionary translates as 'to guard, protect, take under one's wing', 'take care of', 'respect'.[59] The Arabic word is therefore polysemic and allows for multiple interpretations and legal uses.

The 'guardian' is required to 'safeguard the sacred and prohibit any attack on the latter'. What is 'sacred'? And does the term refer exclusively to Islam or also to other religions? The word used in Arabic is *muqaddasāt*, which Wehr translates as 'sacred things'.[60] The root is not unique to an Islamic context, as the verb *qadusa* (sanctify, glorify) is also used by Christians to denote the process of canonization and the celebration of the mass.[61] At the same time, one cannot exclude an interpretation centred on the *res sacrae* of Islam: mosques, Qurᵓans, et cetera.

Inevitably, as these provisions are mere principles, they will be defined in concrete terms by secondary norms and by their jurisdictional implementation.[62] However, as correctly pointed out by the Venice Commission, '[a] state which proclaims itself to be civil (Article 2) should not be competent to determine what is sacred and "protect" that which is held to be so'.[63] Furthermore, such wording could legitimize the criminalization of blasphemy, thereby curtailing freedom of thought, conscience and expression. This risk has been stressed, once again, by the Venice Commission,[64] as well as by Human Rights Watch (HRW): Amna

55 It must also be noted that the Arabic term for 'sacred' is in the plural form (*muqaddasāt*) which seems to corroborate the hypothesis that it is not limited to Islam. However, another possible interpretation is that it merely refers to the 'sanctities' of Islam. *V. infra*.

56 Horchani, 'Islam and the Constitutional State', 205.

57 Venice Commission, 'Opinion on the Final Draft', 8. Spigno, 'Diritti e doveri', 100.

58 Bousbih and Yaalaoui, 'The Interplay of Politics and Religion', 20.

59 Wehr, 'رعى'.

60 Wehr, 'مقدس'.

61 Wehr, 'قدس'.

62 'The ambiguity of this constitutional provision (Article 6), as it appears in the chapter on "General Principles", allows maximum capture of the varied real-life situations involving religion. The actual process of pin-pointing will then take place via other legal provisions, which will act empirically, on an "as and when" basis. This is the core function of "principles" in law: they take the form of programmatic norms that require the creation of further norms to bring about their own implementation.' Bousbih and Yaalaoui, 'The Interplay of Politics and Religion', 20.

63 Venice Commission, 'Opinion on the Final Draft', 9.

64 Venice Commission, 9.

Guellali, former director of HRW's Tunisian office, remarked that the protection of the sacred could lead to the imposition of an orthodox interpretation of the sacred texts and their immutable dogmas, thereby undermining any possibility of 'critique and dispute'.[65] Such risks grow if we consider that, while the state is assigned responsibility for the 'protection of religion', there is no actual mention of *freedom* of religion. Article 6 grants citizens 'freedom of belief' and the right to engage in 'religious practices', but it does not refer to the freedom of religion or the right to express non-religious convictions. Combined with the privilege granted to Islam in different parts of the Constitution[66] and with the shariatic prohibition of apostasy, this may have worrying implications.

The above-mentioned panel of experts also criticized Article 6 on several grounds. First, they observed, it is not the task of a democratic state to protect one religion to the exclusion of the others; therefore, the experts suggested the replacement of *rāᶜiyat al-dīn* with the plural *rāᶜiyat al-adyān*, that is, 'guardian of religions'.[67] Second, they pointed to another crucial part, namely, the safeguarding of places of worship from all '*partisan* [*ḥizbī*] instrumentalization': as the panel correctly observes, this formulation does not guarantee a safe space from *political* (*siyāsī*) instrumentalization by imams with a political agenda. They therefore suggested that the article be amended accordingly.[68] Regrettably, these proposals did not find their way into the final draft.

Freedom of conscience also constituted a minefield within the ANC. This right is an evolution of the freedom of religion, so that it not only includes the protection of non-religious convictions but also implicitly covers the criticism of religious tenets when the latter are at odds with individuals' conscience.[69] As such, it has both an internal and external dimension.

It is interesting to note that the amendment to suppress the clause was presented and supported by a plethora of different deputies representing the entire political spectrum.[70] The reason why lawmakers coming from such different ideological, religious and political backgrounds all wanted to suppress freedom of conscience is not immediately clear, and my interviewees provided differing explanations. According to Chawki Gaddes, secretary general of the Tunisian Association of Constitutional Law and president of the Tunisian Privacy Commission, participants played political games within the Assembly that were inconsistent with rigid ideological distinctions: votes were also cast as part of political trade-offs.[71] In the opinion of Yadh Ben Achour, who personally conducted a campaign in favour of freedom of conscience, the latter is regarded by some as a vehicle for blasphemy and apostasy – a possibility that is unacceptable, even to

65 Guellali, 'The Problem with Tunisia's New Constitution'.
66 Venice Commission, 'Opinion on the Final Draft', 9.
67 Ben Achour et al., 'Muqtarahat Hawla Mashruᶜ Al-Dustur', 4.
68 Ben Achour et al., 4.
69 Ben Achour and Jelassi, 'Lecture analytique', 23.
70 See 'Vote sur un amendement de l'article 6'.
71 Interviewed by the author, Tunis, July 2016.

some non-Islamists.[72] According to Ferchichi, president of the Tunisian Association Defending Individual Liberties, there is no single explanation, because the reasons to vote against freedom of conscience were multiple and personal: some might have done it for the aforementioned religious reasons or conservatism; others may have acted out of political calculations; still others may have done so paradoxically, lest Islamists might invoke it to justify their adherence to the Qurʾanic verses discriminating against women, Jews or homosexuals.[73] This is precisely, in fact, what Rached Ghannouchi did during a public exchange I had with him concerning those issues: in response to my question regarding Ennahdha's position on three controversial issues, namely the decriminalization of homosexuality, the right of Muslim women to marry non-Muslim men and the equality between men and women under inheritance law, he avoided replying by invoking the 'freedom of conscience' that the constitution bestows on every member of parliament.[74]

Furthermore, in spite of freedom of conscience, the president of the republic (Art. 76), the members of the government (Art. 89) and the members of parliament (Art. 58) must take an oath 'by God Almighty' (*bi-Allāh al-ʿadhīm*): this represents a serious violation of freedom of conscience and patent discrimination against atheists, agnostics and potentially non-Muslims – following the common interpretation of the word 'Allah' as referring to the God of Islam, as one would be inclined to do in light of Article 1.

The last section of Article 6 is split into two linked parts. The first reads: 'The state undertakes to disseminate the values of moderation and tolerance'. This part builds upon the preamble, in particular on the Tunisian people's 'commitment to the teachings of Islam and its aims characterized by openness and moderation'. A reading of the two provisions in combination, as per Articles 145[75] and 146,[76] reveals that 'the sole purpose of the teachings of Islam would be to foster openness and tolerance'.[77] Such 'openness' and 'tolerance' are clearly intertwined with the ban on *takfir*, which constitutes the last part of Article 6. By means of these provisions, secularists aimed to secure an interpretation of Islam antithetical to the extremism and exclusiveness typical of Salafism and Wahhabism and to forestall dangerous threats to unorthodox individuals.

The prohibition of *takfir* is a unique provision which was added at the last minute due to an incident within the Constituent Assembly: a prominent Ennahdha leader publicly accused a socialist of unbelief after the latter requested

72 Ben Achour, Interview.

73 Ferchichi, interview.

74 2016 Euromediterranean Dialogues, organized in Rome by the Italian Ministry of Foreign Affairs and the Istituto per gli Studi di Politica Internazionale (ISPI). ISPI, *Med 2016 – What Role for Islam?* Min. 40.

75 'This Constitution's preamble is an integral part of the Constitution.'

76 'The Constitution's provisions shall be understood and interpreted in harmony, as an indissoluble whole.'

77 Bousbih and Yaalaoui, 'The Interplay of Politics and Religion', 22.

an amendment to Article 1 to read that Islam is 'the religion of the people'. As stressed above, the accusation of unbelief is particularly serious in an Islamic context, not only for the reputation of a Muslim but also for their very safety. This is why, following the incident, the secular opposition demanded an explicit prohibition of excommunications.[78]

While the intention and the spirit behind the promotion of 'moderation' and the prohibition of *takfir* are commendable, not all liberals are happy with it. Gaddes, in criticizing the whole article as a 'terrible compromise, which did not satisfy anybody', has added that the 'prohibition of *takfir*' has no concrete meaning whatsoever.[79] Ferchichi has also warned against introducing such purely religious elements into the state's constitution, as this creates a dangerous mixture between heterogeneous elements.[80] In other words, the attribution of legal relevance to religion, albeit with the best intentions, puts the 'civil state' on a slippery slope.

Women vs men: not equal, but 'complementary'

Tunisia has traditionally been a very advanced state for women's rights compared to the rest of the Arab world. Since 1956, the 'Code of Personal Status' has abolished polygamy, established the principle of freedom of consent to marriage and granted women the right to divorce.

Ennahdha has taken an ambivalent stance on this issue: despite public declarations of support for women's rights and for the Code of Personal Status,[81] the party's proposals in the constituent phase and some written statements by Rached Ghannouchi tell quite a different story.

Beginning with the latter, Ghannouchi expressed highly controversial views on the matter in a 2000 essay published by the Maghreb Center for Research and Translation. In a chapter devoted to the Code of Personal Status (significantly entitled 'The destruction of the family in Tunisia and the Code of Personal Status'),[82] he criticized the code for being '"dangerous" and "against the intellectual, cultural and legal heritage" of Tunisia, and for being a clear influence of the "Western wave"'.[83] He also attacked the egalitarian idea behind it, which he accused of giving women access to any societal role and thereby creating social trouble: 'Woman was pushed into the police creating many problems, in the army, women became drivers of buses and planes [...] all this to demonstrate that our regime was really civilised [...] and that the Tunisian woman was free!'.[84] He contrasts the ideology underlying this effort with one based on the

78 Longo, 'L'islam nella nuova Costituzione', 115.
79 Gaddes, interview.
80 Ferchichi, interview.
81 Colombo, *Tunisia: A Nascent Democracy under Siege*, 48.
82 Colombo, 48.
83 Colombo, 49.
84 Colombo, 49.

complementary roles of men and women, and on the Islamic *authority* of the former over the latter.[85]

The idea of complementarity between men and women is, in fact, what Islamist parties tried to insert into the first draft of the Constitution. It should be noted that Ennahdha's own constitutional project did not even mention women. The section focusing on equality (Art. 3) merely referred to the equality of all 'Tunisians' before the law, using only the male adjective *tunisiyyīn* without naming the forbidden grounds for discrimination (sex, race, religion, ethnicity, and so on). Subsequently, in the first constitutional draft of August 2012, religious parties advanced an article on women's rights that was strikingly similar to one in the Egyptian Constitution under discussion at the same time:[86]

> The state shall guarantee the protection of the rights of women and shall support the gains thereof as true *partners to men* in the building of the nation and as having a role *complementary* thereto within the family. The state shall guarantee the provision of equal opportunities between men and women in the bearing of various responsibilities. The state shall guarantee the elimination of all forms of violence against women.[87]

Ennahdha voted against an alternative version that would have bound the state to guarantee women's rights and their advancement in all fields and prohibited the adoption of any laws undermining them.[88] According to Faridah al-Abidi – Ennahdha chair of the Committee on Rights and Freedoms within the ANC – 'there is no absolute equality between men and women'.[89]

Why did Islamists push for this idea, and how should 'complementarity' be understood from an Islamic perspective? The concept has its roots in the Qurʾan itself, 2.228: '[...] And women shall have rights similar to the rights against them, according to what is equitable; but men have a degree (of advantage) over them. And Allah is Exalted in Power, Wise'. It is interesting to read the explanation for this verse provided by Hamza Roberto Piccardo in the Italian edition of the Qurʾan he edited:

> This verse may give rise to misunderstandings, because it might give the impression that [it] enshrines a disparity between the rights of men and women. [...] It is therefore a relative superiority in certain fields [...] but it has to be understood in terms of the intrinsic value of being male and female, and never to be discharged in the direction of a hateful domain or blind imposition. [...] The physiological and psychological differences between male and female should, in respect of their diversity, create a harmonious development

85 Colombo, 49.
86 See Chapter IV.
87 Charrad and Zarrugh, 'Equal or Complementary?', 235. Emphasis added.
88 Gallala-Arndt, 'Tunisia after the Arab Spring', 612.
89 Gallala-Arndt, 611.

of the family and society. Male sensibility is mostly exterior, projected in a field outside the family that tends to become public and political. The female one is mostly interior, attentive to itself, aiming at the protection of the acquired or the acquisition of simple means of sustenance and security [...] Within the family the respect of the Law and the Tradition of Allah means to avoid creating situations that require an affirmation of power that mortifies the complementarity of spouses. [...] Being different and complementary also implies the assumption by man of the lead, which exercised in the right way, does not undervalue the female, but completes her.[90]

Tunisian women were not quite convinced by such reasonings. The reference to them as 'partners' of men, as if they had no autonomous function in society, and especially the downgrading from 'equality' to 'complementarity', caused an uproar within civil society,[91] and the article was eventually withdrawn. In the final version adopted by the Constituent Assembly, Article 21 stipulates:

> 'All citizens, male and female, [*al-muwāṭinūn wa-al-muwāṭināt*] have equal rights and duties, and are equal before the law without any discrimination'.

Furthermore, Article 46 ensures the protection and reinforcement of women's accrued rights, and requires the state to guarantee equal opportunities between men and women 'to all levels of responsibility in all domains'. In terms of positive actions, it stipulates that 'The state works to attain parity between women and men in elected Assemblies' and 'to take all necessary measures in order to eradicate violence against women'.

Although the wording is generally considered very advanced, some concerns for women's rights may arise from Article 49, in that this allows restrictions of rights for the sake of public morals – a vague and open provision that could have a discriminatory impact.

To conclude on women's rights, a positive development took place in 2014, when Tunisia dropped all reservations to the Convention on the Elimination of Discrimination Against Women (CEDAW).[92] Such reservations concerned Article 9, on acquiring nationality based on matrilineal descent; Article 15, on a woman's right to choose her domicile; and Article 16, on the equality of rights in the field of marriage, family law and succession.[93] Ennahdha tried to oppose the move, claiming that CEDAW would 'encourage promiscuity and a chaotic sex life',[94] but eventually, the reservations were dropped, although with the specification that the country 'shall not take any organizational or legislative decision in conformity with the requirements of this Convention where such a decision

90 Hamza Roberto Piccardo in Colombo, *Tunisia: A Nascent Democracy under Siege*, 49.

91 Abbiate, 'La partecipazione popolare', 69. Moussa, 'Dalle tre paure', 80.

92 'Tunisia: Landmark Action on Women's Rights'.

93 Gallala-Arndt, 'Tunisia after the Arab Spring', 604. It is interesting to note that such reservations had been presented as a temporary measure before adapting the Tunisian legislation to the CEDAW.

94 Gallala-Arndt, 608.

would conflict with the provisions of Chapter I of the Tunisian Constitution'.[95] This could be problematic in light of the constitutionalized role of Islam, as discussed above. However, we must also take into account Article 20, which grants international treaties supremacy over ordinary laws: now the latter will have to comply with the CEDAW provisions.[96]

Light and shadows of the 2014 Tunisian Constitution: The *Code des Libertés* as a crucial but unlikely step forward

Overall, the Tunisian Constitution can be considered a progressive text, with a significant potential in terms of democratic development for the country, and perhaps for the region as a whole. Tunisia, indeed, is not just the initiator of the Arab Spring, but also the only country that has survived the winter that followed: its authentic, albeit imperfect, democracy and its strong and pugnacious civil society are good starting points to bring the constitutional principles from paper to reality.

At the same time, the text contains several ambiguities that could ultimately trigger open conflicts between secularists and Islamists: while the two groups share a preference for democratic procedures, this concord does not extend to the substantive principles of a liberal democracy. As M'rad notes, '[i]n a way, the fight against Islamic tyranny has supplanted the fight against the dictatorship. The same is true of Egypt. Islamists have traditionally and fundamentally put religion above democratic values and institutions, even if they do proclaim their respect for democracy and their attachment to the values of modernity'.[97] The establishment of the Constitutional Court, prefigured by Article 118 of the Constitution, will arguably represent a crucial step in dispelling the ambiguities and bringing the country in one direction or the other.

For these reasons, in 2017, late President Béji Caïd Essebsi established the 'Individual Freedoms and Equality Committee', known by the French acronym COLIBE,[98] whose task was 'preparing a report on the legislative amendments required to implement individual freedoms and equality in Tunisia pursuant to the 2014 Constitution and to the international human rights standards'.[99]

The committee's final report contains crucial recommendations for legislative amendments. These have been included in a Draft Code of Rights and Individual Freedoms (*Code des Libertés Individuelles – CODLI*) officially tabled at the Tunisian Parliament in 2018 by 16 deputies from different political groupings. The code aims to bring about an overall reform of the Tunisian legal system so

95 'Tunisia: Landmark Action on Women's Rights'.
96 Ceccherini, 'La questione dell'eguaglianza uomo-donna', 127. On Article 20 see also *infra*, Chapter VIII.
97 M'rad, 'The Process of Institutional Transformation', 72.
98 *Commission des libertés individuelles et de l'égalité.*
99 Ben Achour and Jelassi, 'Analytical Reading', 12.

as to remove any provisions – whether civil, criminal or administrative – that impede the full enjoyment of individual freedoms as foreseen by the Constitution.

In the next chapters, as anticipated, I will focus on the case studies of homosexuality and freedom of conscience, to show how steep a hill remains to be climbed in achieving a full recognition of individual liberties, even in the presence of a formally advanced constitutional text. The CODLI also takes crucial steps in these controversial matters. Concerning homosexuality, it recognizes sexual orientation as an illegitimate ground for discrimination and mentions the respect for sexual life and personal identity within the right to privacy. In conjunction with the principle of dignity, these provisions require amending those articles (226, 226 bis and 230) that criminalize homosexuality and curtail freedom of conscience.[100] Concerning the latter, the code takes on board the definition of the ICCPR and recognizes the right to atheism and non-religious convictions, albeit stopping short of explicitly allowing the *expression* of atheist sentiments (which is the real issue, as I will show).[101] The code also provides wide coverage for artistic freedom, specifying that it cannot be restricted for ideological, political or religious reasons.[102] Furthermore, it mentions sexual life, as well as religious and non-religious convictions, in connection with the right to privacy.[103]

Islamists have reacted vehemently to the CODLI: Ennahdha has named the reform proposal a 'threat to the family's structure and society's cohesion';[104] a former minister of religious affairs, Noureddine Khadmi, has even spoken of *fitna*, while Salafists have targeted COLIBE's president, Bochra Bel Haj Hamida, with insults and physical threats.[105] Secular forces, on their part, did not race to support the cause, with only 16 MPs ready to sponsor it, many of whom were not re-elected in the following parliamentary elections. Even less was the project successful at winning the hearts and minds of the Tunisian public.[106] For all these reasons, the CODLI seems to be destined to remain, at least for now, a beautiful but fruitless monument to good intentions.

100 Ben Achour and Jelassi, 'Lecture analytique', 40–41.
101 Ben Achour and Jelassi, 21.
102 Ben Achour and Jelassi, 30.
103 Ben Achour and Jelassi, 46.
104 Virgili, '"Arab Spring" Yesterday and Today'.
105 Virgili.
106 Bhira, 'Code des libertés individuelles en Tunisie'.

Introduction to the case studies

The following three chapters concentrate on two major social taboos in Tunisia and Egypt, namely homosexuality and blasphemy – with the latter being widely understood as including heresy and apostasy or any expression that is perceived to go against the dominant religious doctrine and mores.

In spite of the political turmoil, societal upheaval and constitutional processes these countries have undergone, any attacks, real or imagined, on religion, and on the sexual heteronormativity entrenched in religion (or at least perceived as such[1]), are still considered intolerable wounds inflicted to society and its values. This represents a major obstacle to the legal acceptance of sexual rights and full freedom of conscience, belief and expression; therefore, in spite of the constitutional guarantees, homosexuality and blasphemy are still chastised, in courts and in the larger society.

Starting from the assumption that the rights in question fully fall within the civil liberties protected both at domestic constitutional and international legal terms, and that they should be limited only according to strict criteria,[2] I will examine criminal prosecutions of homosexual acts and expressions offending religion and public morals. In both cases, I will briefly introduce the main penal provisions in the books, and present some relevant case law, additionally using interviews conducted with relevant experts and civil society actors to better

1 *Inter alia*, is notorious in Tunisia the case of Sfax's imam calling for the execution of homosexuals on religious bases. See Monceau, 'En Tunisie'. In so doing, he follows the path of more famous Islamic scholars such as the well-known Yusuf al-Qaradawi. See 'Sheik Yousuf Al-Qaradhawi'. See also Kugle and Hunt, 'Masculinity, Homosexuality and the Defence of Islam', 274. For this and other examples of 'neo-orthodox' homophobic Islamic scholars, Zollner, 'Mithliyyun or Lutiyyun? Neo-Orthodoxy and the Debate on the Unlawfulness of Same-Sex Relations in Islam'.

2 E.g., Art. 49 Tunisian Constitution, based on human rights international covenants: 'The limitations that can be imposed on the exercise of the rights and freedoms guaranteed in this Constitution will be established by law, without compromising their essence. Any such limitations can only be put in place for reasons necessary to a civil and democratic state and with the aim of protecting the rights of others, or based on the requirements of public order, national defence, public health or public morals, and provided there is proportionality between these restrictions and the objective sought'.

DOI: 10.4324/9780429259418

define the legal issues or to contextualize the topics. Finally, in order to verify my initial hypotheses, I will assess the compatibility of such restrictions with the parameters set by the constitutions in force in Egypt and Tunisia and by international human rights law.

I will show that the two issues share noteworthy similarities: the same *ratio legis* for prosecution prevails; and the same constitutional and international guarantees protect both rights. In other words, gays, atheists, blasphemers and their kind are persecuted under laws that respond to the same logic, in that they all vaguely protect public morals; at the same time, these laws violate several constitutional and international provisions protecting individuals' autonomy and pursuit of self-fulfilment from interference by both the state and society.

As clarified in the introduction, one of the main assumptions underlying this study is that human rights are universal. To quote Samar Habib, 'rights discourses can be universally applicable with respect to torture and persecution, since these constitutionally affect human beings in similar ways, irrespective of cultural differences or social constructions'.[3]

3 Habib, 'LGBT Activism in the Middle East', 1.

VI (Il)legal persecution of freethinkers

Introduction

In this chapter I am going to focus on the right to hold and express unconventional beliefs in Egypt and Tunisia, especially looking at how freethinkers' rights are curtailed for religious reasons. I use 'freethinkers' as an umbrella term covering a plethora of non-conformist manifestations of individual conscience. These may include the following: atheism, i.e. 'a lack of belief or a strong disbelief in the existence of a god or any gods'; apostasy, i.e. 'the act of refusing to continue to follow, obey, or recognize a religious faith'; heterodoxy, i.e. what is 'contrary to or different from an acknowledged standard, a traditional form, or an established religion'; heresy, i.e. 'dissent or deviation from a dominant theory, opinion or practice'; and blasphemy, i.e. 'the act of insulting or showing contempt or lack of reverence for God' and 'irreverence toward something considered sacred or inviolable'.[1]

Evidently, these notions are as heterogeneous as interwoven with each other: a heterodox opinion on religion may be perceived as blasphemous, and its author in turn designated an apostate. This confusion of terms and ideas is reflected in the legislation and case law of Tunisia and Egypt, where vague clauses and legal aporias are exploited to expel undesired individuals from society. The specific case studies I have selected reflect the attempt to show different facets of the spectrum of 'freethinkers' and the treatment they face.

To quote Brian Whitaker, 'the treatment of non-believers [...] becomes the ultimate test: when an atheist can be accepted as a normal human being, liberty will have truly arrived'.[2]

Tunisia

Statutory provisions

In Tunisia there are no laws against either apostasy or 'blasphemy' as such – that is, laws directly criminalizing the contempt for the sacred. Ennahdha attempted

1 Definitions from the Merriam-Webster dictionary.
2 Whitaker, *Arabs Without God*, 7.

DOI: 10.4324/9780429259418-VI

to introduce an explicit 'blasphemy law' both in the Constitution and in ordinary legislation,[3] but a vigorous reaction from civil society forced the proponents to step back. However, this does not mean that provocative, non-conformist speech is permitted: rather, it is criminalized under different labels, showing how broad the concept of 'contempt for religion' is.

Within the section of the Penal Code dedicated to the 'offenses against morals', a subsection refers to 'public offenses against decency'. Therein, Article 226 criminalizes any action tantamount to 'public indecency' with a six-month prison term and a fine.[4] Article 226bis further expands:

> Anyone who publicly undermines good morals [*al-akhlāq al-ḥamīda / bonnes moeurs*] or public decency [*al-adab al-ʿāmma / morale publique*] through words or deeds, or intentionally disturbs others in a way that offends modesty [*al-hayāʾ/ pudeur*], shall be punished with a six-month term of imprisonment and a fine of one thousand dinars.
>
> The same penalties apply to anyone who publicly draws attention to an opportunity to commit debauchery [*fujūr/débauche*] through printed, recorded, audio or visual, electronic or optical material.[5]

It is important to note that the criminalization of homosexuality is located in the same section of 'offenses against morals', and that the 'debauchery' (*fujūr*) of Article 226bis is the same word used in the Egyptian criminal law to condemn homosexuals. These are just two of many instances of proximity between homosexuality and blasphemy that I will highlight in this and the following chapters.

In addition to Article 226bis, Article 121ter (whose validity has been questioned[6]) stipulates a penalty of imprisonment of up to five years for the publication or distribution of any kind of material liable to harm public order or decency. Other norms curtailing free speech in the name of decency, morals and

3 Habib Ellouz, a hard-liner of Ennahdha, argued in favour of a law against blasphemy (two-year prison for first-time offenders, four years for repeat offenders), in favour of shar'ia as the main source of legislation, and against freedom of conscience. Likewise, in the drafting process, several Ennahdha leaders argued for more restriction on free speech. In June 2012 Ennahdha proposed an Art. 3 reading 'The state guarantees freedom of religious belief and practice and criminalizes all attacks on that which is sacred'. *V.* Human Rights First, 'Blasphemy, Freedom of Expression, and Tunisia's Transition to Democracy'. McCarthy, 'Protecting the Sacred'. Whitaker, *Arabs Without God*, 163.

4 *Outrage public à la pudeur* in the French version; ***kull man yatajāhir ʿamd^{an} bi-fuḥsh*** (lit. 'those who publicly and intentionally declare obscenity').

5 Own translation from Arabic and French. Al-Majalla al-jazaʾiyya [Tunisian Criminal Code]. Code Pénal [Tunisian Criminal Code].

6 This article is particularly problematic as regards its current legal validity. Indeed, the Decree-Law 115/2011, which has renovated the press code, has also explicitly abrogated all those laws having modified the old one. Considering that Article 121ter penal code was previously part of the press code, and has been transferred to the penal code by the 'Organic Law 2001-43 of 3 May 2001, amending the press code', such law should also be considered abrogated, thereby including those articles that it transferred from the press code to the penal code. See Eddhif, 'Le Code pénal à la lumière du Décret-loi 2011-115'.

public order come from equally vague criminal law provisions contained in the Telecommunications Code and the Press Code. For instance, Article 86 of the Telecommunications Code punishes any person who knowingly harms others or disturbs their peace of mind through public telecommunications networks with imprisonment of one to two years and a fine.

The vague and broad nature of such laws, containing clauses hard to define and to distinguish from one another,[7] has led to arbitrary decisions in courts. Several cases arose in the aftermath of the revolution, testifying to the clash between opposite worldviews. I am going to examine some which are particularly interesting from a legal perspective, in that they show how broad the judges' interpretation of 'public decency' and 'public morals' is.

Ils ne sont pas Charlie: *Muhammad's cartoons as a threat to social peace*

The first case I address is that known as '*Affaire Mahdia*'. It concerned two atheist freethinkers, Jabeur Mejri and Ghazi Béji, who were found guilty of posting sexual caricatures of the Prophet Muhammad on their Facebook pages.[8] Further to the publication, a lawyer decided to lodge a legal complaint based on the 'offense to the Prophet, to the Islamic religion and to Muslim believers' and 'incitation to discord [*fitna*]'.[9] Another plaintiff followed suit, lamenting an attack against the Islamic community (*umma*) and 'a grave moral damage'[10] to him personally. In consequence, a formal investigation was opened against Mejri and Béji, for alleged violation of Articles 121ter and 226 of the Penal Code, and 86 of the Telecommunications Code.

The verdict fully endorsed the allegations. At first, it paid formal tribute to the defendants' freedom of belief, by saying that 'religious beliefs or the absence thereof [...] cannot be the object of a criminal proceeding, as this pertains to the individual religious freedom guaranteed by international conventions, notably by the Universal Declaration of Human Rights'.[11] However, the judgment added that depicting the Prophet in a sexual or degrading way goes beyond the boundaries of the licit, because such an act 'provokes other people's sentiments and its diffusion has the consequence of disrupting public order', under Article 121ter of the Penal Code.[12] Furthermore, such images are liable to violate decency and public morals under Article 226bis. The judge then addressed a very sensitive point: 'the Tunisian legislator has not provided a definition of decency/

7 It is even difficult to find in English a univocal translation for each of them, as there are no specular expressions and the ones employed here ('offense to public decency', 'offense to public morals', 'indecent behavior'...) are quite interchangeable.

8 For an account of the events, see Riahi, '"Affaire Mahdia"'.

9 Riahi. Own translation from Arabic.

10 *Dhurur m'anwy had.*

11 'Dossier Juridique'. Own translation from French.

12 For a critique of the 'provocation' argument, *v. infra*. On 'defamation of religion' in general, see Leo, Gaer, and Cassidy, 'Protecting Religions from "Defamation"'.

good morals [*bonnes moeurs* in French, *al-akhlāq al-ḥamīda* in Arabic]'. This vagueness is in fact the very problem of the various clauses criminalizing free speech in the Tunisian legislation, and is responsible for abuse and misuse of the principle of legality in criminal law. Despite acknowledging the legislative gap, the judge filled it by referring to a consistent jurisdictional interpretation: 'The jurisprudence dealing with the issue has considered *bonnes moeurs* as the whole of moral rules, traditions, mores, religious prescriptions *prevailing* [*dominantes*] in society and which may not be contravened.'[13]

This claim shows three important facts: (1) the interpretation given to the clause is a very broad and vague one; (2) it is loosely grounded on a hotchpotch of moral and religious customs that, albeit not binding by law, are assumed to be mandatory; (3) such moral and religious rules are those *prevailing* in society: in other words, those defined by the majority. In sum, according to this reading, the penal code contains a clause allowing a judge to deprive individuals of their personal freedom if they disregard undefined, non-legal rules based on morals and religion as defined by the majority.

The detrimental effect on the principle of legality was enshrined in the final statement of the judgement concerning Article 226bis: 'As per the constant jurisprudence, the legal system represses any attempt to attack what people consider sacred (as is the case for blasphemy, which is a verbal offense against God), *for this is equivalent to defiling good morals*'.[14] Such an 'equivalence' is a clear breach of the principle of legality, as it creates by analogy a crime of blasphemy which is not statutorily provided for, notwithstanding the prohibition of analogic reasoning in criminal law. As jurists criticizing the verdict rightly commented:

> The Mahdia Tribunal could not, in the absence of a law criminalizing the alleged offense to the 'sacred', condemn the defendants on such a basis. The legal label employed here is a ruse that nullifies the judgment's unproved assumption [*pétition de principe*] according to which the accused are not prosecuted for their religious convictions. [...] In so doing, this label not only breaches the principle of legality which regulates the offenses and penalties, but also the guiding principles of interpretation in criminal law. For the sake of people's freedom, it is not permitted to extend the application of criminal laws through analogic reasoning, *a fortiori* or *a contrario*. Criminal statutes require the so-called strict construction.[15]

Furthermore, the same jurists observed that the tribunal had omitted to demonstrate the interest of the plaintiffs in being part of the trial – since obviously nobody had forced them to endure the pain of such a sight – as well as their capacity

13 Emphasis added.

14 Emphasis added. Own translation from French

15 These considerations are developed by Ali Mezghani, Kalthoum MeziouDoraï, Monia Ben Jémia, Souhayma Ben Achour, law professors, and Mokhtar Trifi, lawyer and former president of the *Ligue Tunisienne des Droits de l'Homme*. 'Dossier Juridique'. Own translation from French.

to act as custodians of the general will of society. According to the critics, this is a typical procedure following the Islamic principle of *ḥisba*, whereby any believer has the right and the duty to impose the good and stop evil.[16] I will delve more into this concept with reference to Egypt, where *ḥisba* was, in fact, the legal principle invoked in the infamous trial of the alleged apostate Abu Zayd.

Ni Allah Ni Maître, *or 'the crime of atheism'*

Another interesting case, which is relevant due to the public scandal it provoked and for its legal implications, concerned the 2011 film *Ni Allah ni maître*[17] by Nadia El Fani. The movie shows the hardship non-fasting Tunisians endure during Ramadan, and represents an accusation against Islamists, who seek to impose their mores upon others, and against state authorities who are often complicit with Islamists' demands – even outside of any legal framework.

First the screening theatre was raided by Salafists during the première,[18] and then three lawyers filed a legal complaint, whereupon the public prosecutor, finding it *prima facie* well grounded, ordered an investigation.[19] Although the legal proceeding did not continue, and the statute of limitations has since elapsed for that crime,[20] it is very relevant to examine the reasoning behind the accusations. The very title of the movie was brought as evidence of El Fani's deliberate intent to offend Allah, 'the most sacred entity for the Tunisian people [...], *by explicitly denying his existence*' (emphasis added).[21] The same malicious intent was demonstrated, according to the legal proceeding, by El Fani's public profession of atheism (*ilḥādahā*) in a Tunisian TV show. In other words, the body of the crime did not even consist here in offensive, vulgar or blasphemous speech, as in the *Mahdia* case, but in a mere declaration of atheism.

The complainants showed an awareness of the conflict thus created with freedom of belief, and reaffirmed that 'everybody is bestowed with the freedom of belief'. However, according to them, El Fani's 'faith or absence thereof shall remain a personal matter', whereas the offender:

> first, has intentionally chosen to make it public in the media, and secondly to use a shocking title, thus injuring [*khādish*] our people's beliefs, religion and norms. In so doing, she has exceeded the boundaries of her private

16 'Dossier Juridique'.

17 'Neither Allah nor master', AKA *Laïcité Inch'Allah*.

18 I received a personal account of this story from an activist of the feminist and pro-lesbian organization *Chouf*, who was inside the cinema when the Salafists attacked. For a detailed report and videos, see 'Attaque du Cinéma Africart par des Islamistes'.

19 Mounir Baatour (El Fani's lawyer), interview. According to Article 30 of the Tunisian Code of Criminal Procedure, the prosecutor freely considers the appropriate follow-up for complaints and information he receives. Code de Procédure Pénale [Tunisian Code of Criminal Procedure].

20 Mounir Baatour, interview.

21 Office of the Public Prosecutor of Tunis, 'Legal Complaint against Nadia El Fani, Doc. n. 7032915/2011 [in Arabic]'. Courtesy of Mounir Baatour. See also Zeghidi, 'Tunisie: La Liberté Inch'Allah!'

sphere of beliefs, and she has committed an enormous offense [*taᶜdiya*] and provocation [*istifzāz*] against the entire society.

In other words, freedom of conscience, belief and speech succumb to an overbroad interpretation of a vague, collective and non-legal interest such as society's 'sensitivity'. This proves that the real taboo is atheism per se: manifesting unbelief, no matter the means or the tone, is considered by itself an infraction, a provocation trespassing the limits of the licit.

Another accusation brought against El Fani was that, with her statements, she had 'created discord [*fitna*]', exciting violent reactions from 'tens of thousands of people taking to the streets to express their profound rejection and anger over this gratuitous provocation and harm to their sentiments and the most sacred things'. The hypothesized crimes were two articles of the former Press Code,[22] 44 and 48, having a penal character. Article 48 punished with imprisonment those who, by using the media, committed offense against decency and 'one of the cults whose exercise is admitted'; Article 44 referred specifically to the hypothesis of, *inter alia*, incitation to hatred between religions and spread of ideas based on religious extremism. By using these arguments, the complainants on the one hand equated a declaration of atheism with a form of 'religious extremism'; on the other hand, they held Nadia El Fani responsible for the riots against her movie, as if she had 'incited' them.

The same pattern, based on such a distorted concept of 'provocation', applies to other post-revolutionary cases, which have gained public attention. Article 121ter, namely the accusation of disruption of public order, was used, for instance, against two artists performing in the exhibition *Printemps des Arts*: Nadia Jelassi, who denounced in her artwork the Qur'anic penalty of stoning; and Mohamed Ben Slama, who portrayed the name of Allah made by ants. An Islamic preacher called for their murder, and Salafists erupted in violent riots. Yet, political condemnations and legal charges for disruption of public order were raised against the victims of such irrational rage.[23] In other words, the constitutional protection of minorities yielded to the 'law of the strongest'.

According to relevant figures I have interviewed, the situation has recently been improving compared to the immediate post-revolutionary period: many Salafists have been arrested under terrorist charges, and Ennahdha does not seem to have a political interest in backing certain manifestations of religious extremism any more.[24] However, recent occurrences seem to point to a worrying trend.

22 Now abrogated by a new one established with Law-Decree 115-2011 of 2 November 2011, although some provisions remain identical.

23 Abrougui, 'Tunisia's Red Lines'. The Troika condemned the provocation, and Ennahdha proposed a law against blasphemy. Ziad Krichen, journalist at *Le Maghreb*, interviewed by the author, Tunis, July 2016.

24 Ziad Krichen, interview. Amna Guellali, Former Director Human Rights Watch Tunisia, interviewed by the author, Tunis, July 2016. Both mentioned the detrimental role of Ennahdha at that time in fostering religious violence. Krichen referred in particular to the Leagues for the protection of the revolution, linked to Ennahdha, which ignited a generalized political violence. (Cf. Cavalliès, 'La Ligue de Protection de la Révolution: Le bras armé d'Ennahdha?')

Mounir Baatour and Emna Chargui: 'blasphemous extremists'?

In a sadly ironic twist, El Fani's lawyer, Mounir Baatour, has also been forced to flee Tunisia due to death threats and a legal prosecution for blasphemy. A prominent figure in the country's human rights landscape, Baatour is also the founder of *Shams*, the first openly pro-LGBT organization in the Arab world (see next chapter), and the president of the Tunisian Liberal Party – in which role he even filed a candidature for the presidential elections of September 2019.[25]

Just a few months after the elections, the counterterrorism public prosecutor at the Court of First Instance of Tunis opened an investigation against him, based on a Facebook post where he decried the Prophet Muhammad as a paedophile, a rapist and a killer.[26] In the indictment file, Baatour is charged with: 'accusation of apostasy [*takfir*] and its solicitation, incitement to hatred and to animosity between races, doctrines, and religions', under Article 14 of Law 26/2015 on the fight against terrorism; 'incitement to hatred, violence, and segregation toward persons or groups of persons based on racial discrimination' as per Articles 3 and 9 of Law 50/2018 on the elimination of all forms of racial discrimination; and 'directly calling for hatred between races, religions, and populations' via audio-visual and electronic means, under Articles 50 and 52 of Decree-Law 115/2011 on freedom of the press.[27]

The fact that the investigation was initiated by the *counterterrorism* section of the tribunal evidences the abnormality of the accusations with respect to the conduct prompting it. Furthermore, the prosecutor distorted the terms of the laws s/he invoked. For instance, the reference to *takfir* in theory should conform to Article 6 of the Constitution, having the purpose, as mentioned, of banning the hideous Islamist practice of censoring unwelcomed ideas by menacing their authors with an implicit (and sometimes explicit) death threat. This is precisely what Baatour was a *victim* of, targeted as he was with accusations of apostasy and death threats by a multitude of social media users and even by a renowned Tunisian preacher.[28] In other words, the accused in this case is actually a victim of *takfir*, not an offender. Similarly, Article 3 of Law 50/2018 engages the state to 'spread the culture of human rights, equality, tolerance and acceptance of others among the different components of society': indicting an individual for blasphemy goes diametrically against this provision, in that it represents a human rights violation, and the negation of tolerance toward diversity. This case shows that even well-intentioned laws, if not specific enough, may turn victims into culprits.

While the new Press Code was saluted as a crucial advancement compared to the previous one (and rightly so, from many points of view), Baatour has

25 AFP and Le Figaro, 'Tunisie: le candidat défendant les droits des LGBTQ exclu de la présidentielle'.

26 'Tunisia: Halt Prosecution of Prominent Activist'.

27 'Tunisia: Halt Prosecution of Prominent Activist'. Prosecutor's Office at the Counterterrorism Section of the Court of First Instance of Tunis, Case 3860/31.

28 'Tunisia: Halt Prosecution of Prominent Activist'.

not been the only one who fell foul of Article 52 on 'inciting hatred between religion'. In the midst of the 2020 coronavirus pandemic, a joke on social distancing cost the openly atheist Tunisian blogger Emna Chargui a sentence of six months in prison. Her fault: posting on her Facebook profile an ironic text titled 'Surat Corona' mimicking the Qur'an. Like Baatour, Chargui has fled Tunisia since.[29]

These cases, enjoying media resonance, are just a few among many others having a lower profile. In particular, the Civil Collective for Individual Freedoms, in its yearly reports on the state of individual freedoms in Tunisia, documents ongoing harassment and legal prosecutions by public authorities against non-fasters and restaurant owners during Ramadan.[30]

As long as laws of this kind are in the books, and prosecutors and judges maintain an ideological mindset giving those laws a liberticidal interpretation, atheists and freethinkers will remain under constant threat of persecution.

Egypt

Legislation criminalizing apostasy and blasphemy

Egypt persecutes atheists, blasphemers and freethinkers to an even larger extent than Tunisia. A comparative analysis of the Tunisian statutes and case law and the equivalent Egyptian ones shows similar patterns in the legal basis and ideological reasoning behind the repression, despite some relevant differences.

Starting with apostasy, Egypt has no formal ban on it, while the 2014 Constitution even states that 'Freedom of belief is absolute'[31] (thus implicitly including atheism) and prohibits discrimination based on, *inter alia*, religion.[32] At least theoretically, this far-reaching recognition represents an improvement over the 1971 Constitution, which did not frame freedom of belief as a natural right, but as a concession by the state.[33]

However, these inclusive and liberal provisions are limited (and even contradicted) by the privilege enjoyed by the 'Heavenly religions', namely Islam, Christianity and Judaism: these are the only ones explicitly mentioned in the Constitution, which grants them a special status by making their canons[34] legally

29 Foroudi, 'Blogger Flees Tunisia after Arrest'; Boukhayatia, 'Affaire Emna Chergui, Nième Duel Entre Liberté de Conscience et Atteinte au Sacré'.

30 Le Collectif Civil pour les Libertés Individuelles (CCLI), 'Les Libertés Individuelles en 2019: Le Danger des Populistes!', 17. Le Collectif Civil pour les Libertés Individuelles (CCLI), 'État des Libertés Individuelles 2018: Bas les Masques !', 14.

31 Art. 64.

32 Art. 53.

33 'The State shall guarantee the freedom of belief and the freedom of practice of religious rites', Art. 46. 'The Constitution of the Arab Republic of Egypt, 1971'.

34 Art. 2: 'Islam is the religion of the state and Arabic is its official language. The principles of Islamic Sharia are the principal source of legislation'. Art. 3: 'The principles of the laws of

relevant and restricting the right to practise religious rituals to their followers.[35] Hence, only Muslims, Christians and Jews are entitled to manifest and practise their faith, in spite of the principle of equality and non-discrimination enshrined in Article 53. Furthermore, they are bound by the rules of their respective religions, even when these contradict individual rights.

Despite the lack of a specific provision, prohibitions of apostasy and 'idolatry/paganism' have *de facto* been created in court using three tools: (1) the concept of public order; (2) the criminal ban on blasphemy, mainly *ex art.* 98(f) of the Penal Code; and (3) inconsistencies and gaps in civil law, which have permitted a direct reference to Islamic jurisprudence.[36] I will come back to this third way of criminalizing apostasy and idolatry, that is, by direct reference to shariatic rules in the civil legal system, when I analyse the Abu Zayd case *infra*. For now, I will concentrate on the first two tools, namely the concept of public order and the criminal ban on apostasy.

The Egyptian Court of Cassation has made the prohibition of apostasy a fundamental element of public order since 1975.[37] This argument has been used, *inter alia*, to deny followers of the Bahai faith the right to practise their religion.[38] It is premised on the idea that leaving Islam or believing in a creed other than the 'religions of the book' falls under the rules of 'public policy' rather than personal belief.[39] Public policy is defined as '"the social, political, economic or moral principles in a state related to the highest (or essential) interest (*maslaha 'ulya, or: masalih jawhariyya*) of society", or as "the essence (*kiyan*) of the nation"'.[40] In the words of the renowned Islamic legal scholar al-Sanhuri, general interests must always prevail over individual ones.[41] Yet, nowhere are these interests clearly outlined, and it is up to the courts to concretely define them on an *ad hoc* basis. The only general guideline is that they must correspond to the 'essential principles of Islamic law', as per consistent Egyptian jurisprudence.[42] Consequently, the absence of an explicit law against apostasy is not an obstacle to the criminalization thereof, because the prohibition is considered to be one of the very foundations of the Egyptian legal order.

The second tool utilized to punish apostasy is by considering the abjuration of Islam as a form of 'contempt' for religion.[43] This leads me to address blasphemy

Egyptian Christians and Jews are the main source of laws regulating their personal status, religious affairs, and selection of spiritual leaders'.

35 Art. 64: 'The freedom of practicing religious rituals and establishing places of worship *for the followers of revealed religions* is a right organized by law'. Emphasis added.

36 El Fegiery, 'Islamic Law and Freedom of Religion', 6–7.

37 Faraj, 'Religious Minorities under Pressure', 642.

38 El Fegiery, 'Islamic Law and Freedom of Religion', 6.

39 Berger, 'Apostasy and Public Policy', 725.

40 Berger, 725.

41 Berger, 726.

42 Berger, 726.

43 Whitaker, *Arabs Without God*, 133.

in Egyptian legislation. Unlike the Tunisian case, the Egyptian criminal code has an explicit ban on blasphemy, in Article 98(f):[44]

> Whoever exploits religion in speech, in writing or any other means for the promotion of extremist ideas with the intent of stirring discord [*fitna*] or disdaining and disrespecting any of the heavenly religions or the communities belonging thereto, or harming national unity, shall be punished by imprisonment for not less than six months and not more than five years, or a fine of not less than five hundred pounds and not exceeding one thousand pounds.[45]

The analysis of the Arabic wording is very revealing, as it exhibits some marked similarities with the accusations against Tunisian freethinkers examined above. It is impossible to circumscribe *a priori* the spectrum of Article 98(f). An attempt to better define the crime was made in 2006, when legislators removed some obscure references to 'favouring' *fitna* and 'harming social peace'.[46] Despite this, the wording remains so vague and the matter so sensitive that anything that falls outside of the accepted orthodoxy is a fair target. Such vagueness goes against the principles outlined by the Supreme Constitutional Court of Egypt on matters of penal law: the SCC has reaffirmed that criminal statutes are governed by strict standards and that the definition of criminalized conduct must be clear, categorical, univocal and unambiguous, as per the principle of *nullum crimen sine lege*.[47]

Starting with 'extremist ideas' (*afkār mutaṭarrifa*), its meaning is as ambiguous in Arabic as it is in English, and refers, according to different dictionaries, to ideas which 'incite violence' or are 'brought to the extremes' or 'exceed the limits of moderation'.[48] Egyptian courts have acknowledged the vagueness intrinsic to this formulation, but their attempts to define it have led to an even worse outcome, namely an interpretation of 'extremism' derived from the 'common shariᶜa' as any opinion that deviates from the 'known truths' of religion.[49] This reading criminalizes freethinkers while absolving radicals who advocate violence on the basis of Qurᵓanic verses and hadiths, in that they do not deviate from established sources and interpretations.[50] As has been correctly stated,

> [t]he law does not specify what constitutes an 'insult' or amounts to 'inciting', leaving it almost fully to the judge's discretion and, hence, the dominant cultural influences. This could lead to such absurd situation in which

44 Sometimes transliterated as 98(w), because of the letter و used in the Arabic text.
45 Qanun al-ᶜUqubat [Egyptian Criminal Code]. Own translation from Arabic.
46 Ramadan, 'Asbab ᶜAdam Dusturiyyat', 6.
47 Ramadan, 7.
48 Ramadan, 9. Own translation from Arabic.
49 Ramadan, 9.
50 Ramadan, 9.

> the Egyptian state is a member of an international military coalition against ISIS but its judiciary jails people who mock ISIS[51]

– as happened to four Christian teenagers convicted for ridiculing prayers of ISIS warriors.[52]

The clause referring to 'exploitation of religion' is not any clearer, nor is the concept of 'stirring *fitna*'. The ambiguity surrounding the overall intent of the law emerges from the divergence of judicial interpretations: while certain rulings that read the article teleologically maintain that it aims at preventing sectarian strife, and they thus conclude that the contempt of religion must have this intent in order to be punished, other verdicts have adopted a more literal reading and considered 'disrespecting religions' an autonomous crime, independent of 'stirring sedition'.[53] Under the latter interpretation, religions are the direct object of protection. As a result, novelists, bloggers and intellectuals have been condemned to harsh prison terms for publishing books, articles or blog posts considered blasphemous against Islam or Al-Azhar,[54] or merely for adopting an interpretation of Islam that differs from the orthodoxy – something considered 'offensive'.[55] In certain cases, judges did not even require specific *conduct* to occur for a crime to take place: people have been prosecuted without actually disrespecting any creed, just because their religious identity is considered blasphemous *in re ipsa* in the eyes of Sunni Islam: this has happened to Shiᶜi Muslims, Bahais and atheists, as explained below.

This succinct summary of cases prompted by Article 98(f) highlights two main points: laws of this kind are discriminatory in that they privilege certain creeds over others, and they have a dangerous chilling effect on freedom of thought, expression and religion.

Additional provisions are used against individuals accused of violating religion and public morals; in particular Article 160 of the penal code anticipates a penalty up to five years in prison for the desecration of religious ceremonies, buildings, symbols and graves; Article 161 imposes the same penalties for publishing distorted versions of religious books or publicly mocking religious ceremonies; and Article 178 punishes with detention of up to two years and a fine anyone who publishes, distributes, displays or otherwise promotes any kind of material contrary to 'public morals'.

Patterns of persecution of atheists and blasphemers

There are roughly five main groups persecuted for religious reasons, encompassing an extremely wide spectrum: (1) blasphemers *stricto sensu*, that is, those who

51 Mansour, 'Freedom of Expression in Egypt', 235.
52 'Teens Convicted of Blasphemy for Video Mocking ISIS'.
53 Ramadan, 'Asbab ᶜAdam Dusturiyyat', 12.
54 El Fegiery, *Islamic Law and Human Rights*, 116.
55 Ramadan, 'Asbab ᶜAdam Dusturiyyat', 11.

willingly scorn one of the 'heavenly religions'; (2) those who publish 'obscene' content; (3) 'heretical' intellectuals who take a critical approach to religious matters and to the laws descending from religious principles; (4) atheists and apostates; (5) members of unaccepted sects or religions, such as Shiᶜa and Bahais.

Individuals in all of these categories have been victims of a widespread witch-hunt.[56] Accusations may target all forms of expression (acts, drawings, writings, speeches, etc.), either blasphemous or merely unorthodox according to the dominant doctrine, irrespective of the means of transmission (with the internet being the most frequent medium).[57]

The risk is higher for members of minority groups. Figures show that people belonging to the Christian minority are by far the most targeted in respect to the population,[58] sometimes for trivial reasons, such as private discussions with Muslims that lead to revenge accusations of blasphemy.[59] Shiᶜa[60] and Bahais[61] are also frequently targeted. On the other hand, rare are the cases where a Sunni Muslim is condemned for attacking a minority creed.[62] Another problematic aspect is the equation of atheism with blasphemy, as seen in the Tunisian case: a public declaration of atheism may lead to a conviction, as illustrated below. Furthermore, a judicial declaration of apostasy has civil consequences for marriage, inheritance and custody of children,[63] and apostates who are born Muslim are not allowed to change their religion on their ID cards.[64]

In most cases, legal prosecution is in addition to protests and vigilante actions by the 'offended' populace, which frequently involves acts of violence against the victims and their properties.[65] Far from intervening to halt the assaults, the police tend to join them, searching and arresting the victims without legal grounds and referring their cases to public prosecution.[66] Once a complaint reaches that stage, the case will likely end up in court, as only ten per cent of the files brought before the public prosecutor since 2011 have been dismissed.[67] If this does not happen, the accused is not safe anyhow: on some occasions, especially those involving humble people in rural areas, the controversy is settled through customary reconciliation processes entailing dramatic abuses of the victims' rights, such

56 *Inter alia*, Ibrahim, 'Besieging Freedom of Thought'. Mansour, 'Freedom of Expression in Egypt'. O'Sullivan, 'Egyptian Cases of Blasphemy and Apostasy'. El Fegiery, 'Islamic Law and Freedom of Religion'. El Fegiery, *Islamic Law and Human Rights*. Saber, 'Report'.
57 Ibrahim, 'Besieging Freedom of Thought', 16.
58 The EIPR calculated that, after the 2011 revolution, accusations of blasphemy against Christians accounted for more than 41% of the total, while Christians represent around 10% of the Egyptian population. Ibrahim, 10.
59 El Fegiery, *Islamic Law and Human Rights*, 128.
60 Roberts, 'The State of the Right to Freedom of Expression', 26–29. See also *infra*.
61 El Fegiery, *Islamic Law and Human Rights*, 167–68.
62 El Fegiery, 129.
63 El Fegiery, 174.
64 El Fegiery, 188.
65 Ibrahim, 'Besieging Freedom of Thought', 17.
66 Ibrahim, 17.
67 Ibrahim, 17.

as eviction from their villages, with no compensation for the loss of property and economic activity.[68]

The public prosecutor usually does not protect the suspects from the abuses they suffer. On the contrary, the tendency is to detain them automatically, even when there are no grounds for pre-trial detention. Illegitimate questions, aimed at proving the accused person's faith and observance, often form part of the interrogation.[69] Only well-known figures, usually from Cairo, are sometimes able to avoid being detained (at least before the trial), while ordinary citizens are nearly automatically imprisoned during the trial and later convicted.[70] In the words of Alber Saber, one of the victims of this system, '[t]his gives hatemongers the chance to lock undesirable people away from society with great ease, using a single meaningless piece of paper or sending a complaint to the public prosecutor, turning this unethical law into a weapon that could be used against anyone'.[71]

While the controversial concept of 'public order' is often invoked, in many cases the courts do not even provide evidence of potential unrest to justify convictions, and purely resort to abstract and highly subjective evaluations of the blasphemous nature of the speech in question.[72] The following (rare) opinion against the liberticidal trend is worth noting:

> The judgment in case 529/2012/Agouza misdemeanor, issued on 26 April 2012, stated that the intent of the criminalization was not to protect ideas and beliefs and therefore prohibit a discussion and debate about them; nor is it to protect the sentiments that are naturally inflamed if a person transgresses established intellectual principles, especially religious principles. Rather, the court stated, the provisions provide legal protection for unity and deter civil strife. Faith may be exercised freely as long as it does not impinge on public morals. The protection exists first and foremost for the benefit of society and social peace.[73]

If, on the one hand, this verdict sets down a very important principle, i.e. that the law cannot prevent intellectual discussions and is not intended to protect the feelings of those who may take offense, on the other hand it reasserts the ambiguous concept of social peace as a basis for censoring views unacceptable to the general public. In a highly conservative country in which massive, sometimes violent protests against perceived blasphemers are not uncommon, this transfer of liability from the raging rioter to the peaceful 'provoker' will inevitably have a chilling effect on freedom of conscience and expression.[74]

68 Ibrahim, 22.
69 Ibrahim, 27.
70 Ibrahim, 19. Saber, 'Report'.
71 Saber, 'Report'.
72 El Fegiery, *Islamic Law and Human Rights*, 130.
73 Ibrahim, 'Besieging Freedom of Thought', 31. See also Roberts, 'The State of the Right to Freedom of Expression', 28.
74 Cf. El Fegiery, *Islamic Law and Human Rights*, 132.

Islamists and (un)free speech

Islamist forces constitute relevant protagonists in this picture. The Muslim Brotherhood long claimed that apostasy should be punished by death, before slightly reforming its view and demanding a discretionary punishment unless 'the public actions of apostates pose a high threat to society'.[75] Their conception of apostasy is quite encompassing: according to the Egyptian Islamist scholar Yusuf al-Qaradawi, considered an influential MB ideologue, apostasy does not consist merely in the act of treason against the state or the community (as reformists who intend to soften the rigor of shariᶜa claim), and not even exclusively in the explicit declaration of unbelief, but also in the expression of non-conformist ideas that the state must censor.[76]

Islamist actors have not limited themselves to testifying against the alleged blasphemers in court, but have also harassed them and their defenders in multiple ways.[77] The Muslim Brotherhood in particular, from its parliamentary seats and media outlets, has incited protests, mobs and legal actions against freethinkers.[78] Certain imams have ignited violence against alleged blasphemers, while religious institutions have demanded that undesirable written works be censored and their authors punished.[79] Among the victims of smear campaigns and attacks – sometimes violent, with a deadly outcome – we may include the intellectuals and writers Farag Foda and Sayyid al-Qimni, the academic Nasr Hamid Abu Zayd, the Nobel laureate Naguib Mahfouz and other novelists such as Alaᶜ Hamed, Haider Haider, Tawfiq Abd al-Rahman, Yasser Shaban and Mahmoud Hamid, the judge and scholar Muhammad Saᶜid al-Ashmawy, and the poets Ahmed al-Shawi and Helmi Salim.[80]

In the case of Sayyid al-Qimni, a prominent liberal and rationalist writer who was even awarded Egypt's highest cultural prize in 2009,[81] the attacks from the MB and other Islamist groups[82] were fortified by a fatwa from the Dar al-Ifta demanding the application of Article 98 against him. The religious legal opinion stated:

> The Muslims [believe] unanimously that whoever curses the Prophet or slanders Islam removes himself from the fold of Islam and [from the community] of Muslims, and deserves punishment in this world and torment in the world to come… The statements [from Al-Qimni's writings] quoted by the [individual] who requested the fatwa are heretical, regardless of who wrote them; they remove their author from the fold of Islam … and [also]

75 El Fegiery, 178.
76 El Fegiery, 103.
77 Ibrahim, 'Besieging Freedom of Thought', 25–27.
78 El Fegiery, *Islamic Law and Human Rights*, 109–15.
79 Ibrahim, 'Besieging Freedom of Thought', 24. Saber, 'Report'.
80 El Fegiery, *Islamic Law and Human Rights*, 109–15.
81 Azuri, 'Dispute over Granting of State Award'.
82 Suleiman, 'Egyptians Protest Award to Controversial Writer'.

> constitute a crime according to Article 98 of [Egypt's] penal code. If these depraved, loathsome, and invalid statements were indeed made by a specific individual, then this individual should be convicted rather than awarded a prize, and punished to the full extent of the law.[83]

In a previous fatwa, the Dar al-Ifta had given the following opinion on apostasy:

> Any person who joins Islam by his/her own free will cannot deviate from the public order of society by publicly announcing his/her apostasy and requesting the change of his/her religious affiliation. This prohibition, according to this *fatwa*, is necessary to protect the rights of other citizens, and to avoid any temptation and confusion for the majority.[84]

In the case of Al-Qimni, fortunately, the Court of Administrative Justice refused to revoke the prize, remarking that 'cutting off freedom of reason and thought is the equivalent of cutting a person's throat'.[85] Furthermore, the court stated that 'to reach another outcome would have violated the rights to freedom of belief and the pursuit of knowledge, which are protected inter alia by the international conventions Egypt has ratified'.[86]

Not equally lucky was Helmi Salim, who in 2017 was attacked by MB parliamentarians and by the Islamic Research Academy at Al-Azhar for a poem in which he equated God with a peasant forcibly feeding a duck. The MB judged it more offensive than the Danish caricatures of the Prophet, while Al-Azhar accused Salim of 'propagating atheism' in society.[87] As a consequence, the Court of Administrative Justice cancelled the prize Salim had been awarded by the Ministry of Culture and revoked the license held by the magazine where the poem had been published, invoking the argument that 'press freedom should respect the fundamental religious and moral values of society'.[88]

The Salim case is only one of many where the University of Al-Azhar (often portrayed as a 'moderate' institution) has been in the forefront of vicious hate campaigns against 'blasphemers' and apostates.[89] The former grand imam of Al-Azhar himself, Muhammad Sayyid Tantawi, has stated that apostasy, when it is accompanied by disrespect towards Islam, should be considered tantamount to a 'seditious crime of treason against the Islamic state'.[90] In 2012, Al-Azhar

83 Azuri, 'Dispute over Granting of State Award'.
84 El Fegiery, *Islamic Law and Human Rights*, 180.
85 Ibrahim, 'Besieging Freedom of Thought', 33.
86 Roberts, 'The State of the Right to Freedom of Expression', 28.
87 El Fegiery, *Islamic Law and Human Rights*, 115.
88 El Fegiery, 115.
89 Ibrahim, 'Besieging Freedom of Thought', 24, 42. O'Sullivan, 'Egyptian Cases of Blasphemy and Apostasy', 102, 105, 109.
90 O'Sullivan, 'Egyptian Cases of Blasphemy and Apostasy', 129.

published a document on freedom of expression that required the latter to respect Islamic morals and religious sensibilities.[91]

El Fegiery has detected a consonance of views between Al-Azhar and the Muslim Brotherhood on these matters. For instance, in the case of Egyptian judge and scholar Muhammad Saᶜid al-Ashmawy, Al-Azhar ordered the removal of his books from the Cairo International Book Fair, while the MB conducted a vicious campaign against him, due to his interpretation of the Qurᵓan and the sunna and his views on the place of shariᶜa in modern states.[92]

In the case of writer Alaᶜ Hamed, Al-Azhar was the instigator of the trial that ended with Hamed's conviction and sentencing to eight years of imprisonment due to his novel *A Distance in a Man's Mind*, which the Islamic institution judged blasphemous and, as such, 'a call to revolt against the basic social structure'.[93] The case of Islam El Beheiry followed a similar pattern: a television host and reformist Islamic scholar, in 2015 he was sentenced to a five-year term of imprisonment for violating Article 98f, after Al-Azhar lodged complaints about the content of his TV show.[94]

With the famous writer Farag Foda – an opponent of Islamism and defender of the Coptic minority – Al-Azhar's Scholar Front (a faction close to the Muslim Brotherhood), went as far as to publicly declare him an apostate.[95] One week later, he was shot dead. The killer 'referred specifically to the Al-Azhar statement as providing pure justification for the writer's killing'.[96] Sheikh al-Ghazali, one of Al-Azhar's most prominent scholars, even defended the accused in court, where he stated that 'anyone who objected to the implementation of the Shariᶜa is an excommunicate and an apostate'.[97] He further claimed that 'any individual, or group of people, who killed such a person is not liable to be punished, because in carrying out the act of such a killing, they would be executing the legitimate *ḥudūd* penalty on apostasy, within Shariᶜa'.[98] Al-Ghazali was also part of the Al-Azhar committee that censored novels by Nobel laureate Naguib Mahfouz, once again with vocal support from the Muslim Brotherhood.[99] Al-Azhar's leaders have never disowned him or any other member who issued excommunication fatwas.[100]

As a bitter, final note, we should observe that, while Al-Azhar's *takfirism* has hit freethinkers hard, it has instead spared ISIS, despite vocal calls on the institution to excommunicate the terrorist movement. The argument offered by the university's Sheikh Al-Tayyeb was the lack of grounds to accuse ISIS members of

91 El Fegiery, *Islamic Law and Human Rights*, 122.
92 El Fegiery, 109.
93 Boyle and Sheen, *Freedom of Religion and Belief*, 30.
94 Roberts, 'The State of the Right to Freedom of Expression', 29.
95 El Fegiery, *Islamic Law and Human Rights*, 107.
96 O'Sullivan, 'Egyptian Cases of Blasphemy and Apostasy', 106.
97 O'Sullivan, 106.
98 O'Sullivan, 106.
99 El Fegiery, *Islamic Law and Human Rights*, 111.
100 Fouad, 'Al-Azhar Refuses to Consider the Islamic State an Apostate'.

apostasy, since they had not recanted their faith.[101] Evidently, for the prestigious Islamic institution, massacres, rapes and tortures in the name of Allah do not reach the same threshold of impiety as a novel does.

The Islamist attitude toward (un)free speech is in line with the theoretical framework outlined in Chapter I: 'Islam is conceived as a polity, not just as a religious community. It follows therefore that apostasy is treason'.[102] This reasoning has been scrupulously followed by the Egyptian Courts, as I am going to show in the next section.

Relevant case studies

The 'Abu Zayd case': an unfortunate milestone

The case of Nasr Hamid Abu Zayd remains an unfortunate testament to the worst effects of the mingling of shariatic and secular elements in the Egyptian legal order. It also represents an example of how certain ideas may be considered heretical and consequently condemned as a form of apostasy, despite the lack of clear norms and an explicit disavowal of the faith.

The case dates back to 1994, when Abu Zayd, professor at Cairo University, submitted his theological publications to the internal academic panel in order to obtain a promotion. While most colleagues praised the scientific quality of his scholarship, a member of the examining committee argued that some of the writings contradicted well-established Islamic truths, and initiated a legal proceeding aimed at declaring Abu Zayd an apostate.[103] The legal complaint was based on the principle of *ḥisba*, a religious obligation requiring believers to enjoin good and forbid evil – as such defined by the Egyptian Court of Cassation in line with a well-established religious tradition.[104]

In fact, *ḥisba* per se was not explicitly laid down in the Egyptian legal system; the only indirect references to it were contained in Law 78/1931 on religious tribunals (which had been abrogated by Law 462 of 1955), and precisely in Articles 280 and 110. Article 280 included a clause allowing for direct recourse to the 'main texts of Abu Hanifa's school' as subsidiary sources in the absence of special statutes regulating a case; Article 110 equated 'God's rights' with public order, which had been traditionally guaranteed by the enforcement of *ḥisba*.[105] Part of this framework was the right of a private individual to file a complaint based on *ḥisba*, thereby enforcing at once a religious obligation and public order.[106]

101 Saker, 'Why Does Egypt's Largest Muslim Beacon, Al-Azhar, Refuse to Declare IS "Apostate"?'; Gabra, 'The Ideological Extremism of Al-Azhar'; Fouad, 'Al-Azhar Refuses to Consider the Islamic State an Apostate'; 'Dispute at Al-Azhar's "International Conference on the Renewal of Islamic Thought" Reflects Institution's Long-Standing Rejection of Religious Reforms in Egypt'.

102 Lewis, *From Babel to Dragomans*, 306.

103 An-Na'im, 'The Contingent Universality', 51.

104 al-'Awwâ, 'Un arrêt devenu une "affaire"', para. 17.

105 Castro, 'Diritto Musulmano', 33.

106 Thielmann, 'La jurisprudence égyptienne', para. 24.

In theory Law 462 of 1955 has established a different rule, as its Article 5 states that the right to file a legal complaint must be based on the code of civil and commercial procedure, which requires a direct personal interest to initiate a legal action: since *ḥisba* is eminently a matter of public interest, it is incompatible with a private one, as also clarified in Egyptian case law.[107] However, Law 462 has also created some legal aporias. First, it includes an unclear exception to account for the special rules of procedure that Law 78/1931 established for religious tribunals.[108] Second, Article 6 states that all matters of personal status that would have originally pertained to Islamic courts must be decided in accordance with Article 280 of Law 78/1931. As said, Article 280 mentions the subsidiary recourse to the texts of Abu Hanifa: thereby, Article 6 of Law 462/1955 opened a Pandora's box of the direct access of shariᶜa to the Egyptian legal system, even in antinomy with other norms. This legal intricacy made it unclear, in the Abu Zayd case, which procedure should prevail – the one established by Article 5 or the shariatic rules set forth in Article 6.

This contradiction was highlighted by the First-Instance Tribunal of Giza. Its decision to deny the procedural admissibility of the complaint interestingly quoted the constitutional jurisprudence examined in Chapter III:

> Had the constitutional legislator wished to make the principles of Islamic shariᶜa proper rules enshrined in the Constitution, or had he wanted such principles to be directly applied by the courts with no need to enshrine them in specific legislative texts adopted in conformity with the constitutional procedures, he would not have failed to do so expressly.[109]

The Court of Appeal and the Court of Cassation, however, radically overruled the first-instance verdict. From a procedural point of view, the Court of Appeal admitted the complaint on the basis of the above-mentioned exception laid down in Article 5, which allows the *ḥisba* procedure as *lex specialis* derogating from the Code of Civil Procedure in favour of Article 280 of the Law on the Islamic Tribunals.[110] Strikingly, the court further cited the opinion of Islamic scholars to specify that the ruler's authorization is not a precondition for enforcing *ḥisba* against something religiously inadmissible:[111] in so doing, it reasserted the primacy of shariᶜa over state law, in line with the assumptions outlined in Chapter 1 of this book. In the view of the Court of Appeal, 'any attack against the fundamental

107 Thielmann, para. 24.

108 'The rules of the Code of Procedure will be applicable to the procedure in the matters of personal status and *waqf* that fell previously within the jurisdiction of the religious courts of personal status or of the community assemblies, except for those cases that have been subjected to special rules in the regulations concerning the organization of religious courts of personal status or in other complementary laws', cit. in Thielmann, para. 23. Own translation from French.

109 Dupret and Berger, 'Jurisprudence Abû Zayd', para. 35. Own translation from French.

110 Dupret and Berger, para. 70.

111 Dupret and Berger, para. 148.

tenets of religion equates to attacking the state in its very constitutive nature', for Egypt 'is not a secular, atheist or Christian state; it is Muslim, and its religion is Islam'.[112] The Court of Cassation advanced this reasoning by explicitly establishing a direct connection between apostasy and public order, with a sort of syllogistic reasoning: if Islam is the religion of the state, and apostasy is an attack against Islam, the apostate is also a public enemy, a foe of the state; therefore, it is legitimate to curtail freedoms that undermine the nation's public order:

> To depart from Islam is to revolt against it, and this necessarily finds its reflection in the loyalty of the individual to the *Sharî'a,* the state, and his ties with the society. This is what no law or state tolerates. Hence, the *Sharî'a* and all other constitutions and laws permit freedom of opinion within the public order that prohibits wrong doing [*sic*] or misuse of a right. No individual has the right to call for what contradicts the public order (*al-nizâm al-'âmm*) or morals (*a/-adâb*), or use his opinion to harm the fundamentals upon which the society is built, or to revile sacred things, or to disdain Islam or any other heavenly religion.[113]

From a substantive point of view, the Court of Cassation pointed out that the lack of a norm proscribing apostasy within Egyptian legislation was not to be considered an obstacle: the silence of the law on this matter should not be used to infer the legislator's will to contradict the text of the Sacred Qur'an, the sunna and the Islamic jurisprudence, as the court argued.[114]

Yet, Abu Zayd had not abandoned his faith: the question that then arises is on what grounds it was possible to declare him an apostate. This is another sensitive and troubling aspect of the judgments. The judges in both the Court of Appeal and the Court of Cassation did not take into account the fact that Abu-Zayd's essays did not contain any professions of apostasy and not even anything blasphemous (i.e. derogatory of Islam): rather, they were scientific pieces aimed at critically analysing the sacred texts. However, according to the Court of Cassation, apostasy does not require a patent declaration of unbelief, but 'may be deduced from the meaning of clear wording'.[115] The scholarly intent behind Zayd's writings did not shield him from charges of apostasy, because a researcher should not deviate 'from the fundamentals of the *Sharî'a* and dogma, and their meanings, fundamentals and foundations' under any circumstances.[116] Zayd's fault consisted, *de facto*, in adopting a liberal, rationalist and historicized approach to the scriptures. According to the judges, he dared to deny 'what is axiomatic to any educated Muslim having a religious cultural background'[117] by describing

112 Dupret and Berger, para. 135. Own translation from French.
113 Dupret and Berger, para. 175.
114 Dupret and Berger, para. 145.
115 Dupret and Berger, para. 169.
116 Dupret and Berger, para. 164.
117 Dupret and Berger, para. 163.

the Qurᵓan as a human and cultural product and denying the divine origin of the sunna and the eternal validity of shariᶜa law, by depicting the latter as a cause of backwardness among Muslims, by scorning certain aspects of religion as pure superstition, by decrying slavery and objecting to women's inequality in inheritance rights, and so on. In a word, he had dared to defy a well-entrenched and undisputable orthodoxy. The fact that he had done so for the purposes of scholarly research was deemed totally irrelevant: he had trampled on established dogmata, which no believer is allowed to discuss let alone challenge:

> His pretext that his words are only allegorical interpretations (*ta'wîl*) is rejected, since such interpretation should not deviate the researcher from the fundamentals of the *Sharî'a* and *dogma, and their meanings, fundamentals and foundations.* Interpretation has its rules and criteria *set by Muslim legal scholars.* Otherwise, it would be a means for dissenters (*ashâb al-hawâ*) to deviate from the Law of God, and to escape from any legal text and legislate what God has not allowed, which would lead to *error and misguidance.* Interpretation does not mean to attack the *Sharî'a* texts and scorn them, to consider them invalid, to describe abiding by their stipulations as backwardness, to call for deviation from the Law of God to something else, or to *deny knowledge which is axiomatic to religion.*[118]

As a result, Abu Zayd was declared an apostate and forcefully divorced from his Muslim wife, as per a clear shariatic rule that prevents a Muslim woman from being married to an unbeliever. The Muslim Brotherhood saluted this judgement, stating that 'challenging the beliefs of the Muslim *umma*, the Qur'an and Islamic shariᶜa is not freedom of expression or a practice of *ijtihād*'.[119]

The Abu Zayd case remains a milestone for several reasons. First, it clearly demonstrates the repercussions of a hybrid system that comingles modern codified civil law with archaic, undefined religious rules, especially in the presence of a supremacy clause such as Article 2 of the Egyptian Constitution. Second, this proceeding shows that the concept of heresy is so broadly interpreted that a merely rational epistemology of religion, in contrast to its rigid, century-old orthodox interpretation, may be judged heretical. Finally, the judgement is relevant because it creates an automatic connection between heresy and apostasy, even when the accused has not explicitly rejected the faith.

In addition to the violation of the constitutional principles of freedom of thought, expression, religion and scientific research, the conclusions reached by the Egyptian tribunals also impacted the separation of powers by establishing the principle that a judge can enforce rules and prohibitions based not on state laws but on religious opinions.[120]

118 Court of Cassation, cit. in Dupret and Berger, para. 164. Emphasis added.

119 El Fegiery, *Islamic Law and Human Rights*, 112.

120 Thielmann, 'La jurisprudence égyptienne', para. 25.

The case of Alber Saber: An example of a revolution without freedom

Let us now move on to the aftermath of the 2011 revolution, when the winds of change were blowing so forcefully as to blind many with illusions that would soon be exposed as such. I am going to examine the case of Alber Saber, a Christian-born Egyptian atheist found guilty of criticizing religion and promoting atheism on his personal website,[121] an audacious act that led to a criminal prosecution and a prison sentence.

A long-standing atheist, Saber had already suffered several attacks from Islamist groups at the university even before prosecution, with the police being unable (or unwilling) to protect him.[122] The trigger for the criminal proceeding was Saber's decision to upload the film 'The Innocence of Muslims' – which had caused a worldwide uproar due to its allegedly blasphemous content – on his website, in order to debunk the lies circulating about it.[123] When a mob of enraged Muslims attacked Saber's home, the police, called by his mother for protection, apprehended Saber and put him in custody, allegedly to guarantee his safety. In fact, he was kept in jail and mistreated by both the police and inmates incited by the police, while his file was transmitted to the public prosecutor. Following a 13-hour interrogation focused on his religious beliefs and practices, the prosecutor decided to refer Saber for trial, based on several criminal provisions: Articles 98(f), 102 (on stirring sedition), 160/1 (on perturbing religious rituals), 161/1 (on printing and publishing holy books in a perverted way), and 171/3 (on public incitement to commit crimes).[124] Both the courts of first and second instance upheld all the allegations, sentencing the defendant to three years in prison. However, the appeal verdict was rendered *in absentia*, as Saber had since been granted asylum in Switzerland.

The analysis of the appellate ruling is particularly revealing.[125] First, the judge examined Saber's ideas – spread through Facebook, Twitter and YouTube – and portrayed them in terms of calls for atheism, insult against God, doubts about the holy books and derision of Muslim and Christian rituals and prophets. According to the court, the defendant's intent was 'to evoke turmoil between the Christians and the Moslems in the country, to despise holly [*sic*] religions and to harm national unity'. Furthermore, the tribunal portrayed Saber's views as 'extremist' and found the defendant fully conscious of the 'extremity of the ideology he [was] spreading' by demolishing the founding pillars of Islam and Christianity and demeaning believers.

The court exhibited an awareness of the principle of freedom of belief 'which is protected by the provisions of all the Egyptian Constitutions'. Still, it continued, 'this does not give the excuse to [the one] who argues the principles of a

121 Eltahawy, 'Egypt's War on Atheism'.
122 Alber Saber, telephone interview by the author, May 2017.
123 Saber, interview.
124 Saber, interview.
125 Examined here in the official English translation, courtesy of Saber: Case 1614/2013.

religion to disrespect its sanctity or to degrade it or to disrespect this religion'. The twofold reference to the 'principles' and 'sanctity' of a religion seems to exclude both criticism of religious tenets as well as mere assertions of unbelief. Consistent with this, the court defined itself as a 'sanctuary' and the

> protector for holly [*sic*] religions [...] against everyone who cross [*sic*] the boundaries and limits by abuse [*sic*] these religions through propagating insults, lies and to speak of these publicly. This can lead to grave turmoil that can not be controlled as it storms the society's principles and basics.

Two elements are especially worth noting. One is the usual suspect, namely the disruption of public order: since 'religious sentiments are not easy to calm or to sooth', 'evoking [*sic*] these feelings subjects order and security to the gravest dangers'. Another interesting point is the terminology employed to describe Saber's statements: not only 'insults', but also 'lies'. This argumentation is typical of judgments on blasphemy and is used as a valid reason to censor unwelcome ideas as if they were dangerous 'fake news' – to use an expression in vogue. This clearly follows the path highlighted in Chapter II: in a purely religious perspective, the constitutionally required neutrality between different beliefs is set aside, and an irrefutable religious 'truth', unilaterally identified by the authorities, is counterposed with the 'lies' denying it. The tribunal becomes the guarantor of such truth and assumes a role indistinguishable from that of a religious institution. The final part of the Saber ruling is emblematic in this respect, as it flagrantly shifts the focus from a legal to a religious perspective, underscoring the sacred function of the court:

> Believing in the message that the Court bares [sic], the court was horrified by this extremist thought that the accused propagated [...]. He was led behind the devil, and closed his mind so that he fell by and with the devil.[126]

From these highly mystical premises, it follows that the court is bestowed with the sacred mission to purge the defendant and society of such evil, with a conviction that assumes the form of a judicial exorcism. I will elaborate more on this point in the next chapter.

Blasphemy, heresy, atheism ... even homosexuality: all sides of the same coin

The cases presented above are far from exceptional. Blasphemers, apostates, atheists and freethinkers are under constant threat in Egypt, and lumped together in one basket. While in the two previous sections I have analysed what are, in strict terms, cases of heresy and blasphemy, even a mere declaration of atheism is legitimate grounds for prosecution.

126 Case 1614/2013.

For instance, atheist writer Salah al-Din Mohsen was condemned to three years of hard labour in 2001 for both his criticism of the Qurʾan ('a book of holy ignorance', written not by God but by the self-proclaimed prophet Muhammad[127]) and his open atheism:

> Mohsen has openly stated that he is an atheist. He has also called for the establishment of an Egyptian atheists' association. In Egypt, such blasphemous sentiments are not only illegal, but widely considered to be contemptuous of the great majority of the population.[128]

The parallel with the reasoning of Tunisian judges and prosecutors is striking: the mere expression of *personal* beliefs is deemed 'contemptuous' of the 'majority'. The lip service paid to freedom of expression also follows the same scheme:

> We are not against freedom of expression, but we strongly fight the spread of deviant beliefs in our society [...]. Mohsen was not arrested because of his beliefs; he is free to embrace whatever ideology he pleases, but this freedom should not extend to propagating erroneous beliefs.[129]

Again, the idea emerges of an indisputable 'religious truth' that the state is called to enforce; freedom of belief and expression are only permitted within its tightly constrained boundaries. The state establishes by law the 'right and true' and the 'wrong and false' in the domain of inner beliefs and enforces such irrefutable assumptions in court, considering any deviation illegal and contemptuous of the majority. An antagonism is thereby constructed between 'blasphemy', understood in a broad sense, and public morals, and this antagonism is used as an instrument of oppression against bloggers, artists and writers.[130]

Things have not changed much lately: in 2020, activist and blogger Anas Hassan was condemned to a three-year prison term and fined 300,000 Egyptian pounds for managing the 'Egyptian Atheists' Facebook page, 'that publishes atheistic ideas and criticism of the "divinely revealed religions"'.[131] Renowned Egyptian atheist activist Sherif Gaber met a similar fate – he was sentenced in 2019 to three years in prison for 'contempt of religion' and 'spreading immoral values', namely defending LGBT rights.[132]

Ideological (and even legal) parallels exist between the persecution of freethinkers and homosexuals: both minorities are equally loathed by the average

127 O'Sullivan, 'Egyptian Cases of Blasphemy and Apostasy', 100.
128 O'Sullivan, 100.
129 O'Sullivan, 100.
130 E.g. Haider Haider, in O'Sullivan, 102.
131 'Economic Misdemeanour Appeals Court Upholds Verdict against Blogger, with 3 Years Imprisonment and a 300,000 EGP Fine for Managing the "Egyptian Atheists" Facebook Page'.
132 'Atheist Egyptian Blogger Jailed for Videos Expressing His Views'.

Egyptian, according to all the actors I interviewed.[133] In the next chapter, I am going to describe the legal dimension of this connection, as gay people are often accused not only of 'debauchery' but also of 'insulting religion'. The correlation is bidirectional: even when the defendant is charged with blasphemy and his/her sexual orientation is not questioned, any positive reference to homosexuality is presented in court as evidence of contempt of religion. Indeed, Gaber's ordeal started when he challenged a university *science* lecturer who argued that homosexuals should be crucified in the streets. After he demanded that the lecturer stick to science, Gaber was reported to senior university faculty, who began digging into the student's social media accounts and shared his atheist writings.[134] The case was brought to the attention of the authorities, who ordered his arrest. The police report connected to this arrest is extremely telling:

> The investigations and information proved that the aforementioned defendant [Sherif Gaber] had gone through some conversations and discussions with some of the professors at the Suez Canal University and with some of his fellow colleagues, with regards to the characteristics of the Divine Self and he denied the miracles and the Monotheistic religions and affirmed the rights of homosexuals and gays to have sexual intercourse. [/] The investigations and information also added that he scorned the teachings of the true Islamic Religion. He also denied the divine miracles and the verses of the Holy Quran, in an attempt to promote these ideas at the campus, the ideas, which he was convinced of through the social media, on the internet, claiming that he possessed the material and logical evidences that proved that his ideas and beliefs are correct.[135]

The investigation concluded that Gaber's crime consisted in stating things

> which are considered as *contempt of religion*, insulting the Divine Self, the Holy Quran, and Prophet Muhammed God's prayers and peace be upon him. And his also *calling for spreading debauchery and immorality, homosexuality* and *acknowledging atheism publicly* and calling up the students to perform such acts.[136]

133 Among those I interviewed in 2020: atheist and gay activist Mohamed Hisham Nofal, who obtained asylum in Germany due to the persecution he faced after publicly declaring his atheism in a TV show (see Gaetani, 'Do You Remember Mohamed, the Egyptian Atheist Kicked out from TV?'); Ismail Mohammed, Egyptian host of the pro-atheist Youtube talk show 'Black Ducks' (see Beek, 'Wordt de Arabische Wereld Minder Religieus?'); atheist Egyptian journalist Khaled Diab (see Diab, 'Confessions of an Egyptian Infidel,'); and a member of a Facebook group of Egyptian atheists.

134 'IHEU Raises Concerns for Egyptian Atheist Sherif Gaber'.

135 'IHEU Raises Concerns for Egyptian Atheist Sherif Gaber'.

136 'IHEU Raises Concerns for Egyptian Atheist Sherif Gaber'. Emphasis added.

These few lines condense all the main topics of this book, unveiling the consubstantial connection between heresy (denying what orthodoxy holds for certain), atheism (rejecting religion) and homosexuality (spreading sin), which are all different faces of blasphemy. They are an insult to religion and its sanctity and represent different instances of the same *fitna*. In the next section, I am going to conclude this chapter by spending a few words on this crucial religious concept.

Final reflections on Egyptian and Tunisian freethinkers: public order and *fitna*

The Tunisian and Egyptian cases show similar patterns in the persecution of freethinkers. Both countries use vague norms and polysemous clauses on public morality and public order, interpreted according to the will of the majority, as flexible tools to target unorthodox speech of all kinds. Another pattern is that judges pay lip service to freedom of belief and expression, only to cast aside the substance thereof; indeed, although pretending to respect freedom of belief, including atheism, judges *de facto* radically deny it, decrying atheism or heterodox statements as 'errors' or 'lies' that the court, as the guardian of religion, must amend, and demanding that those beliefs be kept private, in order to avoid three main harms: (1) injuring believers' sentiments; (2) endangering public order; (3) bringing division (*fitna*) in society.

As far as the public order argument is concerned, it is based on the assumption that contempt for religion 'incites' social turmoil. This 'incitation' thesis is not new in the context of blasphemy. In the words of Kamali, an authoritative scholar of Islamic law, 'blasphemy today continues to be a dangerous offence, which can incite violence and loss of life, and pose a threat to law and order in society, as was seen in the aftermath of Salman Rushdie's misguided venture'.[137] This is faulty reasoning that willingly muddies the waters: 'incitement' may be defined as the 'advocacy [...] directed to inciting or producing imminent lawless action and [...] likely to incite or produce such action';[138] in other words, the inciter and the perpetrator play on the same team, to the extent that the latter commits the crime following the input of the former. Our case is the very opposite. Muddling the two cases on the basis of the similar result would entail transferring liability: responsibility for violence would be moved from its direct cause (the actual perpetrator, the exalted crowd or individuals that kill and destroy) to the indirect one (the alleged 'blasphemer'), which makes the explosion of violence inevitable, almost in terms of naturalistic necessity.

Furthermore, paying formal homage to freedom of belief and unbelief but demanding that the latter remain 'private' – just because it is opposed to that of the majority – creates a paradoxical alternative: either one patently discriminates against a specific creed (i.e. atheism) or one should require the same from

137 Kamali, *Freedom of Expression in Islam*, 249.
138 Brandenburg v. Ohio at 447.

any comparable expression in similar conditions, with the ironic consequence that the utterance 'I am Muslim', in a predominantly non-Muslim environment, should be considered tantamount to 'incitation to the disruption of public order', 'insult to public decency' and a manifestation of 'religious extremism'.

In other words, the logic whereby criticism of the largest creeds should be banned because of the greater reactions it can provoke stands in polar opposition to constitutionalism as an instrument of protection of minorities and represents a pure manifestation of surrender to the 'law of the strongest'.[139]

Concerning *fitna*, this is a very sensitive concept: as also touched upon in Chapter I, *fitna* belongs to the religious realm, where it denotes one of the most heinous crimes, first and foremost a 'state of rebellion against God's Law',[140] and the intent to sow the seeds of doubt in the hearts of pure believers. This includes heterodoxy, following the Qurᵓanic warning against those who take advantage of elusive verses to spread doubts [*fitna*] through false interpretations.[141] In its social and political sense, *fitna* likewise has a specific undertone of religious sin, as the first and most terrible *fitna* was the political and religious split that occurred around the fourth caliph, which caused the schism between Sunnis and Shiᶜa. Interestingly, *fitna* has an additional meaning, referring to the dissemination of 'obscenity' and 'licentiousness', with a sexual connotation: those 'agents of immorality' are also guilty of spreading *fitna* and tearing society apart.[142] This contributes to explaining the amalgam of political, religious and morality elements in legislation and case law as well as the lumping together of gays and freethinkers in the same category.

Mejri, Béji, El Fani, Abu Zayd, Saber, Gaber and all the other freethinkers, in other words, are guilty before man and before God of maliciously trying to sow doubts, division and depravity. Hence, law and religion are inextricably linked, and the tribunal must perform the role of both a civil institution enforcing the law and a religious temple enforcing God's will, thereby purifying the twofold treason against God and against the state by issuing convictions that take the form of a judicial exorcism.

In the next chapter, I will show that the same pattern applies to homosexuality and will provide additional evidence to prove the close proximity of this crime with blasphemy.

139 See Virgili, 'Libertà e democrazia nell'Islam'; Colaianni, 'Diritto di satira e libertà di religione'. Furthermore, such an interpretation of a criminal provision is flawed in that it detects the *objective* aspect of the offense in the *subjective* perception that the commission of such crimes may provoke within the public opinion, expressed in the so-called 'social alarm'. Picotti, 'Istigazione e propaganda della discriminazione razziale', 132.

140 Gardet, 'Fitna'.

141 Virgili, 'Libertà e democrazia nell'Islam', 26–30.

142 *Fitna* is also the promotion of immorality, often with sexual implications. See Virgili, 30.

VII (Il)legal persecution of sexual minorities

Introduction

This chapter concentrates on analysing the legal situation LGBT people face in Tunisia and Egypt. In both countries, vague, liberticidal laws and a widespread homophobia combine, resulting in the persecution of many individuals, despite constitutional guarantees. While Tunisia is showing some positive signs of increasing openness towards the issue, which has started to be publicly discussed in the media thanks to civil society activism, in Egypt the situation does not seem to offer any prospect of improvement.

As a preliminary remark, I should state that my analysis will only address the legal treatment of homosexuality, which, in the Muslim world, is sometimes distinct from that of transsexualism.[1] The reason why I use the acronym 'LGBT'[2] is because the laws against homosexuality are used facilely against everyone whose appearance does not conform to the general standards – including transgender individuals and crossdressers – irrespective of their sexual orientation.

Another necessary clarification is that my analysis is purely legal in character and does not address the debate on personal identification and labels. In other words, it is not pertinent to this study to ascertain whether the concept of homosexuality was always present throughout the history of Islam or if it represents instead the imposition of a 'Western taxonomy of sexuality'[3] upon a cultural context which was traditionally characterized by a fluid, non-binary sexuality. What is relevant here is not designations, whether natural or self-perceived, but how certain identities and behaviours are targeted by the law.[4]

To phrase this in different terms, it is not relevant who is a Jew as per the Mosaic law, but who is a Jew as per Hitler's law.

1 An emblematic case is that of Iran, where homosexual behaviours are punished with the death penalty while reassignment of sex is legal.
2 Lesbian, gay, bisexual, transgender.
3 Joseph Massad in Habib, 'LGBT Activism in the Middle East', 1.
4 For an analysis of sexual taxonomies in the Muslim world, see Hamzić, 'A History in the Making', 54 ff.

DOI: 10.4324/9780429259418-VII

Tunisia

Relevant provisions

Criminalization of homosexuality in Tunisia mainly rests on the explicit prohibition in Article 230 of the Penal Code, which is part of the chapter on 'offenses against morals'[5] and its sub-section on 'indecent behaviour'.[6] This immediately points to the clear cultural premise: the criminal norm is not linked to a concrete individual interest but to the collective and undefined honour of society.

While the French version of Article 230 only mentions 'sodomy' (something which has created ambiguities in the West[7]), the official Arabic text – which is the only one to have legal force – reads as follows: 'Male or female homosexuality [*al-liwāṭ aw al-musāḥaqa*], if it does not fall into one of the cases provided by the preceding articles, will be punished with a prison term of three years'.[8] Starting from the less ambiguous element, the exclusion of the conduct envisaged in the preceding articles means that Article 230 only applies to acts which are (1) consensual; (2) private; and (3) between adults.[9]

The term used for male homosexuality, *al-liwāṭ*, has the same root as Lot, the Biblical and Qurʾanic patriarch who escaped the divine destruction of Sodom and Gomorrah. The term is therefore religious in origin, and its meaning markedly ambiguous: although it is often used to refer to the act of 'sodomy', (and paradoxically, in the classical Arabic texts, mostly to active sodomy, including by heterosexuals[10]), it may equally refer to less specific homosexual acts[11] and even to mere homosexual tendencies.[12]

The accusation of *musāḥaqa*, lesbianism, also carries ambiguities, from a conceptual and a legal point of view. Wehr translates it as 'lesbianism' without further indications, which reproduces the same ambiguities of *liwāṭ*.[13] While

5 '*Attentats aux moeurs*' in French.

6 '*De l'attentat à la pudeur*'.

7 Thereby, the French text excludes other forms of male-to-male intercourse and any lesbian behaviour, while it would paradoxically criminalize heterosexual sodomy, given that the French word *sodomie* may equally refer to anal sex between a man and a woman. This discrepancy between the French text and the Arabic one (the latter being the sole official one, it is important to stress again) has sometimes created significant misunderstandings among scholars and activists. As a relevant example, we may consider the 2015 Report on 'State-sponsored homophobia' released by the International Lesbian, Gay, Bisexual, Trans and Intersex Association (ILGA), which, in reviewing the world legislation against homosexuality, mistakenly lists Tunisia as a country where female homosexuality is legal, on the basis of the French version of article 230. *V.* Carroll and Itaborahy, 'State Sponsored Homophobia 2015'. This mistake is corrected in the 2016 Report.

8 Own translation from Arabic.

9 Ferchichi, Article 230 du Code pénal.

10 Bosworth et al., 'Liwāṭ'.

11 The Wehr dictionary translates *liwāṭ* as 'pederasty'. Wehr, 'لواط'.

12 Wehr.

13 Wehr, 'مساحقة'.

Article 230 is much less frequently used against women than against men, both for cultural reasons and because of the absence of forensic evidence,[14] lesbians are charged under Article 230 when they are caught *in flagrante delicto* (especially in prisons), and they are prosecuted under different statutory provisions (such as prostitution, indecency, etc.).[15]

Indeed, the direct criminalization of homosexuality under Article 230 is not the only means of prosecuting individuals having non-conformist sexual behaviours and gender identities: all the provisions described in the previous chapter – that is, those criminalizing attacks on public morals and the incitement to debauchery – are also used to this end. This confusion between sexual orientation, homosexual behaviour and the series of provisions ambiguously targeting 'indecency' under different labels raises serious concerns from a criminal perspective, due to the violation of the principle of legality (which requires criminal provisions to identify specific acts and to be clear and unambiguous). Article 230, as a generic ban on 'homosexuality',[16] fails to identify the material element of the crime; thus, it may target those who merely identify as gay or lesbian, in the absence of any specific act,[17] and it does not specify which kind of same-sex contact is outlawed.[18] Consequently, the boundaries between the specific crime of homosexuality *ex art.* 230 and other kinds of 'attacks against good morals' between members of the same sex are not clearly defined in the law.[19] The Court of Cassation has not contributed to restore the strict construction required by criminal law, having instead expanded the purview of the different crimes against good morals, including Article 230, so as to include any kind of intimate act, even those not explicitly sexual such as kisses or caresses, if committed with lecherous intentions.[20]

In the next sections, I am going to analyse case law against LGBT people based both on Article 230 and on different provisions allegedly protecting 'good morals'.

14 *V. infra* on the anal test.

15 Mounir Baatour, Shams' lawyer and founder of the Tunisian Liberal Party, interviewed by the author, Tunis, July 2016. Member of *Chouf*, a feminist organization also fighting for lesbian rights, interviewed by the author, Tunis, July 2016. Amina Sboui, also known as Amina Tyler, former member of FEMEN arrested for posting on Facebook a picture of herself with naked breast, interviewed by the author, Tunis, August 2016.

16 I use this term as in my view it may encompass the polysemic meaning of *liwāṭ* and *musāḥaqa*. See for instance the entry 'homosexuality' in the Merriam-Webster dictionary, that refers both to 'the quality or state of being homosexual' and to 'erotic activity with another of the same sex'. 'Homosexuality'.

17 This is not a merely theoretical possibility nowadays, given the public appearance of openly homosexual activists on Tunisian mass media; *v. infra*.

18 Cf. Ferchichi: ' As such, these materials can be interpreted variously – one is free to interpret a homosexual act as only "homosexual sex" or as any act involving members of the same gender with a sexual aim or dimension (kissing, oral sex, foreplay, etc.).' Ferchichi, 'Law and Homosexuality', 2.

19 Ferchichi, 'L'homosexualité en droit tunisien', 174.

20 Ferchichi, 176.

Relevant case law on liwāṭ

The first case I examine is one that has been covered extensively by international media, thanks to the NGOs that put it in the spotlight.[21] Six young students were arrested in their student housing in Kairouan, after the police were informed that 'a number of homosexuals are using a house in Kairouan to do sodomy'.[22] It must be noted that there was no *flagrante delicto* and that their private residence was raided without a search warrant, as allowed by the state of emergency law.[23]

Charged with sodomy (under Article 230), and with publicly undermining decency or public morals (under Article 226bis), the students were brought to a forensic physician in order to undergo an anal test aimed at verifying 'whether they [were] used to passive sodomy, and, if so, to ascertain the date of the latest anal intercourse'.[24] Theoretically, they were entitled to refuse the examination and tried to do so, but the police forced them to consent by using violence.[25] The forensic report, far from showing scientific certitude, affirmed that all the defendants presented physical signs demonstrating that they had been 'relatively' [*nisbiyy^{an}*] used to passive sodomy 'in the past', and that in the previous days they had experienced 'anal penetration by a solid and large body compatible with an erect penis'.[26]

In spite of such vagueness and of some of the defendants' denial, first- and second-instance judges used this report as irrefutable proof of the material element of the crime. Additional pieces of evidence presented were a condom, female clothes and a computer storing one video from the pro-LGBT organization Shams and one with homosexual pornographic material. The latter led to one defendant being additionally charged with *publicly* undermining public decency and inciting debauchery, based on the assumption that new technologies would make public access to and diffusion of these recordings easy.[27]

Ultimately, the First-Instance Tribunal of Kairouan sentenced all defendants to a prison term of three years under Article 230, with six additional months for the individual found guilty under Article 226bis. Furthermore, as the offenders showed 'the evident will to mobilize others and spread the vice', they received the ancillary punishment of banishment from Kairouan (Art. 5 Penal Code) so as to avoid 'offense to social identity', 'provocation of public sentiments' and 'reactions' from society.[28] The Sousse Court of Appeal significantly reduced

21 Case 6782/2015. Unless stated otherwise, all Tunisian cases analysed here have been kindly provided by Mounir Baatour, and have been translated from Arabic into French by a professional translator. Own translations from French into English.

22 'Tunisia: Men Prosecuted for Homosexuality'.

23 Samti, 'On Human Rights Day, a Tunisian Court Sent Six Men to Prison for Being Gay'.

24 'Tunisia: Men Prosecuted for Homosexuality'.

25 'Six Tunisian Students Freed from "sodomy" Prison Sentence'. 'Tunisia: Men Prosecuted for Homosexuality'.

26 Case 6782/2015.

27 Case 6782/2015.

28 Case 6782/2015.

the sentences to one and two months, revoked the banishment and acquitted the defendant accused of publicly undermining public decency, since 'the videos were on the defendant's laptop, in his home, and they were neither publicly diffused nor sent to another person'.[29]

These verdicts raise several points for reflection. First, they clearly show that the anal test is inadequate to provide scientific evidence of consensual sodomy:[30] the 'attitude to sodomy' is formulated in merely hypothetical terms, and – as the lawyer Mounir Baatour noted in his appeal to the Court of Cassation – the exam cannot prove that penetration, if it ever occurred, was performed with a penis and not with an object.[31] Nevertheless, neither judgment challenged this element, and even though the appellate court considerably reduced the penalty, it did so by taking into account 'attenuating circumstances',[32] while accepting *in toto* the outcome of the forensic examination. Similarly, the banishment from Kairouan was revoked on appeal on the grounds that it was an 'unreasonable' sanction – but this revocation did not entail any critical reflection on the substance of the argumentation used by the first-instance tribunal.

In sum, the Kairouan conviction was mostly based on anal tests 'proving' passive sodomy. Although the lack of official figures on the number of convictions under Article 230, let alone on the specific grounds of culpability, prevents a rigorous quantitative analysis, this indeed seems to be the prime cause for conviction in such cases.[33] However, it is not the *sole* cause, as the following case shows.

The case in question concerned the conviction of two men *ex art.* 230 by the Tribunal of Sfax in 2016[34] and is relevant for two reasons: (1) no anal test was performed on the accused; (2) no distinction was made between active and passive sodomy.

From the judgment, it emerges that the two culprits had initially admitted engaging in sodomy, with the aggravating circumstance of prostitution; however, the confession was made when the police raided their house without legal assistance and allegedly under duress.[35] Afterwards, both men recanted their confessions and denied all allegations. Considering that the accused persons did not undergo any medical examination and that they recanted their confessions, the prosecution's case remained weak in evidentiary terms. At any rate, per Article 69 of the Code of Criminal Procedure, a confession does not relieve investigating magistrates of their duty to seek additional pieces of evidence. In the case under consideration, that circumstantial evidence was found in an SMS message

29 Case 6693/2016.
30 *V. infra* for more details on this aspect.
31 Baatour, 'Appeal to the Court of Cassation, Case 6693/2015 [in Arabic]'.
32 Probably due to international and civil society pressure. Such a mitigation seems also *contra legem*, as Article 230 'calls for a punishment of "three years" for the perpetrators of "sodomy or lesbianism" and does not allow the judge to mitigate the sentence but only to decide whether or not to impose it.' Ferchichi, 'Law and Homosexuality'.
33 As confirmed by all the sources I consulted.
34 Case 1757/2016.
35 Mounir Baatour, interview.

in which the two men planned their sexual encounters. Condoms and lubricants found in the house also served as additional proofs; these items, according to one of the defendants, were not even his own but belonged to an association fighting HIV where he worked. However, none of these mitigating arguments was taken into account, as the judge simplistically concluded that 'the defendants' denial [was] worthless, given the amount of other circumstantial elements'.[36]

Compared to the Kairouan case, this verdict had some important differences: while in the Kairouan case the possession of condoms was considered non-decisive, circumstantial evidence, in this case purely presumptive elements were deemed sufficient to reach the burden of proof for *liwāṭ*. Convictions of this kind, imposed in the absence of an anal test or even when the result is negative,[37] clearly show that this degrading procedure is more of an anticipated punishment than a forensic tool. The same conclusion applies in the Egyptian case, as I show below.

Non-conformist behaviours outside of the scope of Article 230

Article 230 is not the only means of prosecuting LGBT people. Even when homosexual intercourse is not proven, different types of conduct may be used as indirect evidence of homosexuality or prosecuted as separate crimes. Possession of sexually related objects and male pornography are two possible grounds for prosecution, as seen above. Other forms of conduct may also trigger prosecution under Article 226bis. In a 2017 homosexuality case before the Tribunal of Tunis,[38] the defendant, although acquitted of charges *ex art.* 230 due to lack of evidence, was nevertheless convicted of 'inciting debauchery' and 'undermining public morals' because he had shared a photo of his buttocks in a private online chat. In another case, decided in 2018 by the Tribunal of Sousse,[39] two men were convicted of publicly undermining public morals because they sported female clothes in the public street. The court stated explicitly that 'wearing female clothes is an act which undermines public decency [*atteint à la pudeur*]'.

These judgments, involving the categories of decency and public morals in cases of non-conformist sexual or gender behaviour, underscore the conceptual proximity between offences related to deviant religious beliefs on the one hand, and unconventional sexualities on the other. The moral categories to which these crimes belong and the vagueness of the law make homosexuals and freethinkers particularly vulnerable to societal pressure. For instance, a Tunisian judge, Omar Weslati, told me that his colleague who convicted the Kairouan students had, by his own admission, no other choice but to do so due to strong social pressure. On appeal, the penalty was considerably reduced for an equal and opposite

36 Case 1757/2016.
37 Y.N., 'Tunis: Poursuivi pour homosexualité malgré un test anal négatif'.
38 Case 33570/2017.
39 Case 4292/2018.

reason – due to the uproar coming from progressive sectors of society and from abroad.[40] In both cases, legal arguments played a secondary role. This does not change the fact that, in the opinion of Judge Weslati, Articles 226, 226bis and 230 are clearly unconstitutional.

Strategies for decriminalization

Abrogation of Article 230

A number of civil society organizations are currently fighting for LGBT rights in Tunisia. Each of them has its own approach, but they are all united under the 'Collective for Individual Freedoms', an umbrella group for 29 organizations defending individual liberties.[41]

Among those NGOs, Shams was the first to explicitly mention the 'rights of sexual minorities' in its statute. The organization has a legal focus – it wishes to abrogate Article 230. To this end, it has prepared a draft bill citing both international law and the Tunisian Constitution.[42] The association's members have also taken a very direct approach to the issue, by publicly appearing in Tunisian mass media in order to defend their sexual identity and publicize their fight against Article 230. While this has been a dramatic step forward for Tunisian gays, who, for the first time, have spoken of their existence publicly, proudly and with their faces uncovered – something unthinkable until a very few years ago – it has also provoked a backlash.[43] At the same time, sadly, very little support has come from so-called progressive and secular politicians, with the notable exception of former minister of justice Mohamed Salah Ben Aissa, who in 2015 called for the abrogation of Article 230 – a call which was immediately disowned by the president of the republic in person and allegedly cost Ben Aissa his post.[44] For these reasons, other organizations for the protection of minorities – such as *Damj*

40 Omar Weslati, Judge at the Court of Appeal of Tunis and Secretary General of the *Observatoire Tunisien de l'"Independence de la Magistrature*, interviewed by the author, Tunis, July 2016.

41 ATFD: Association Tunisienne des Femmes Démocrates; EuroMed Droits; Beity; ADLI: Association de Défense des libertés individuelles; ASF: Avocats Sans Frontières; Damj: Association Tunisienne pour la Justice et l'Egalité; Association Shams; LTDH: Ligue Tunisienne pour la Défense des Droits de l'Homme; Kelmti; FIDH: Fédération internationale des Droits de l'Homme; Chouf; OMCT: Organisation Mondiale Contre la Torture; Free Sight; CALAM: Coexistence with Alternative Language and Action Movement; Association Tunisienne pour la défense des valeurs universitaires; Mawjoudine; Waai; Jamaity; Mnamti; Oxfam; Horra; Association Tunisienne de la Santé Reproductive; Fanni Raghman anni; Association Tunisienne de Lutte contre les MST et le SIDA; Tahadi; Groupe Tawhida Béchikh; Association Art Rue; Association Tunisienne pour l'égalité sociale et la solidarité; ATP +: Association Tunisienne de Prévention Positive. See EuroMed Rights, 'Tunisie: Recommandations du "Collectif Pour Les Libertés Individuelles"'.

42 Shams, 'Projet de loi présenté par l'association Shams au Parlement visant l'abrogation de l'article 230 du Code Pénal'.

43 McCormick-Cavanagh, 'Is Homophobia at All-Time High in Tunisia?'; Monceau, 'En Tunisie'.

44 AFP, 'Tunisie – L'homosexualité coûte son poste au ministre de la Justice'.

and *Mawjoudin-We Exist* – have adopted a more nuanced approach that focuses less on publicity and more on cautious activities such as awareness campaigns, training, psychological and logistical support and so on. It goes without saying that, despite tactical differences, all these NGOs share the hope of seeing Article 230 repealed.[45]

Although not directly concerning Article 230, a positive sign, possibly paving the way for a different judicial approach to the matter, came from the Tunis Court of Appeal in May 2019, when the Court rejected a request by state authorities to dissolve the association Shams. The action brought by the officer in charge of state litigation aimed to shut down Shams on the grounds that its activities deviated from the objectives of its statute and promoted illegal behaviour.[46] In particular, the complaint accused Shams of drifting away from its stated purpose of defending 'sexual minorities' by instead encouraging homosexual relations and the 'adoption of homosexual opinions', in contravention of Article 230 of the criminal code and 'against Islam [and] social values'.[47]

While the anti-Shams case confirms the trend of using religion and undefined social values for the purpose of censorship, the verdict rejecting the complaint represents a game-changer. Ironically, the innovative element of this judgment came as a direct consequence of the wording of the complaint against Shams. Indeed, facing the allegation that Shams was defending 'homosexuals' instead of 'sexual minorities', the court was compelled to define the latter and concluded that this term comprises 'any sexual affinity between the two parties that is beyond the natural norm (male and female)', that is, homosexuality. The crucial implication of this reasoning is that homosexuals have thereby been conferred the protected status of minorities.[48] Interestingly, the court referred to international documents, such as the 'Declaration of Montreal on Lesbian, Gay, Bisexual, and Transgender Human Rights' and the 'Yogyakarta Principles' on the application of international human rights law in relation to sexual orientation and gender identity. Even more strikingly, in response to the argument that defending the rights of homosexuals violates Article 230 and promotes relations which are 'against Islam' and 'social values', the tribunal rejected it and affirmed that Shams' work is meant to 'preserve human dignity and prevent aggression for having different sexual orientations'.[49] With this statement, the court stopped short of issuing a direct opinion on Article 230 (which would have been beyond its competence); however, according to Ferchichi, it unequivocally recognized that Article 230 is incompatible with human dignity.[50]

45 Ali Bousselmi, president of the association *Mawjoudin-We exist*, interviewed by the author, Tunis, July 2016. Shams Radhouani Abdi, former member of the same organization, interviewed by the author, Tunis, July 2016. Hafedh Trifi, member of the association *Damj*, interviewed by the author, Tunis, July 2016.

46 Ferchichi, 'Tunisian Court Defends Advocacy of Homosexual Rights'.

47 Ferchichi.

48 Ferchichi.

49 Ferchichi.

50 Ferchichi.

Judgment of a prospective Constitutional Court

The establishment of the Constitutional Court, a crucial advancement anticipated by the new Constitution, could potentially represent a significant step forward towards advancing fundamental freedoms, according to all the sources I have consulted with. Especially when it comes to LGBT rights, given that the parliamentary road to reform is blocked, the Constitutional Court raises high expectations for the removal of Article 230 on the grounds of unconstitutionality.

Having said that, nothing can be taken for granted as much depends on the justices' cultural, religious and political background. Indeed, as Ferchichi warns, along with multiple arguments against Article 230, the Constitution also contains legal elements in its favour.[51] One might be Article 1, which enshrines Islam as the religion of Tunisia, due to the prevalent view of homosexuality as going against Islamic values. Other obstacles include 'public morals' and 'public health', identified by Article 49 as legitimate limitations on the enjoyment of rights. Considering the deeply rooted rejection of homosexuality in Tunisian society[52] and the stereotypes surrounding homosexuals as plague spreaders, this hypothesis cannot be hastily dismissed.

Ban on the anal test

From a procedural point of view, three means of evidence are used to prove someone's homosexuality: confession, *flagrante delicto*, and the medical examination of the male anus for the signs of passive sodomy. Tunisian authorities largely rely on anal tests,[53] which are performed by forensic physicians, as seen above.

From a medical point of view, such tests are devoid of any scientific value,[54] and they also raise problems regarding their compatibility with medical ethics rules. This conflict may strongly affect the entire edifice of the criminalization of homosexuality: if doctors were found in violation of the ethical code while performing anal tests, they would no longer be allowed to conduct them. For this reason, Guellali, former director of Human Rights Watch Tunisia, has argued that the fight for a ban on anal tests may be, in the short term, a strategically wiser goal than the abrogation of Article 230 by parliament, which is very

51 Ferchichi, interview.

52 According to a poll of the Pew Research Center, 94 per cent of Tunisians consider homosexuality unacceptable. 'The Global Divide on Homosexuality'.

53 'Tunisia: Men Prosecuted for Homosexuality'. Vinchon, 'L'enfer du "test anal" en Tunisie'.

54 'According to Physicians for Human Rights, anal exams have no medical or scientific value in determining whether consensual anal sex has taken place.' 'Tunisia: Men Prosecuted for Homosexuality'. According to a Tunisian forensic doctor I have interviewed, it is possible that a recent sodomy leaves some physical signs, but it is impossible to reach a scientific certitude on that, unless violence was involved (interviewed by the author, Tunis, July 2016). See also the detailed criticism against anal tests coming from a Lebanese medical association: Lebanese Medical Association for Sexual Health, 'Anal Tests in Lebanon'.

unlikely.[55] This path, in fact, has been successfully followed in Lebanon, where steps have been taken to end this practice thanks to the conjoint efforts of the Lebanese Order of Physicians and the Ministry of Justice.[56]

From this perspective, a positive development occurred in 2017, when Tunisia's minister for human rights formally announced the end of forced anal tests, following a recommendation from the UN Human Rights Council.[57] However, this reform is insufficient, both *de jure* and *de facto: de jure*, because the tests are still legal as long as the person consents; and *de facto*, because prosecutors continue to order them and the victims in police custody are often pressured to give their consent.[58]

The Tunisian Council of the Order of Physicians has also intervened on this matter. In 2015, it released an official communiqué in which it, 'as the guarantor of respect for medical ethics, strongly condemn[ed] any forensic examination without consent or not justified, against the dignity and the physical or mental integrity of the person examined'. Furthermore, the council declared that it would conduct 'an investigation in order to assess a possible breach of the code of medical ethics'.[59] In 2017, the same body released an additional communiqué reiterating the condemnation for any unjustified medical exam that infringes on the physical or moral integrity of the examined person. It further stressed:

> [t]he order of physicians considers the practice of a genital or anal examination to verify or confirm the nature of a person's sexual practices, *without their free and informed consent*, as an attack on their dignity and calls on requisitioned doctors to inform the people they have to examine about their right to refuse such an examination.[60]

This statement, and especially the clause stressing the need for informed consent, can be assessed in two ways. On the one hand, it is clearly unsatisfactory for the aforementioned reason: it neither recognizes the medical uselessness of the anal exams nor imposes a ban on them on ethical grounds. On the other hand, it is more relevant and innovative than it might appear at first glance, considering that, in the Tunisian Code of Medical Ethics, quite surprisingly, no norm requires a patient's consent to medical treatment.[61] It must be said that other rules from the Code apply. First, the patient must be informed of the nature of the examination before it is undertaken (Art. 73). The doctor must also refuse to

55 Interviewed by the author, Tunis, July 2016.
56 Ghoshal, 'Dignity Debased'.
57 AFP, 'Tunisia Bans Forced Anal Exams for Homosexuality'.
58 'Beginning of End for Forced Anal Exams'; 'Tunisie: Achever les réformes en matière de droits humains'.
59 Conseil National de l'Ordre des Médecins de Tunisie, 'Communiqué'. Own translation from French.
60 Conseil National de l'Ordre des Médecins de Tunisie, 'Communiqué: Le Consentement dans le Cadre de l'expertise Médicale'. Own translation from French; emphasis added.
61 Code de déontologie médicale [Tunisian Code of Medical Deontology].

perform an examination in certain circumstances, namely if he assesses that the interests of his patient are at risk (Art. 72), or 'if he considers that the questions posed to him are extraneous to strictly medical techniques' (Art. 74).[62] Despite the ambiguity of these provisions, a Tunisian forensic physician[63] confirmed to me that ethical issues arise when a judicial authority requires an examination to prove somebody's homosexuality, as it may be tantamount to degrading and discriminatory treatment.[64] Although he remarked that the patient's free and informed consent exempts the doctor from liability, he added that the physicians themselves ought to dissuade the patient from submitting to the examination if they deem it discriminatory. Furthermore, in no case should the doctor allow the police to be present, as this could result in psychological (or even physical) pressure to accept the examination.

An additional element has to be taken into account, namely the conflict between the code of ethics and the norms regulating the duties of the forensic physician before the judge.[65] There is no scope here to address this issue in depth; but it should be noted that the judge's request is formulated in terms of 'order' (*maʾmūriyya*) to the doctor.[66] This explains why the last paragraph of the 2017 communiqué of the Order of Physicians focuses on this point, stressing that a doctor, while acting as a court assistant, is never a substitute for the judge, and must always 'bear in mind the respect of the law and of his deontological duties'.[67] With this hendiadys, the Order seemingly aimed to reiterate that the deontological norms are on an equal footing with the other legal requirements, meaning that a physician cannot obey court orders that contravene medical ethics. Given the legal intricacy of this matter, a joint decision from the Order of Physicians, the Ministry of Health and the Ministry of Justice would nevertheless be desirable.

Comprehensive revision of the penal code

A comprehensive approach that tackles liberticidal laws would be, according to some,[68] more strategically productive than a fight focused exclusively on Article 230, as this would reduce conservative social pressure on a plethora of different issues.

An overall reform of the penal code, aimed at harmonizing it with the new constitution and the new democratic order, has been on the table for a few years,

62 Own translation from French.

63 *V. supra* note 54.

64 More on this in Chapter VIII.

65 I thank Dr. Sami Ben Sassi for brainstorming with me on these intricate matters. Interviewed by the author, Tunis, August 2016.

66 Based on an official court document, Order of medical examination [in Arabic].

67 Conseil National de l'Ordre des Médecins de Tunisie, 'Communiqué: Le Consentement dans le Cadre de l'expertise Médicale'.

68 Antonio Manganella, Tunisia office director of *Avocats sans Frontières*, interviewed by the author, Tunis, July 2016. Amna Guellali, interview. Yadh Ben Achour, interview.

according to Antonio Manganella, director of *Avocats sans Frontières* (ASF) in Tunis.[69] ASF is part of the 'Observatory of Tunisian Justice', a body aimed at scrutinizing Tunisian criminal law in order to harmonize it with international legal standards. The above-mentioned Collective for Individual Freedoms was similarly founded with the explicit intent of pushing for a comprehensive reform of the Penal Code and the Code of Criminal Procedure, so as to comply with the Constitution.

While all these attempts have yet to produce objective results, they also testify to the dynamism of the Tunisian landscape with regard to human rights issues, even the most controversial ones. This is a relevant difference to Egypt, where the situation is much less promising, as I am about to show.

Egypt

The witch-hunt against the 'debauched'

Unlike Tunisia, Egypt does not have an explicit legal ban on homosexuality. However, the crackdown against LGBT people is even more egregious here than in the 'Jasmine country', due to Article 9(c) of the Law 10 of 1961 'on the Combating of Prostitution'. This reads as follows:

> Punishment by imprisonment for a period not less than three months and not exceeding three years and a fine not less than 25 LE and not exceeding 300 LE in the Egyptian administration and not less than 250 Lira and not exceeding 3000 Lira in the Syrian administration or one of these two punishments applies in the following cases: [...]
>
> C) Whoever habitually engages in debauchery [*fujūr*] or prostitution.[70]

Fujūr is interpreted as referring to male homosexuality. However, there is debate among scholars and activists about whether this wording directly refers to homosexuality or not. According to the International Lesbian, Gay, Bisexual, Trans and Intersex Association (ILGA), *fujūr* merely refers to generic 'debauchery', meaning that, in ILGA's view, there is actually no ban on same-sex relations per se in the Egyptian penal system.[71] Wehr translates *fujūr* as 'immorality, iniquity, depravation, dissolution, debauchery, licentiousness, profligacy, dissolute life, fornication, whoredom';[72] there is no explicit mention of sodomy or male-on-male acts, although of course they may be implicitly included in a genus-species relation. According to Scott Long, instead, *fujūr* is not any more ambiguous than 'sodomy' or 'unnatural acts' in the English legal tradition – both used to

69 Antonio Manganella, interview.

70 The law dates back to the time of the United Arab Republic. All translations of Law 10/1961 are taken from 'Egypt: Law No. 10/1961, on the Combating of Prostitution'.

71 Carroll, 'State Sponsored Homophobia 2016', 11.

72 Wehr, 'فجور'.

variably punish bestiality, homosexuality and also anal sex between a man and a woman.[73] As stressed above, it should be noted that Arabic lacks an exact equivalent of 'homosexuality' in all its facets. Furthermore, according to Long, Egyptian jurisprudence made clear a long time ago that *fujūr* unambiguously refers to homosexuality.[74]

Even so, Baudoin Dupret correctly notes that the criminalization of homosexuality in Egypt is based on the use of analogy, which is clearly forbidden in criminal law.[75] The vague text of the law, only defined by an unpublished ruling of the Court of Cassation, has paved the way for legal uncertainty, which has been addressed by drawing on a common-sense (non-legal) understanding of what is 'normal' and 'natural', in a mixture of juridical, moral and stereotypical arguments.[76] It is worth recalling what was stated in the previous chapter regarding the requirements outlined by the Supreme Constitutional Court for criminal law statutes: they must be univocal, unambiguous and not based on analogy.[77]

Another problematic element in the letter of the law is the association between debauchery and prostitution – which has raised doubts on whether payment between sexual partners is necessary for the crime to be committed. In a 1975 landmark decision, the Court of Cassation stated that *fujūr*, when committed between two men, is punishable even if non-commercial (unlike sexual intercourse between a man and a woman).[78] In the judgment, the court condemned the passive partner, caught *in flagrante*, and rejected his argument that he had not had sex for payment:

> The legislator explicitly stated that this crime [the habitual practice of debauchery] happens when one practices vice [*fasha'*] with people with no distinction, and when this happens habitually. He did not necessitate for this charge that the practice of debauchery [*fujur*] … happens in return for a payment.[79]

However, a certain confusion on the commercial nature of *fujūr* has continued to resurface. This happened, for instance, in the 2001 Queen Boat affair – one of the most egregious debauchery cases, which is analysed in more detail below, involving the arrest of 52 men aboard the floating nightclub Queen Boat docked on the Nile in Cairo. The Court of Misdemeanors stated:

> The crime designated in [this text] is only committed when a man or a woman fornicates (*mubasharat al-fasha'*) with people without distinction, habitually. When a woman fornicates and sells her virtue to whomever asks

73 Stewart, 'How "Debauchery" Law Set up Egypt's Gay Crackdown'.
74 Stewart. Long, 'Entrapped! How to Use a Phone App to Destroy a Life'.
75 Dupret and Ferrié, 'Morale ou nature', 49.
76 Dupret, *Adjudication in Action*, 313.
77 Ramadan, 'Asbab ʿAdam Dusturiyyat', 7.
78 Human Rights Watch, 'In a Time of Torture', 14.
79 Court of Cassation, case 683 of 1975, cit. in Human Rights Watch, 14.

> for it without distinction, she commits prostitution (*da'ara*) […]; *fujur* occurs when a man sells his virtue to other men without distinction.[80]

Another element emerging from the Queen Boat affair, and from the landmark case of 1975, is that passive sodomy is the only form considered relevant as it is the only type to be purportedly detectable by a forensic physician;[81] there is also an evident cultural subtext of loathing for male feminization associated with the phenomenon.[82] This reflects a pattern that was originally typical of all instances of *fujūr*, although such distinctions have faded over time, and defendants have been convicted irrespective of their sexual roles (*v. infra*).[83]

In sum, in the application of Law 10/1961, we can notice a threefold discrimination, based on sex, sexual orientation and sometimes on sexual role. First, only the woman who sells her body is liable for prosecution, while the man who buys it is not even considered an accomplice or an inciter: Law 10/1961 makes it a crime to incite or assist a woman in prostitution, but the person who procures a sexual service is exempted from this accusation.[84] Second, in the case of homosexual intercourse, the payment criterion is dropped. Third, the passive partner has been traditionally more exposed to conviction than the active one. These three elements indicate a clear legal privilege for heterosexual males.

As concerns the requirement of 'habituality', this has been interpreted in case law as meaning that the act must be 'indiscriminate', namely, per the Court of Cassation, performed 'more than once in three years, with more than one person',[85] and in different circumstances.[86] *De facto*, this is an element which is almost impossible to prove, and even the Court of Cassation has stated that this should be 'left to the given court to determine […] as long as this determination is reasonable'.[87] At the same time, the Court of Cassation has also stressed that clear evidence is needed – a mere suspicion being insufficient to press charges of debauchery.[88] In practice, however, these guarantees are often circumvented by lower courts.[89]

To make things even more ambiguous, the vaguely worded Law 10/1961 makes collateral conduct – such as allowing one's premises to be used for the

80 Case 182/2001, Qasr al-Nil, in Dupret, *Adjudication in Action*, 313.
81 Dupret and Ferrié, 'Morale ou nature', 45.
82 Confirmed by many other indicators examined below.
83 Human Rights Watch, 'In a Time of Torture', 15. Human rights activist at the Egyptian Initiative for Personal Rights, phone interview by the author, May 2017.
84 Abdel Hamid, 'The Trap', 39.
85 Human Rights Watch, 'In a Time of Torture', 16.
86 Abdel Hamid, 'The Trap', 37.
87 Human Rights Watch, 'In a Time of Torture', 137.
88 Abdel Hamid, 'The Trap', 38.
89 Abdel Hamid, 40.

purpose of debauchery[90] or inducing someone to commit debauchery – a prosecutable offense:

> Whoever incites a person, be they male or female, to engage in debauchery or in prostitution, or assists in this or facilitates it, and similarly whoever employs a person or tempts him or induces him with the intention of engaging in debauchery or prostitution, is to be sentenced to imprisonment for a period not less than one year and not more than three years and a fine between 100 and 300 LE in the Egyptian administration and between 1000 and 3000 Lira in the Syrian administration.[91]

This provision mirrors Article 269bis of the Criminal Code:

> Whoever is found on a public road or a frequented place inciting the passersby to commit indecency with signals or words shall be punished with imprisonment for a period of no less than three months. If the perpetrator commits this crime again within one year of the date of the first judgment against him for the first crime, the penalty shall be imprisonment for a period of no less than a year and a fine of no less than five hundred and no more than three thousand pounds. Further to a ruling of conviction, the convict shall be placed under police surveillance for a period equal to that of the penalty.[92]

An additional provision of Law 10/1961 (Article 2) makes it a crime to 'induce' someone into debauchery 'by means of deception, force, threats, abuse of authority or other means of coercion'. This is especially relevant in connection with the practice of 'internet entrapment' by the Egyptian police, as I am going to show below.

Besides the laws directly addressing debauchery, we also have to consider the more generic range of crimes related to public decency. A relevant one is Article 178 of the Penal Code, on the manufacture and possession of material against public morals:

> Whoever publishes, manufactures or possesses, for the purpose of trade, distribution, leasing, posting or displaying publications, manuscripts, drawings, advertisements, carved or engraved pictures, hand drawings, photographs, symbolic signs, or other objects or pictures in general, if they are against public decency [*al-ḥayāʾ al-ʿām*], shall be punished with imprisonment for a period not exceeding two years and a fine of not less than five thousand pounds and not exceeding ten thousand pounds or either penalty.[93]

90 Arts. 8 and 9.
91 Art. 1(a) Law 10/1961.
92 Qanun al-ʿUqubat [Egyptian Criminal Code]. Own translation from Arabic.
93 Qanun al-ʿUqubat [Egyptian Criminal Code]. Own translation from Arabic.

This article is used to target possession of pornographic materials or sexual conversations on the internet, and even non-sexual internet advertisements are criminalized under this provision if they occur between gay men.[94] Recently, a new statute on cyber-crimes has further widened the scope of the crimes addressed by the statute with specific regard to online content: as per Article 25 Law 175/2018, 'Anyone who publishes online content that threatens society's and family's values shall be punished for at least six months of prison and a fine of at least fifty thousand pounds'.[95]

Furthermore, following the public display of rainbow flags during a concert held in Cairo in 2017, which caused public hysteria, the Supreme Media Regulatory Council issued an order preventing the appearance of 'homosexuals and their slogans in the media', so as 'to preserve order and public decency and out of respect for the values and correct beliefs of society'.[96] The order calls homosexuality 'a sickness and disgrace that would be better hidden from view and not promoted for dissemination', 'a blatant sin' and an 'aberration from all monotheistic faiths and from the canon of nature and the universe, a deviation that should not be codified or afforded any legitimacy that could help it spread or grow', on the assumption that 'Egyptian society's view differs from that of western societies in that we have social and religious tenets'.[97]

All these provisions are invoked and combined with no attempt at accuracy against homosexuals and activists. This enables judges to impose more than one penalty on the same conduct, in explicit violation of the judgments of the Constitutional Court, which has reaffirmed the general principle of law that a person cannot be punished more than once for the same act.[98]

Elements of evidence

In terms of evidence, the techniques used to prove homosexual conduct are the same in Egypt as in Tunisia: *flagrante delicto*, confession, circumstantial evidence and forensic expertise.[99] Regarding the last-mentioned, Egyptian prosecutors and judges – like their Tunisian peers – require anal examinations, which are carried out by the Forensic Medical Authority, a department of the Ministry of Justice.[100] This happens despite the fact that forensic reports are far from showing scientific certitude regarding the regularity of penetration,[101] as discussed above. Even the director of the Egyptian Forensic Medical Authority, interviewed by Human Rights Watch, admitted that 'the test cannot prove

94 Human Rights Watch, 'In a Time of Torture', 137.
95 Ramón Mendos, 'State-Sponsored Homophobia 2019', 518.
96 'Unofficial Translation of Statement by Egypt's Supreme Council for Media Regulation'.
97 'Unofficial Translation of Statement by Egypt's Supreme Council for Media Regulation'.
98 Abdel Hamid, 'The Trap', 27.
99 Dupret, *Adjudication in Action*, 307.
100 Ghoshal, 'Dignity Debased', 24.
101 Human Rights Watch, 'In a Time of Torture', 44.

criminal behavior according to the letter of the law'.[102] In his own words, 'there is no way to determine through the forensic examination whether the vice is practiced "without discrimination", with multiple partners. [...] Circumstantial or other evidence is needed.'[103] As a consequence, doctors rarely certify in a forensic report that an individual is habituated to sodomy.[104] At the same time, a negative test is no guarantee of acquittal: 'doctors routinely add a caveat in medical reports that concealment of signs of anal intercourse is possible through the use of lubricants and cosmetics'.[105] Thus, like Pontius Pilate, forensic physicians can wash their hands of the defendants' destiny without taking responsibility for either a medical lie or the acquittal of an individual presumed 'debauched'. As in the Tunisian case, the anal exam becomes therefore redundant – an inhuman and degrading treatment that purely functions as an anticipated penalty. It must be stressed that, in agreeing to perform this exam, Egyptian doctors are violating their own Code of Ethics, which prohibits physicians 'from carrying out positively or negatively any acts that constitute participation in torture operations and other kinds of cruel or inhumane treatment and from colluding or instigating these acts'.[106]

As regards circumstantial evidence, the bar is set very low and is based on gross stereotypes: an 'effeminate' appearance,[107] a profession seen as typically feminine or 'perverted',[108] possession of female clothes or beauty products, wigs, condoms, lubricants, hormonal medications[109] and even a certain hair style or underwear colour[110] can be sufficient to reach the burden of proof. A sad paradox that should be noted here is that condoms, while listed as evidence in more than ten debauchery cases examined by the Egyptian Initiative for Personal Rights (EIPR – arguably the main NGO working on this issue) are actively promoted by the Ministry of Health as a means to prevent HIV.[111] Another common pattern in evidence collection is the extortion of confessions with torture and inhuman and degrading treatments.[112]

With the rise of the internet and especially with the emergence of dating apps, an additional trend has emerged, namely the use of conversations and photos taken from dating applications and websites as crucial evidence in court cases.

102 Human Rights Watch, 112.
103 Human Rights Watch, 112.
104 Abdel Hamid, 'The Trap', 30.
105 Ghoshal, 'Dignity Debased', 28.
106 Egyptian Medical Code of Ethics, mentioned in Abdel Hamid, 'The Trap', 31.
107 Dupret, *Adjudication in Action*, 308.
108 In the Queen Boat case, for instance, the profession of masseur was seen as an element of proof. Dupret, 308.
109 Abdel Hamid, 'The Trap', 22.
110 Human Rights Watch, 'In a Time of Torture', 18.
111 Abdel Hamid, 'The Trap', 22. Egyptian Initiative for Personal Rights, 'Universal Periodic Review of Egypt 34th Session'.
112 Human Rights Watch, 'In a Time of Torture', 2. 'Egypt: Security Forces Abuse, Torture LGBT People'.

Often, these elements are obtained by police officers who infiltrate dating apps and lure gay men into fake sexual encounters arranged with the intention of arresting them. The controversial phenomenon of 'internet entrapment', which was documented by Human Rights Watch as early as in 2004, has now become systematic.[113] EIPR has noted that this practice constitutes a breach of the law:

> It is legally established that practising deceit to uncover a crime does not affect the legitimacy of the arrest but this is only in cases where a crime actually occurs, such as a vendor selling a counterfeit product to an undercover police officer. However, when the crime – practising debauchery in this case – does not occur, and the only evidence is electronic conversations, this constitutes a crime of incitement of debauchery.[114]

In other words, according to EIPR, the police in these cases induce people to commit debauchery by using deception – a crime punishable under Article 2 of Law 10/1961. It is unanimously established, in the Egyptian legal doctrine and case law, that it is illegitimate for the police to induce people to commit a crime (which they would not have otherwise committed) in order to arrest them.[115]

For their part, the police claim that a crime in these cases is, in fact, being committed: the arrested individuals have been caught in the *flagrante delicto* of inciting people to vice in the public streets, under Article 269bis of the Penal Code. Yet there are at least two evident fallacies in this line of argumentation: first, when officers apprehend the entrapped individuals, such individuals are not engaged in 'inciting the passersby', but are quietly waiting for the people with whom they have arranged a date; second, they would not be there in the first place had the police not incited them to come.

Religious grounds for prosecuting homosexuality

For the purposes of this study, it is crucial to note that Egyptian case law on debauchery often refers to 'offense against religion'. This corroborates my claim of a consubstantial connection between homosexuality and blasphemy, heresy or apostasy, all of which share a common denominator: any deed, irrespective of its aim and content, that is perceived as a threat to the dominant culture shaped around Islam will be criminalized.

The notorious Queen Boat case is an emblematic example of this attitude, as some of the defendants were convicted of blasphemy and in some cases also debauchery.[116] Article 98(f) of the Criminal Code was explicitly invoked, with

113 Abdel Hamid, 'The Trap', 12.
114 Abdel Hamid, 13.
115 Abdel Hamid, 24.
116 Dupret and Ferrié, 'Morale ou nature', 45.

defendants being accused of exploiting religion by advocating and propagating extremist thoughts with the aim of instigating sedition and division.[117] According to the court, one of the accused 'adopted deviant (*munharifa*) ideas inciting others to hold revealed religions in contempt (*izdira'*) and to call to abject (*radhila*) practices and sexual acts contrary to revealed laws'.[118] The UN Working Group on Arbitrary Detention reported that the defendants were charged with 'making homosexual practices a fundamental principle of their group in order to create social dissensions, and engaging in debauchery with men'.[119] 'Social dissensions' is the *fitna* of Article 98(f), that is, a religious crime, as explained previously. Debauchery, in other words, becomes an epiphenomenon of contempt for 'revealed religions' and their laws.

Hence, in the Queen Boat affair, different elements came together in a mixture of moral, legal and political categories.[120] The judge's attitude was the same as seen in judgments on blasphemy: the crime is a sin requiring a sort of judicial exorcism that should show the defendants the abnormality of their perversion, make them repent for their 'sexual perversion' and cleanse them of their 'sins' through the punishment.[121] In Dupret's words:

> Religious morality works here as the ultimate criterion for the evaluation of human action. Human justice [...] proceeds from this superior authority: forgiveness belongs firstly to God, and secondly to the judges; pity belongs to God, and secondly to the judges; pity belongs to God, so as to soften the judges' hearts afterwards; mistakes must be confessed to God, and only after to the judges.[122]

From this point of view, it should not be surprising that the debate around the Queen Boat case mobilized the idea of an authentic Egyptian culture under threat from the West, with homosexuality depicted as a Western plague maliciously spread to bring moral corruption.[123]

According to Jeffrey Redding, the accusations of crimes against religion in homosexuality cases actually come before accusations of debauchery and assume a greater relevance: '[...] it has often been overlooked that "debauchery" and "gayness" actually entered into the picture later than what is commonly understood: the original charges against the "Queen Boat 52" concerned not "debauchery," but "contempt of heavenly religion".'[124] Indeed, the entire case began with the

117 Dupret and Ferrié, 50.
118 Case 182/2011 in Dupret, *Adjudication in Action*, 306.
119 U.N. Working Group on Arbitrary Detention, 'Yasser Mohamed Salah et al. v. Egypt'.
120 Dupret, *Adjudication in Action*, 300.
121 Dupret and Ferrié, 'Morale ou nature', 55. The use of this religious jargon recurs throughout the verdicts. See Dupret, *Adjudication in Action*, chs. 11–12.
122 Dupret, *Adjudication in Action*, 311.
123 Dalacoura, 'Homosexuality as Cultural Battleground in the Middle East', 1296.
124 Redding, 'Human Rights and Homo-Sectuals', 444. Whitaker, *Unspeakable Love*, 61.

discovery of a purported satanic cult that aimed to destroy Islam and replace it with an evil cult allowing the worst indecencies:

> [S]everal Egyptian government officials who were involved with the (public) trials of the 'Queen Boat 52' attempted to portray it as a matter of 'religiosity' and 'religious' morals. Thus, not only did Judge Hassan al-Sayes [...] attempt to link the 'Queen Boat 52' with violations of Islamic religious/moral norms, but so did an Egyptian prosecutor [...]. [T]he prosecutor submitted that there were '[a] number of those who submitted to vice, until they became its servants with no conscience, have hurried towards all that God has prohibited, ridding themselves of all morals. They strayed from the straight path that God has drawn for man and through which He organized his desires.' Finally, the Prosecutor General of Egypt himself, responding to international condemnation of Egypt's conduct in relation to the 'Queen Boat 52', has emphasized that '[w]e are dedicated to protecting society against perversion, from a *religious*, social, and cultural point of view'.[125]

Attempts to connect homosexuality and religion have not ceased. In recent reports on state-sponsored homophobia, ILGA has repeatedly found that the accusation of 'contempt of religion' is still used to prosecute homosexuals and even mere sympathizers with their cause.[126] In 2019, for instance, a TV presenter was sentenced to one year in prison for contempt of religion and incitement to debauchery just for interviewing a gay man on his TV show.[127] All Egyptian activists and homosexuals I interviewed confirmed that the general hostility against gay people has a strong religious component.

While EIPR did not find that Article 98(f) was explicitly invoked in the cases they analysed, they nonetheless confirmed that religious passages from the Qurᵓan and the sunna are regularly quoted in the rulings and used to justify convictions of homosexual and transgender people,[128] with documented sentences such as 'These cases shake the Throne of God', 'God curses men who dress like women' and 'Homosexuality is a transgression against humanity and contravenes nature hence God has made it a major sin'.[129]

It is pertinent to note that Egyptian courts have asserted the existence of a connection between 'debauchery' and 'Satanism' also in cases that do not involve homosexuals but rather a different type of 'debauched' individual – as an additional proof of proximity between the 'crimes' of homosexuality, blasphemy and atheism. This is well exemplified by the case of novelist Ahmed Naji,

125 Redding, 'Human Rights and Homo-Sectuals', 445. Emphasis in the original.

126 Mohamed, 'Sexuality, Development and Non-Conforming Desire', 12. Carroll and Itaborahy, 'State Sponsored Homophobia 2015', 52. Ramón Mendos, 'State-Sponsored Homophobia 2019: Global Legislation Overview Update', 13.

127 Ramón Mendos, 'State-Sponsored Homophobia 2019: Global Legislation Overview Update', 13.

128 EIPR representative, interview.

129 Abdel Hamid, 'The Trap', 36.

who was charged with 'obscenity' under Article 178 of the Penal Code (punishing the publication of materials which undermine 'public morals', as discussed above).[130] After his initial acquittal, on the grounds of the artistic nature of the work, the Court of Appeal issued a differing judgment and sentenced Naji to a two-year incarceration for 'undermining public morality'.[131] The judge concluded that:

> [t]he law was meant to protect *public morality, religion, patriotism, and the family*. This way, Naji's writing, the judge argued, undermined the society itself. He accused the writer of ignoring the values and ethical boundaries of Egyptians in a '*diabolical* way' that incited *debauchery*. The judge called on parliament to increase prison terms for such offenses 'because spreading vice in an attempt to destroy the values and the *moral code* of society is such a grave matter requiring a harsh reprisal.' He then severely criticized all those who think that the moral code is relative and not immutable and unchangeable. It was shameful, he said, to leave 'the fate of our nation at the mercy of those who would treat it lightly and scandalously as if they were playing cards.' He concluded: 'Down with such freedom that brought to us corruption, loss of ethics, and moral looseness since the incidents that hit our beloved Egypt.'[132]

Several elements require attention here. First, the judge mentions all the pillars of Egyptian collective morality that, as argued above, curtailed individual rights in the Constitution of 2012: 'public morality', 'religion', 'patriotism' and the 'family'. To that, he adds an extremely relevant element, namely the reference to the 'diabolical', in connection with 'debauchery'. This evidently allocates the crime, once more, to the theological realm and casts it as a sin to be atoned for via a form of modern, judicial exorcism.[133] We must also highlight that 'debauchery' here is not used in its legal meaning, but in a non-technical way to characterize expressions which are perceived as being outside the boundaries of public morality.

Once again, homosexuals and freethinkers are put in the same basket, as pariahs who threaten religion and society.

Recent trends in persecution

EIPR has documented a dramatic increase in the number of anti-LGBT legal cases in recent years: while 185 men were charged with debauchery in the 13 years between 2000 and 2013, 232 were charged in the four-year period between

130 'Ahmed Naji'.
131 Mansour, 'Freedom of Expression in Egypt', 234.
132 Mansour, 237. Emphasis added.
133 Mansour, 238.

2013 and 2017 alone.[134] The NGO 'Solidarity with Egypt LGBT' has noted that in the aftermath of the 2011 revolution, during the rule of the SCAF[135] and Mohammed Morsi, making accusations of homosexuality was a way to tame public protests: 'the most famous charge which revolutionists and human rights activists were accused with, was being homosexual, or their political opinions support homosexual rights'.[136] The reasons for the persecution under al-Sisi seem equally political, and driven by the quest for easy consensus within the religious and conservative society of Egypt: 'he has wanted to show Egyptians that he is as conservative as the ousted Muslim Brotherhood'.[137]

The political motives go hand in hand with the exploitation of highly publicized scandals involving 'sexual deviants' by sensationalist media outlets. Two episodes in particular have made waves in recent years: the first is the 'deviants' wedding' of September 2014, concerning the arrest and subsequent trial of some men who had appeared on a YouTube video celebrating a fake gay marriage. The second is the 'Bab al-Bahr bathhouse' case a few months later, which concerned the live-streamed arrest and public shaming of a group of men at a public bathhouse. Both cases show the collusion between media and police in creating sexual scandals and invoking exemplary punishment for the 'debauched'. Indeed, the witch-hunt against the participants of the 'deviant's wedding' was prompted by TV host Tamer Amin, who aired parts of the video and called upon the police to chase the participants; the police followed suit, identified them by blackmailing one of their acquaintances, and arrested them. They stood trial and were eventually acquitted of the habitual practice of debauchery, but they were convicted for publicizing it.[138] Even more egregious was the role of the media in the Bab al-Bahr bathhouse case, which saw the television presenter Mona Iraqi accompany the police during the raid and film the nearly-naked men during their arrest. Eventually, after being beaten, insulted, humiliated and forced to undergo an anal test, the unfortunate protagonists were all acquitted due to the illogicality of the police report, which was so embellished that the police claimed to have witnessed sexual intercourse *during* the arrest. However, the court victory did not make up for the trauma and the social distress the victims have endured ever since. One has even attempted suicide.[139]

Among the most publicized cases was the one I described at the outset of this book. In September 2017, a concert by the Lebanese band Mashrouᶜ Leila, whose singer is openly gay, took place in Cairo. During the concert, someone in

134 Abdel Hamid, 'The Trap', 8. Egyptian Initiative for Personal Rights, 'Universal Periodic Review of Egypt 34th Session'. A document produced by the NGO 'Solidarity with LGBT in Egypt' speaks of 91 to 150 cases only in the biennium 2013–2015. Abdella, 'From Mubarak to Sisi', 2.

135 Supreme Council of the Armed Forces.

136 Abdella, 'From Mubarak to Sisi', 4.

137 Abdella, 4.

138 Abdel Hamid, 'The Trap', 20.

139 Abdel Hamid, 46.

the audience raised a rainbow flag, and this was widely shared on social media. This action was enough to ignite generalized hysteria, and the matter was treated as a high security issue. Authorities responded with an unprecedented crackdown, which led to the identification and arrest of 76 individuals – those who raised the flag and others who were considered to be LGBT or mere supporters – with the moral support of Al-Azhar, the Coptic Church and state media. Trials, detention, torture and anal examinations followed.[140]

So far, Sarah Hegazi has paid the highest price – at least as far as we know publicly – but it is impossible to determine how many lives have been destroyed, and in how many ways, by this egregious homophobia at all levels of the state and society. It is even more difficult to determine how many victims it will cost in the future, as there is no prospect of improvement on the horizon.

Strategies for decriminalization

Compared to the situation in Tunisia, in Egypt things look much darker, with no prospect of progress in the near future. While the more conservative social fabric is part of the reason, the lack of democracy is undoubtedly another factor, since human rights organizations and NGOs have been hit by a generalized crackdown that has left them with considerably less room for manoeuvre. The result is that all Egyptian homosexuals and human rights activists I interviewed painted a very gloomy picture; they not only mentioned the law but also a very conservative and hostile society.

In spite of these almost insurmountable difficulties, the Egyptian Initiative for Personal Rights is pursuing a multi-strategy campaign based on four main pillars. The first is a draft law aimed at decriminalizing sexual relations between consenting adults. The second aims at involving the Order of Physicians and the doctors' associations in issuing deontological guidelines prohibiting the anal test. The third is joint action with the United Nations Programme on HIV/AIDS (UNAIDS), which aims to prevent condom use from being exploited in court to obtain convictions; in fact, Egypt is in the paradoxical situation of receiving UNAIDS funds for condom promotion, while *de facto* encouraging sexual partners not to use them lest they face criminal prosecution. The fourth action consists in an advocacy campaign targeting dating apps, with a view to getting such companies to adopt measures to protect users, such as end-to-end encryption, fast deletion, possibility to flag suspect individuals, and others.[141]

For the moment, unfortunately, the situation seems far from improving, and actually there are worrying signs of an opposite trend, to the point that the

140 Soliman, 'Two Years after Egypt's "Rainbow Flag Arrests"'. 'EIPR Demands the Immediate Release of Detainees'. Egyptian Initiative for Personal Rights, 'Universal Periodic Review of Egypt 34th Session'.

141 EIPR representative, interview.

Egyptian authorities have gone so far as to target LGBT people and their supporters with terrorism charges.[142]

Final consideration on anti-gay laws in Egypt and Tunisia

The Egyptian and Tunisian laws against homosexuality follow the typical pattern for moral crimes: they do not identify a 'victim' of the violation, because the victim is society itself.[143] They are also shaped using vague and polysemic words, which pave the way for arbitrariness by the use of analogical reasoning and purely moral categories of interpretation. Such categories, furthermore, are based on strongly religious grounds, either implicitly or explicitly mentioned in the verdicts.

Dalacoura has observed that

> if hostility towards homosexuality in the Middle East may not be exclusively associated with Islamism, there is no doubt that the latter's rise and expansion after the 1970s exacerbated the tendency to vilify homosexuality and depict it as part of the West's corrupting cultural influence.[144]

The religious factor is evident also in the social revulsion at homosexuality.[145] According to a study by the Pew Research Center,[146] only 2 per cent of Tunisians and 3 per cent of Egyptians declare that society should accept homosexuality, while 94 per cent of Tunisians and 95 per cent of Egyptians believe it should not. These figures are not much different from those in Jordan, Pakistan, the Palestinian Territories and Indonesia – to mention just a few. The situation is slightly better, albeit not much, in Turkey and Lebanon,[147] where, as Jaspal notes, 'Islam arguably plays a less central role in social and political life'.[148] The Pew poll, in fact, shows a clear inverse correlation between the countries' religiosity scale and the tolerance for homosexuality, with Islamic states scoring the worst.[149] The trend of rejecting homosexuality does not change even among Muslim communities in Europe, where homophobic attitudes are considerably more prevalent than among the average population.[150] This explains why

142 Ramón Mendos, 'State-Sponsored Homophobia 2019', 521. 'Egypt: Security Forces Abuse, Torture LGBT People'.

143 What has been defined as a *ratio socialis* for incrimination. Ferchichi, 'L'homosexualité en droit tunisien', 182.

144 Dalacoura, 'Homosexuality as Cultural Battleground in the Middle East', 1295.

145 Berkouwer, Sultan, and Yehia, 'Homosexuality in Sudan and Egypt', 17. 'The Global Divide on Homosexuality'.

146 'The Global Divide on Homosexuality'.

147 9 per cent of Turks and 18 per cent of Lebanese declare that society should accept homosexuality. 'The Global Divide on Homosexuality'.

148 Jaspal, 'Islam and Homosexuality', 3.

149 'The Global Divide on Homosexuality'.

150 Virgili, 'Lifting the Integration Veil', 37.

targeting homosexuals 'is thought to be an easy way to gain religious credentials and to distract people from the state's other failures',[151] as explained above with regards to Sisi's crackdown.

This social attitude is reflected at the legal level: of the eleven states that impose the death penalty on homosexuals, all are Muslim-majority countries, and they explicitly do so on the grounds of compliance with shariᶜa law.[152] Even when gays and lesbians do not face execution, persecution in different forms is endemic.[153] Given this, it should not be surprising that the Organisation of Islamic Cooperation has constantly been in the forefront of the battle against the protection of sexual minorities in international fora.[154]

This picture contributes to explaining the striking similarities – at the social, ideological and legal levels – in the persecutions against sexual minorities and freethinkers: they are both perceived as different instances of the same threat to religion. In the next chapter, I am going to show that the legal grounds for protection are likewise mostly the same.

151 Mohamed, 'Sexuality, Development and Non-Conforming Desire', 12.
152 Ramón Mendos, 'State-Sponsored Homophobia 2020: Global Legislation Overview Update', 31.
153 'Straight but Narrow'.
154 Hamzić, 'A History in the Making', 105. Rehman and Polymenopoulou, 'Is Green a Part of the Rainbow?', 38.

VIII Constitutional and international freedoms

In the present chapter, I am going to address the main provisions pertaining to the issues at hand as they are enshrined in the Tunisian and Egyptian Constitutions as well as in international law. I will structure this analysis by identifying the key freedoms connected to the topic and presenting the constitutional provisions and the norms deriving from international treaties that protect each of them.

Constitutional obligation to abide by international law

First, I wish to highlight the overarching legal framework: the international norms analysed below, besides being binding for Egypt and Tunisia at the *international* level – in that they derive from treaties ratified by the states, or belong to customary, even *jus cogens*, law[1] – also obligate both countries at the *internal constitutional* level, although to different degrees.

In Tunisia, Article 20 of the Constitution reads: 'International agreements approved and ratified by the Assembly of the Representatives of the People have a status superior to that of laws and inferior to that of the Constitution'. Consequently, as the Penal Code is ordinary legislation, it must conform to the international treaties ratified by Tunisia.

In Egypt, the preamble proclaims that the Constitution is 'in line with the Universal Declaration of Human Rights'. Furthermore, Article 5 obligates the state to respect 'human rights and freedoms, as set out in the Constitution'. Several other generic references to human rights are contained in different *loci* of the text.[2]

1 On the international law obligations incumbent upon states see, *inter alia*, Shaw, *International Law*. Cassese and Gaeta, *Diritto internazionale*. Dailler, Nguyen and Pellet, *Droit international public*.

2 Art. 24: ' The Arabic language, religious education, and national history in all its stages are core subjects of pre-university public and private education. Universities are committed to teaching human rights, and professional morals and ethics relating to various academic disciplines'. Art. 91: ' The state shall grant political asylum to any foreigner who has been persecuted for defending the interests of peoples, human rights, peace or justice. Extradition of political refugees is

DOI: 10.4324/9780429259418-VIII

Regarding the effective legal force of international law, there is a significant difference between the Egyptian and Tunisian cases: although the 2014 Egyptian Constitution, for the first time in Egypt's history,[3] calls on the state to respect international law, it does not confer on the latter a status superior to domestic legislation. Indeed, Article 93 states: 'The state is committed to the agreements, covenants, and international conventions of human rights that were ratified by Egypt. They have the force of law after publication in accordance with the specified circumstances'. This means that international treaties will not be held superior to ordinary statutes unless ratified by a constitutional act. Consequently, conflict between international and national norms is to be resolved by applying the mere chronological criterion (*lex posterior derogat priori*), and any law adopted after an international treaty will prevail over that treaty itself.[4] Even if this solution, at the domestic level, is consistent with a dualist approach regarding national and international legal orders as independent entities,[5] at the international level it may raise doubts regarding the compatibility with Article 27 of the Vienna Convention of the Law of Treaties, whereby 'A party may not invoke the provisions of its internal law as justification for its failure to perform a treaty'.[6] It must be added, at any rate, that the issue of the rank of treaties remains ambiguous:

> There have been statements by the Egyptian government that the judiciary in Egypt 'gives precedence to international treaties over Egyptian domestic legislation in the event of conflict between the two'. Furthermore, the Supreme Constitutional Court has 'accorded treaty provisions a special status' by asserting that 'the human rights clauses of Egypt's Constitutions be interpreted in accordance with those human rights standards generally recognized and applied by democratic States, as reflected in international human rights instruments'.[7]

forbidden. All of the above is according to the law'. Art. 206: 'The police force is a statutory civil body that is in the service of the people. Its loyalty is to the people. It ensures safety and security to citizens, preserves public order and morality. It is committed to undertake the duties imposed on it by the Constitution and the law, and to respect human rights and basic rights. The state guarantees that members of the police force perform their duties. Guarantees for that are organized by law'. Art. 214: 'The law specifies independent national councils including the National Council for Human Rights, the National Council for Women, the National Council for Childhood and Motherhood, and the National Council for Persons with Disability. The law sets out their structures, mandates, and guarantees for the independence and neutrality of their members. They have the right to report to the public authorities any violations pertaining to their fields of work'.

3 Bernard-Maugiron, 'La Constitution égyptienne de 2014 est-elle révolutionnaire ?', 7.

4 Bernard-Maugiron, 7. El-Haj, 'The Relationship between International Law and National Law', 786.

5 The dualist approach considers the international and the national orders as independent and distinct. Conversely, the monist approach views national and international law as forming a single legal order. El-Haj, 'The Relationship between International Law and National Law', 765–66.

6 El-Haj, 786.

7 El-Haj, 786.

Another controversial issue is the broad reservation entered by Egypt at the ratification of the ICCPR as well as the International Covenant on Economic, Social and Cultural Rights (ICESCR): 'Taking into consideration the provisions of the Islamic Sharia and the fact that they do not conflict with the text annexed to the instrument, we accept, support and ratify it'.[8]

Although this is not technically a reservation but only an interpretative declaration, it gives rise to an important ambiguity: while it seems to merely affect the interpretation of the treaty and not allow exceptions or deviations from it,[9] *de facto* it states that Egypt considers itself exempt from any provision that is incompatible with Islamic law.[10] This argument has been invoked more than once by Egyptian courts to deny 'controversial' rights such as apostasy.[11] However, it is not an acceptable one. Although the ICCPR does not contain an explicit prohibition on reservations of a general character, as is the case with the European Convention on Human Rights (ECHR), Article 19 of the Vienna Convention on the Law of Treaties interdicts reservations that are incompatible with the object and purpose of the treaty: hence, a reservation giving generic pre-eminence to shariᶜa – i.e. to a legal system that may contain several provisions antithetical to human rights norms – can be inferred to be incompatible with the object and purpose of ICCPR. Although not legally applicable to the countries under consideration, it is relevant to recall the opinion on shariᶜa issued by the European Court of Human Rights (ECtHR) in the case *Refah Partisi v. Turkey*:

> The Court concurs in the Chamber's view that sharia is incompatible with the fundamental principles of democracy, as set forth in the Convention: 'Like the Constitutional Court, the Court considers that sharia, which faithfully reflects the dogmas and divine rules laid down by religion, is stable and invariable. Principles such as pluralism in the political sphere or the constant evolution of public freedoms have no place in it. The Court notes that, when read together, the offending statements, which contain explicit references to the introduction of sharia, are difficult to reconcile with the fundamental principles of democracy, as conceived in the Convention taken as a whole. It is difficult to declare one's respect for democracy and human rights while at the same time supporting a regime based on sharia, which clearly diverges from Convention values, particularly with regard to its criminal law and criminal procedure, its rules on the legal status of women and the way it intervenes in all spheres of private and public life in accordance with religious precepts.'[12]

While not judging shariᶜa in abstract terms like the ECtHR, the Human Rights Committee (HRC), namely the 'body of independent experts that monitors

8 'International Covenant on Civil and Political Rights: Declarations and Reservations'.

9 Brems, *Human Rights*, 272.

10 Bhala, *Understanding Islamic Law*, 1267.

11 El Fegiery, 'Islamic Law and Freedom of Religion', 13.

12 Refah Partisi and Others v. Turkey, paragraph 123.

implementation of the International Covenant on Civil and Political Rights by its State parties',[13] has also stated that certain interpretations of shariᶜa law are incompatible with the covenant. In particular, the Committee has condemned the enforcement of *ḥudūd* penalties, the discrimination against women and the legalization of female genital mutilation following religious fatwas.[14] At any rate, whatever one may think of shariᶜa in the abstract, concrete grounds for deeming it in conflict with human rights arise from the interpretation given to it by Egyptian courts, which have used Islamic law to deny basic and indisputable rights, as shown above.

Furthermore, discussions on the compatibility of Islamic law and human rights cannot change one inherent characteristic of shariᶜa, namely that is an undefined concept, an umbrella term covering multiple meanings. Therefore, a reservation based on it is necessarily indeterminate, and this makes it illegitimate due to the *carte blanche* it gives to states to decide whether or not to respect the treaty[15] (in clear breach of Art. 19 of the Vienna Convention). Additionally, broad and vague reservations based on shariᶜa law violate the principle of good faith in international treaties.[16]

Non-discrimination

Article 21 of the Tunisian Constitution clearly stipulates that

> 'All citizens, male and female, have equal rights and duties, and are equal before the law without any discrimination'.

The provision enshrined in Article 53 of the 2014 Egyptian Constitution is even broader:

> Citizens are equal before the law, possess equal rights and public duties, and may not be discriminated against on the basis of religion, belief, sex, origin, race, color, language, disability, social class, political or geographical affiliation, or for any other reason.
>
> Discrimination and incitement to hate are crimes punishable by law.
>
> The state shall take all necessary measures to eliminate all forms of discrimination, and the law shall regulate the establishment of an independent commission for this purpose.

At the international level, this fundamental principle is enshrined in the UDHR. Article 1 states that 'All human beings are born free and equal in dignity and rights'; this is complemented by Article 7: 'All are equal before the law and are entitled without any discrimination to equal protection of the law. All are entitled to equal protection against any discrimination in violation of this Declaration and against any incitement to such discrimination.'

13 'OHCHR | Human Rights Committee'.
14 U.N. Human Rights Committee, 'Concluding Observations on the Initial Report of Indonesia'.
15 Abiad, *Sharia, Muslim States and International Human Rights Treaty Obligations*, 79.
16 Abiad, 70.

The ICCPR and the ICESCR, both ratified by Tunisia and Egypt, reiterate these principles and make them legally binding. In particular, Article 2 ICCPR states:

> Each State Party to the present Covenant undertakes to respect and to ensure to all individuals within its territory and subject to its jurisdiction the rights recognized in the present Covenant, without distinction of any kind, such as race, colour, sex, language, religion, political or other opinion, national or social origin, property, birth or other status.

In addition, Article 26 ICCPR stipulates:

> All persons are equal before the law and are entitled without any discrimination to the equal protection of the law. In this respect, the law shall prohibit any discrimination and guarantee to all persons equal and effective protection against discrimination on any ground such as race, colour, sex, language, religion, political or other opinion, national or social origin, property, birth or other status.

Similar provisions are contained in Article 2 ICESCR.[17]

Under international law, the equality of citizens and the prohibition of discrimination should be understood as including sexual and religious (or non-religious) minorities.

Concerning homosexuality, in a ground-breaking 1994 decision, the HRC held that reference to 'sex' in Article 2 as a forbidden ground for discrimination should be interpreted as including sexual orientation[18] – an interpretation that has subsequently been reiterated.[19] The UN Committee on Economic, Social and Cultural Rights and the Committee on the Rights of the Child[20] have stated the same principle. The Committee on the Elimination of Discrimination against Women[21] has likewise made it clear that discrimination based on sex and

17 '1. Each State Party to the present Covenant undertakes to take steps, individually and through international assistance and co-operation, especially economic and technical, to the maximum of its available resources, with a view to achieving progressively the full realization of the rights recognized in the present Covenant by all appropriate means, including particularly the adoption of legislative measures. 2. The States Parties to the present Covenant undertake to guarantee that the rights enunciated in the present Covenant will be exercised without discrimination of any kind as to race, colour, sex, language, religion, political or other opinion, national or social origin, property, birth or other status. 3. Developing countries, with due regard to human rights and their national economy, may determine to what extent they would guarantee the economic rights recognized in the present Covenant to non-nationals'.

18 U.N. Human Rights Committee, 'Toonen v. Australia' (Communication No. 488/1992, CCPR/C/50/D/488/1992, 1994), para. 8.7.

19 Hamzić, 'A History in the Making', 99.

20 U.N. Committee on the Rights of the Child, 'General Comment No. 4'.

21 It is pertinent to recall here that Tunisia has withdrawn all reservations to this Convention.

gender is 'inextricably linked' with other factors, including sexual orientation and gender identity.[22]

On this basis, the Working Group on Arbitrary Detention (WGAD) has issued a crucial opinion: arrests and detentions on the grounds of sexual orientation are discriminatory per se, and therefore illegal under Articles 2 and 26 ICCPR *regardless of the laws under which they are performed*. In other words, the fact that arrests and detentions are based on established legislation does not make them less arbitrary. This means that the criminalization of homosexuality itself is essentially discriminatory and illegitimate,[23] because 'international human rights law prohibits discrimination on grounds of sexual orientation, gender identity and sex characteristics; in the same way as race, sex, colour, or religion, they are not permissible reasons for making distinctions'.[24]

As regards freethinkers, the Human Rights Committee has stated clearly that theistic, non-theistic and atheistic beliefs are all equally protected by Article 18 of the International Covenant on Civil and Political Rights,[25] and that, consequently, the legal guarantees adopted by states have to respect 'equality and non-discrimination on all grounds specified in articles 2, 3 and 26'.[26]

Freedom of conscience and belief

The right of individuals to live their life in accordance with their personal inclinations and convictions, without interference from the dominant social, cultural and religious beliefs, is an expression of freedom of conscience.

In Tunisia, this fundamental principle is enshrined in Article 6 of the Constitution, along with freedom of belief, as extensively discussed in Chapter V. In the context under consideration, freedom of conscience has a particular value with respect to its 'sisters' (freedom of thought and belief). As Ben Achour has put it,

> [f]reedom of conscience [...] guarantees philosophical and metaphysical freedoms. More profound than freedom of thought, it affects religious beliefs and philosophical convictions. It implies, in particular, one's possibility to choose a religion, to change or modify it, or to have no religion at all according to one's conscience. In this perspective, what was considered in

22 U.N. Committee on the Elimination of Discrimination Against Women, 'General Recommendation No. 28'. For a comprehensive overview of these issues, Hamzić, 'A History in the Making'. O'Flaherty and Fisher, 'Sexual Orientation, Gender Identity'.

23 Office of the United Nations High Commissioner for Human Rights (OHCHR), 'Born Free and Equal', 2012, 36. Office of the United Nations High Commissioner for Human Rights (OHCHR), 'Born Free and Equal', 2019, 45.

24 Office of the United Nations High Commissioner for Human Rights (OHCHR), 'Born Free and Equal', 2019, 54.

25 U.N. Human Rights Committee, 'General Comment 22', para. 2.

26 U.N. Human Rights Committee, para. 8.

> the past as the crime of apostasy, *irtidâd*, blameworthy innovation, *bid'a*, disbelief, *zandaqa*, dissidence, *khourouj*, now becomes the expression of a person's creativity and of the power of her intellectual potential.[27]

As has been noted, this principle has extraordinary novelty and importance in an Islamic context.[28]

The Egyptian Constitution, unfortunately, does not explicitly mention freedom of conscience, but it does mention freedom of thought in Article 65 and freedom of belief in Article 64. The latter reads: 'Freedom of belief is absolute. The freedom of practicing religious rituals and establishing places of worship for the followers of revealed religions is a right organized by law'.

It is immediately evident that this article violates religious freedom and the right not to be discriminated against for all those not belonging to the 'religions of the Book'.

At the international level, freedom of conscience and religion are guaranteed by Article 18 UDHR:

> Everyone has the right to freedom of thought, conscience and religion; this right includes freedom to change his religion or belief, and freedom, either alone or in community with others and in public or private, to manifest his religion or belief in teaching, practice, worship and observance.

A relevant difference characterizes the homologous Article 18 of the ICCPR:

> 1 Everyone shall have the right to freedom of thought, conscience and religion. This right shall include freedom to have or to adopt a religion or belief of his choice, and freedom, either individually or in community with others and in public or private, to manifest his religion or belief in worship, observance, practice and teaching. 2. No one shall be subject to coercion which would impair his freedom to have or to adopt a religion or belief of his choice. 3. Freedom to manifest one's religion or beliefs may be subject only to such limitations as are prescribed by law and are necessary to protect public safety, order, health, or morals or the fundamental rights and freedoms of others.

While the UDHR explicitly recognizes the freedom to *change* religion or belief, the ICCPR does not contain a similar statement due to the opposition of some Muslim countries in the drafting phase.[29] However, it mentions the right of an individual to 'have *or adopt* a religion or belief of his choice', which, according to the HRC, cannot be subjected to 'any limitations whatsoever', just like freedom

27 Ben Achour, 'La force du droit'. Own translation from French.

28 Hédia and Belhassine, *Ces Nouveaux Mots Qui Font la Tunisie*, 143. Jabeur Mejri is explicitly mentioned here as a case of prisoner of conscience in violation of this constitutional principle.

29 *V. supra*, Chapter II.

of thought.[30] Furthermore, the Special Rapporteur on freedom of religion or belief has specified: 'The right to change religion is absolute and is not subject to any limitation whatsoever. Any legislation that would prohibit or limit the right to change one's religion would be contrary to international human rights standards'.[31]

Concerning the freedom to express one's religion or belief, Article 18.3 ICCPR specifies that it may encounter limitations 'as are prescribed by law and are necessary to protect public safety, order, health, or morals or the fundamental rights and freedoms of others'. Yet, the HRC has observed that 'the concept of morals derives from many social, philosophical and religious traditions; consequently, limitations on the freedom to manifest a religion or belief for the purpose of protecting morals must be based on principles not deriving exclusively from a single tradition'.[32] In other words, the state may not invoke dominant religious principles or the socio-cultural views of the majority to trample on the rights of minorities, be they sexual or religious.

The link between freedom of conscience and LGBT rights is made explicit in the Yogyakarta Principles – a comprehensive compilation of international law obligations on sexual orientation and gender identity, drawn up in 2007 by a group of human rights experts. At the same time, the Yogyakarta Principles add a caveat to avoid what we discussed in Chapter V, namely the exploitation of freedom of conscience to discriminate against LGBT individuals. Principle 21 reads:

> Everyone has the right to freedom of thought, conscience and religion, regardless of sexual orientation or gender identity. These rights may not be invoked by the State to justify laws, policies or practices which deny equal protection of the law, or discriminate, on the basis of sexual orientation or gender identity.[33]

Freedom of expression

In the Egyptian Constitution, both freedom of expression and freedom of thought are addressed by Article 65. No limitation is explicitly provided there: 'Freedom of thought and opinion is guaranteed. All individuals have the right to express their opinion through speech, writing, imagery, or any other means of expression and publication.'

The Tunisian Constitution guarantees freedom of thought and expression in broad terms in Article 31: 'Freedom of opinion, thought, expression, information and publication shall be guaranteed. These freedoms shall not be subject

30 El Fegiery, *Islamic Law and Human Rights*, 192.
31 El Fegiery, 192.
32 U.N. Human Rights Committee, 'General Comment 22', para. 8.
33 'The Yogyakarta Principles'. Hamzić notes that this is in line with the HRC's and ECtHR's interpretation of this right. Hamzić, 'A History in the Making', 110. On the Yogyakarta Principles, see O'Flaherty and Fisher, 'Sexual Orientation, Gender Identity'.

to prior censorship'. In addition, we have to consider Article 42, which protects 'the right to culture' and 'the freedom of creative expression' and calls on the state to promote 'the values of tolerance, rejection of violence, openness to different cultures and dialogue between civilizations'. On the other hand, Article 6 could represent a justification for laws prohibiting blasphemous speech, in that it calls on the state to 'safeguard the sacred'.

In international law, Article 19 UDHR states: 'Everyone has the right to freedom of opinion and expression; this right includes freedom to hold opinions without interference and to seek, receive and impart information and ideas through any media and regardless of frontiers.'

Article 19 ICCPR is more precise, and also sets limits on freedom of expression:

1 Everyone shall have the right to hold opinions without interference.
2 Everyone shall have the right to freedom of expression; this right shall include freedom to seek, receive and impart information and ideas of all kinds, regardless of frontiers, either orally, in writing or in print, in the form of art, or through any other media of his choice.
3 The exercise of the rights provided for in paragraph 2 of this article carries with it special duties and responsibilities. It may therefore be subject to certain restrictions, but these shall only be such as are provided by law and are necessary:

    (a) For respect of the rights or reputations of others;
    (b) For the protection of national security or of public order (*ordre public*), or of public health or morals.

Although it lists the legitimate grounds for restrictions, Paragraph 3 also makes it clear that they are an exception to the rule, under the principle of proportionality. The most problematic reference is the protection of 'public morals' – a vague clause that authorities widely abuse, as I have shown. In that regard, however, the HRC has firmly maintained:

> Prohibitions of displays of lack of respect for a religion or other belief system, including blasphemy laws, are incompatible with the Covenant, except in the specific circumstances envisaged in article 20, paragraph 2, of the Covenant. Such prohibitions must also comply with the strict requirements of article 19, paragraph 3, as well as such articles as 2, 5, 17, 18 and 26. Thus, for instance, it would be impermissible for any such laws to discriminate in favour of or against one or certain religions or belief systems, or their adherents over another, or religious believers over non-believers. Nor would it be permissible for such prohibitions to be used to prevent or punish criticism of religious leaders or commentary on religious doctrine and tenets of faith.[34]

34 U.N. Human Rights Committee, 'General Comment 34', para. 48.

The reference to Article 20.2, which prohibits 'any advocacy of national, racial or religious hatred that constitutes incitement to discrimination, hostility or violence', does not imply an equation between 'racism' and 'defamation of religion'. A joint statement by three UN Special Rapporteurs has actually stated the opposite: 'racism is often based on demonstrably false ideas of racial superiority and religions often make claims of superiority for themselves'.[35]

In other words, 'freedom of religion does not encompass the right to respect for one's religious feeling',[36] and the safeguard of the sacred must be read in a very restrictive sense (for instance, concerning material protection for places of worship), and never in such a way as to impede the free circulation of ideas. Subordinating freedom of expression to norms against blasphemy, heresy and apostasy means curtailing legitimate ideas and leaving 'Muslim reformers, atheists and members of unrecognised religious minorities [...] vulnerable to persecution'.[37]

Furthermore, from a formal point of view, any law restricting free speech 'must be formulated with sufficient precision to enable an individual to regulate his or her conduct accordingly and it must be made accessible to the public. A statute may not confer unfettered discretion for the restriction of freedom of expression on those charged with its execution'.[38] In this book I have shown that unfettered discretion is precisely the defining characteristic of Egyptian and Tunisian provisions based on general and vague principles such as 'public morals', 'public decency' and 'public order'.

The same constitutional and international norms bestow on LGBT people and their defenders the right to manifest their sexual identity and the arguments associated with the struggle for sexual identity privately, publicly and with various means.

As already observed, there are noteworthy similarities in prosecutions of blasphemers and homosexuals. Any move to overcome a broad interpretation of concepts such as 'public morals', 'decency' and 'good mores' will benefit individuals in both categories.[39]

Right to privacy

The right to establish sexual and romantic relationships is a fundamental component of an individual's private sphere. Public authorities are not entitled to interfere arbitrarily with domestic privacy.

Respect for private life is ensured by Article 24, Section 1 of the Tunisian Constitution: 'The state protects the right to privacy and the inviolability of the home, and the confidentiality of correspondence, communications, and personal information'.

35 Whitaker, *Arabs without God*, 157.
36 El Fegiery, *Islamic Law and Human Rights*, 99.
37 El Fegiery, 103.
38 U.N. Human Rights Committee, 'General Comment 34', para. 25.
39 Cf. International Council on Human Rights Policy, 'Sexuality and Human Rights', 38.

Similar guarantees are present in the Egyptian Constitution. Article 57 states: 'Private life is inviolable, safeguarded and may not be infringed upon'. The same article also guarantees privacy of communications, while Article 58 ensures the inviolability of private homes, 'except by causal judicial warrant'.

In international law, the right to private and family life is guaranteed by Article 12 UDHR and Article 17 ICCPR. The latter, using a language almost identical to the former, states:

1. No one shall be subjected to arbitrary or unlawful interference with his privacy, family, home or correspondence, nor to unlawful attacks on his honour and reputation.
2. Everyone has the right to the protection of the law against such interference or attacks.

A reading of this provision ('No one shall be subjected') combined with the principle of non-discrimination leaves little doubt that the guarantee applies irrespective of sexual orientation and gender. This is made explicit in the above-mentioned HRC decision on sexual orientation: 'It is undisputed that adult consensual activity in private is covered by the concept of "privacy", and that [the complainant] is actually and currently affected by the continued existence of the Tasmanian laws [criminalizing homosexuality]'.[40] The WGAD has affirmed the same concept.[41]

Yet, Article 17 ICCPR does not ensure absolute protection – it merely requires that interference be not 'arbitrary or unlawful'. While Tunisia and Egypt respect the second requirement – as provisions criminalizing homosexuality do exist – what constitutes 'arbitrary' interference? Are there some legitimate grounds for the state to interfere with same-sex intercourse? From this viewpoint, the HRC has likewise been clear in rejecting arguments based on public health or public morals.[42] On public morals, in particular, it has firmly denied that 'moral issues are exclusively a matter of domestic concern. As this would open the door to withdrawing from the Committee's scrutiny a potentially large number of statutes interfering with privacy.'[43]

In other words, social, cultural and religious mores are not valid reasons to deprive individuals of the rights granted by Article 17 ICCPR. This reasoning is consistent with the principle of non-discrimination examined above.

40 U.N. Human Rights Committee, 'Toonen v. Australia', para. 8.2.

41 '[T]he existence of laws criminalizing homosexual behaviour between consenting adults in private and the application of criminal penalties against persons accused of such behaviour violate the rights to privacy and freedom from discrimination set forth in the International Covenant on Civil and Political Rights. Consequently, the Working Group considers that the fact that the criminalization of homosexuality in Cameroonian law is incompatible with articles 17 and 26 of the International Covenant on Civil and Political Rights'. U.N. Working Group on Arbitrary Detention, 'François Ayissi et al. v. Cameroon', para. 19.

42 U.N. Human Rights Committee, 'Toonen v. Australia', para. 8.5–8.6.

43 U.N. Human Rights Committee, para. 8.6.

Protection of human dignity, freedom from torture and inhuman treatments

Anal examinations to prove an individual's homosexuality 'constitute a form of torture or cruel, degrading, and inhuman treatment, prohibited under the Convention against Torture, the International Covenant on Civil and Political Rights (ICCPR), and the African Charter on Human and Peoples' Rights'.[44] For this reason, such examinations have been condemned by the UN Committee against Torture (CAT), the WGAD and the Special Rapporteur on torture, who have also called them 'medically worthless'.[45] Hence, the CAT has explicitly called on Tunisia to abrogate Article 230 and halt anal tests.[46] In a more generic way, the Committee has expressed concern about Egypt over the 'ill-treatment inflicted on men because of their real or alleged homosexuality'.[47]

At this juncture, it is worth recalling that, under international law, the prohibition of torture is considered a peremptory norm of *jus cogens*: as such, it is universally valid and cannot be subject to any derogation.[48]

The Tunisian Constitution, Article 23, firmly protects dignity and prohibits torture, thus making anal tests unconstitutional:[49] 'The state protects human dignity and physical integrity, and prohibits mental and physical torture. Crimes of torture are not subject to any statute of limitations'.

The Egyptian Constitution likewise prohibits torture in the broadest possible terms. Article 52 reads: 'All forms of torture are a crime with no statute of limitations'. The ban is further developed in Article 55, on due process:

> All those who are apprehended, detained or have their freedom restricted shall be treated in a way that preserves their dignity. They may not be tortured, terrorized, or coerced. They may not be physically or mentally harmed, or arrested and confined in designated locations that are appropriate according to humanitarian and health standards. The state shall provide means of access for those with disabilities.
>
> Any violation of the above is a crime and the perpetrator shall be punished under the law.
>
> The accused possesses the right to remain silent. Any statement that is proven to have been given by the detainee under pressure of any of that which is stated above, or the threat of such, shall be considered null and void.

44 'Tunisia: Men Prosecuted for Homosexuality'. See also Ferchichi, 'L'homosexualité en droit tunisien', 188.

45 U.N. Human Rights Council, 'Discriminatory Laws and Practices', para. 37.

46 U.N. Committee Against Torture, 'Concluding Observations on the Third Periodic Report of Tunisia', para. 42.

47 U.N. Committee Against Torture, 'Conclusions and Recommendations of the Committee against Torture: Egypt', para. 5 (e).

48 Bassiouni, 'International Crimes'. On the definition of *jus cogens*: 63; on the prohibition of torture as a peremptory norm: 68.

49 Cf. Ferchichi, Article 230 du Code pénal.

The treatment of homosexuals in Egyptian prisons and the anal tests they are forced to undergo are a clear breach of these provisions.

Legitimate restrictions of rights

Both the Tunisian and the Egyptian Constitutions anticipate legitimate limitations of rights on certain grounds. While a few rights, such as freedom of thought and prohibition of torture, are intangible, as argued elsewhere in this book, others may be derogated in specific circumstances and weighted in a balancing test with other constitutional interests.

Article 49 of the Tunisian Constitution reads:

> The limitations that can be imposed on the exercise of the rights and freedoms guaranteed in this Constitution will be established by law, without compromising their essence. Any such limitations can only be put in place for reasons necessary to a civil and democratic state and with the aim of protecting the rights of others, or based on the requirements of public order, national defence, public health or public morals, and provided there is proportionality between these restrictions and the objective sought,
>
> Judicial authorities ensure that rights and freedoms are protected from all violations.
>
> No amendment may undermine the human rights and freedoms guaranteed in this Constitution.

This provision is based almost word for word on the language used in the ICCPR and in the ECHR in relation to certain rights.[50] From a formal point of view, therefore, Article 49 may boast an impeccable international pedigree. Of course, its concrete application (and abuse) depend on the interpretation given to abstract principles such as 'public order', 'public health' or 'public morals', as stressed above.

In Gaddes' opinion, the full reading of Article 49 suggests an overall liberal meaning due to its strict requirements. Therefore, according to him, an individual's right to enjoy his/her own body, including sexual freedom, cannot be limited on the grounds of 'public morals' or 'public health', for this would mean depriving the right of its essence with no necessity for a civil and democratic state.[51] Additionally, as far as Article 230 is concerned, 'it only applies to acts committed in private. It is therefore illogical to attack homosexuality speaking of public morality'.[52]

50 ICCPR: Freedom of movement (art. 12); freedom to manifest one's religion (art. 18); freedom of expression (art. 19); freedom of association (art. 22). ECHR: Privacy and family life (art. 8); freedom to manifest one's religion (art. 9); freedom of expression (art. 10); freedom of assembly and association (art. 11).

51 Gaddes, interview.

52 Ferchichi, Article 230 du Code pénal. Own translation from French.

This reading of Article 49 is reflective of international law. The HRC has clearly stated that restrictions may not jeopardize the right itself, that they may never reverse the relation between the rule (the right) and exception (the restrictions) and that they have to respect necessity, proportionality and non-discrimination.[53]

Article 92 of the Egyptian Constitution formally reasserts such conditions:

> 'Rights and freedoms of individual citizens may not be suspended or reduced. No law that regulates the exercise of rights and freedoms may restrict them in such a way as infringes upon their essence and foundation.'

Formally, the logic of this provision is the reverse of the relevant Tunisian one: while Article 49 moves from the perspective of identifying legitimate grounds for restricting constitutional protections, Article 92 aims to impede legislative abuses.

Final considerations

From this analysis, two main points emerge. First of all, in the previous chapters I have already stressed the commonalities between homosexuality and blasphemy in terms of the legal bases and rationale for prosecution. In this chapter, I have confirmed my thesis from the opposite angle: similar arguments apply to the assertion of sexual freedom and freedom of conscience. The second consideration is that, on paper, both the Tunisian and the Egyptian constitutions would be altogether adequate to guarantee the respect of those rights as required by international law.

It remains to be seen whether the crucial transition from pure theory and constitutional clichés to actual implementation – which would concretely benefit citizens' lives – will be possible in the face of social, political and religious pressure.

53 *Inter alia*, U.N. Human Rights Committee, 'General Comment 27: Article 12 (Freedom of Movement)', paras 11–18. U.N. Human Rights Committee, 'General Comment 22', para. 8. and U.N. Human Rights Committee, 'General Comment 34', para. 22.

IX Conclusions

Constitutions and individual freedom: the unbreakable bond

This book started on a dark note. The final words of Sarah Hegazi, innocent victim of a Kafkaesque system, were certainly not a beacon of hope. Still, I do not wish to completely shut the door on positive expectations, knowing that past experience is not necessarily a good guide to the future. For homosexuals and freethinkers in Egypt and Tunisia the spring is yet to come, but no winter is eternal.

Perhaps naively, I wrote this book guided by the idea that constitutions are not collections of empty lines merely intended to tick some formal boxes. Based on many autocrats' behaviour, one might be inclined to reach this pessimistic conclusion; however, not even a dictator can always dismiss those powerful words with the snap of his fingers, as the fiercely contested battles around constitution-making testify.

But what exactly is the position of the constitution in a Muslim country? What is intended to prevail: a human-made charter or God's law? And what happens when the two collide? These are the main questions I have tried to address. If we solely consider the classical Islamic and contemporary Islamist mindset, the answer is easy: the legitimacy of power is contingent on respecting the Law of God; as such, it is predicated on shariᶜa, to which a human-made constitution, whenever it exists, will always remain hierarchically subordinate. This conclusion has profound consequences: it deeply affects the rule of law in all its components, which are not limited to formal democracy but include checks and balances and substantive individual freedoms.

This impact is not benign, and this seems to be a direct consequence of religious norms, or of a certain interpretation thereof. Shariᶜa is certainly a polysemous concept, but its prevalent, orthodox interpretation is simply incompatible, under many respects, with the modern understanding of universal human rights. Severe discrimination against non-Muslims and women continues to be justified or even invoked based on religious arguments, and it has a concrete impact on basic rights such as the freedom to pray to one's preferred deity or not to pray at all, to marry the person of one's choosing, and to enjoy equal rights in the private and public sphere. Muslim men are not spared either, as harsh injunctions,

DOI: 10.4324/9780429259418-IX

enforced with draconian punishments, affect the life of every citizen irrespective of sex, religion or any other characteristic, determining how they should conduct their lives, what they should wear, eat or drink, whom they should love, and what they should write, say, believe or even think.

Throughout this analysis, I have highlighted these detrimental outcomes. They are especially evident in the Islamic charters of rights and the Al-Azhar constitutional project but are also apparent in the preparatory works and final texts of the Egyptian and Tunisian Constitutions. The shariᶜa supremacy clause of the Egyptian Constitution is a *de facto* Trojan horse, jeopardizing not only fundamental rights but also the overall stability of the legal system. The marked Islamist influence on the 2012 version further affected individual freedoms in all postulated domains – namely women's rights, non-Muslim rights, criminal law, freedom of belief and expression. And despite the absence of a shariᶜa supremacy clause in the Tunisian Constitution, similar conclusions can be drawn in that case too. After all, as Islamists argue, shariᶜa need not be mentioned explicitly to find its way into a constitutional text: their attempts to enforce Islam as the religion of the state, to criminalize blasphemy, to abolish freedom of conscience and make women complementary to men – all spring from a deference to shariᶜa law and serve to surreptitiously enforce it.

The issue would not be so compelling if shariᶜa could be adapted to the spirit of the times. Unfortunately, attempts to bring about reforms have often foundered in the face of a powerful orthodoxy, thus remaining fruitless and minoritarian at best, or even imposing a high legal and personal price on reformers at worst – up to and including their lives. This is a facet of the persecution of 'freethinkers': vague laws defending 'public morals', 'decency', 'public order' and so on, interpreted according to the religious sensibility of the majority, render any form of criticism, mockery, rejection or mere reinterpretation of Islam punishable. Homosexuals are trapped within the same legal, moral and religious categories: besides the criminal provisions directly targeting homosexuality (in more or less specific terms), LGBT people and their supporters are often prosecuted for defying public morals and religion, which judges explicitly evoke in the trials.

Indeed, for Tunisia and Egypt, homosexuals, atheists and heretics of all kinds represent two sides of the same coin: they are a wound inflicted on the good morals of a decent society, a threat unleashed on its public order. Indelible and ingrained taboos, both LGBT behaviours and expressions of atheism or criticisms of religion remain punished by vague laws and legal aporias – used, misused and reinvented at the whim of judges, in violation of the freedoms guaranteed by the new Constitutions. The examination of case law and the interviews I conducted with experts and activists confirmed that social conservatism and religious norms conspire to give these laws a liberticidal interpretation.

Certainly, Egypt and Tunisia are not the only culprits here, nor are they the worst oppressors of gays and freethinkers: eleven countries in the world punish apostasy[1] or blasphemy[2] with death, and they almost entirely coincide with the eleven states that ambiguously or unequivocally prescribe capital punishment on homosexuals.[3] All of these are Muslim-majority countries that explicitly base their criminal legislation on shariᶜa.[4]

Furthermore, the rights of homosexuals and freethinkers are not the sole issues at stake in Egypt and Tunisia: the enduring discrimination against women and non-Muslims in the private and public sphere and the enforcement of various morality rules (such as the compulsory closure of restaurants and cafés during Ramadan, or the indiscriminate criminalization of 'immoral clothing' and public displays of affection) are all contentious matters ascribable to the same religious root.

It would be naïve to expect the wording of a constitutional article to change things by itself. In these domains, social pressure can be stronger than legal principles and rules, and no change from the top can take root if the ground is hermetically sealed. In fact, many activists – and even jurists – reckon that social pressure can be stronger than the law in these cases. This problem is acutely felt in Egypt, which has a deeply conservative society where 'atheist' and 'gay' are the worst conceivable insults[5] and an authoritarian government that exploits this hostility with political malice. Yet, democratic Tunisia is not immune either, if we consider that all of the Tunisian court cases examined in this book were triggered and influenced by public scandals.

The recognition that the law is a by-product of society is hardly a new insight in legal theory, as I noted in the introduction. But it would be a mistake to regard this influence as unidirectional: legal and constitutional changes are not purely cosmetic developments, good for lawyers' abstruse disquisitions. Legal words have a power that should not be underestimated, and while imposing radical new laws on a reluctant and unready public may provoke acute rejection, such changes, if enacted properly, may also prompt an evolution in mentality that will stand the test of time. In a less ideal and more practical sense, legal words have a power insofar as gays and freethinkers simply could not be locked away (or worse), whatever the opprobrium of society, if the provisions criminalizing homosexuality, blasphemy and apostasy were not on the books.

Constitutions are different, as their norms, in most cases, are not directly applicable. This does not mean, however, that constitutions are nothing more than perfunctory declarations of principles: for the good or for the bad, they

1 Afghanistan, Brunei, Iran, Malaysia, Maldives, Mauritania, Qatar, Saudi Arabia, United Arab Emirates and Yemen. See 'The Right to Apostasy in the World'.

2 Pakistan. See 'Uphold Human Rights'.

3 Afghanistan, Brunei, Iran, Mauritania, Nigeria (12 Northern states), Pakistan, Qatar, Saudi Arabia, Somalia, United Arab Emirates and Yemen. See Ramón Mendos, 'State-Sponsored Homophobia 2020: Global Legislation Overview Update', 31.

4 Whitaker, *Unspeakable Love*, 124.

5 Idea expressed almost identically by various actors. According to Ismail Mohammed, instead, the social acceptance of atheism is slightly increasing compared to homosexuality. Mohammed, interview.

stand atop the hierarchy of sources, and the entire edifice of the national legislation depends on those few articles. More profoundly, constitutions define what I called the 'soul' of a country, its profound identity, and they can perform a transformative role in society.

For all these reasons, law matters, and constitutions matter above all. The use of one word in lieu of another can decide on the very life of a person and change the destiny of a people. And for constitutions to accomplish their supreme mission, they must protect the rule of law and individual freedoms – especially those of the most vulnerable individuals.

As centuries-long struggles worldwide have demonstrated, a religious *Grundnorm* is hardly compatible with the primacy of a human-made constitution and with the full recognition of equal and inalienable individual rights that is central to the constitutional mission. Shariʿa is no exception. Its heavily loaded legal content is made of archaic norms that inevitably clash with internationally recognized universal liberties. Hence, as long as attempts to reform their interpretations are obstructed or repressed due to theological or political motives, these norms can have no place in a modern constitutional system.

It is not my intention to conceal the main purpose of this book, and indeed it would hardly have been possible. This work has not merely sought to theorize and describe, but it has proceeded from a well-defined conceptual mindset with a precise normative intent. In other words, it was not simply meant to analyse *in vitro* the new constitutions drafted in the two main epicentres of the Arab Spring, but also to undertake a human rights-based critique of those texts with a view to a comprehensive implementation of fundamental freedoms.

There is an evident tension between the majoritarian rule intrinsic to a democratic system and the protection of individual liberties abhorred by the majority. A constitution is in fact the supreme barrier between democracy and its degeneration into the infamous tyranny of the majority: it is the 'anti-majoritarian' instrument *par excellence*, called on to temper the general will by ensuring it stops short of violating inalienable individual rights:

> constitutionalism, as a concept, is not the same as a majoritarian democracy. In fact, as several commentators note, constitutionalism is antimajoritarian and therefore exists in tension with democratic practice. Constitutionalism mandates that there are fundamental social values and individual entitlements that may not be negated by the will of the majority. The will of the majority is respected as long as it does not trump the fundamental rights of the minority.[6]

The Constitutions of Egypt and Tunisia mark important steps in the path to freedom, but the road to ensure the protection of individual liberties that clash with values, conventions and anathemas deeply rooted in society is still long

6 El Fadl, 'The Centrality of Sharīʿah', 37.

and treacherous. Yet, however long and treacherous it may be, and whatever pitfalls lurk beneath, constitutional wayfarers must continue until they reach their destination, namely the accomplishment of a true democracy that respects all its minorities. And in every part of the globe, no matter the latitude, religion or culture, 'the smallest minority on earth is the individual',[7] whose inherent liberties no majority has the right to infringe.

This is the authentic meaning of that freedom, *ḥurriyya*, invoked by the people in the streets and squares of Egypt and Tunisia in 2011. This is what their Constitutions are now called on to achieve.

7 'The smallest minority on earth is the individual. Those who deny individual rights, cannot claim to be defenders of minorities', as famously wrote Ayn Rand. See 'Minority Rights'.

Bibliography

Books and scholarly papers

Abbiate, Tania. 'La partecipazione popolare al processo costituente'. In *Tunisia: la primavera della Costituzione*, edited by Tania Groppi and Irene Spigno, 66–74. Roma: Carocci, 2015.

Abdelaal, Mohamed. 'Religious Constitutionalism in Egypt: A Case Study'. *Fletcher Forum of World Affairs* 37 (2013): 35–51.

Abiad, Nisrine. *Sharia, Muslim States and International Human Rights Treaty Obligations: A Comparative Study*. London: British Institute of International & Comparative Law, 2008.

Abrougui, Afef. 'Tunisia's Red Lines'. *Index on Censorship* 41, no. 4 (2012): 148–51.

Abu-Odeh, Lama. 'Egypt's New Constitution: The Islamist Difference'. In *Constitutional Secularism in an Age of Religious Revival*, edited by Michel Rosenfeld and Susanna Mancini, 160–74. Oxford; New York: Oxford University Press, 2014.

Abu-Sahlieh, Sami A. Aldeeb. 'L'apostasia nel diritto musulmano. Il caso dell'Egitto'. *Veritas et Jus* 6 (2013): 63–90.

———. *Les musulmans face aux droits de l'homme: étude et documents*. CreateSpace Independent Publishing Platform, 2013.

———. *Projets de constitutions islamiques et déclarations des droits de l'homme: dans le monde arabo-musulman*. CreateSpace Independent Publishing Platform, 2012.

Ahmed, Dawood I., and Tom Ginsburg. 'Constitutional Islamization and Human Rights: The Surprising Origin and Spread of Islamic Supremacy in Constitutions'. *University of Chicago Public Law & Legal Theory Working Paper*, no. 447 (2014).

Ahmed, Dawood I., and Moamen Gouda. 'Measuring Constitutional Islamization: The Islamic Constitutions Index'. *Hastings International and Comparative Law Review* 38, no. 1 (2015).

Ali, Abdullah Yusuf, trans. *The Holy Quran*. Ware: Wordsworth Editions Ltd, 1997.

Anello, Giancarlo. '"Plural Sharīʿah". A Liberal Interpretation of the Sharīʿah Constitutional Clause of the 2014 Egyptian Constitution'. *Arab Law Quarterly* 31, no. 1 (2017): 74–88.

An-Naʿim, Abdullahi Ahmed. 'The Contingent Universality of Human Rights: The Case of Freedom of Expression in African and Islamic Contexts'. *Emory International Law Review* 11 (1997): 29–66.

———. 'The Legitimacy of Constitution-Making Processes in the Arab World'. In *Constitutionalism, Human Rights, and Islam after the Arab Spring*, edited by Rainer Grote and Tilmann J. Röder, 29–42. Oxford; New York: Oxford University Press, 2016.

———. *Toward an Islamic Reformation: Civil Liberties, Human Rights, and International Law*. Syracuse University Press, 1996.

Anselmo, Daniele. *Shariʿa e diritti umani*. Torino: G. Giappichelli, 2007.

Arzt, Donna E. 'Heroes or Heretics: Religious Dissidents under Islamic Law'. *Wisconsin International Law Journal* 14, no. 2 (1996): 349–421.

'Awwâ, Muhammad Salîm al-. 'Un arrêt devenu une "affaire"'. *Égypte/Monde arabe*, no. 29 (1997): 155–73.

Baderin, Mashood A. *International Human Rights and Islamic Law*. Oxford Monographs in International Law. Oxford; New York: Oxford University Press, 2003.

Barberis, Mauro. *Breve storia della filosofia del diritto*. Bologna: Il Mulino, 2004.

———. 'Diritto e morale: la discussione odierna'. *Revus*, no. 16 (10 December 2011): 55–93.

Bassiouni, M. Cherif. 'International Crimes: Jus Cogens and Obligatio Erga Omnes'. *Law and Contemporary Problems* 59, no. 4 (1996): 63–74.

Berger, Maurits S. 'Apostasy and Public Policy in Contemporary Egypt: An Evaluation of Recent Cases from Egypt's Highest Courts'. *Human Rights Quarterly* 25 (2003): 720–40.

Berkouwer, Susanna, Azza Sultan, and Samar Yehia. 'Homosexuality in Sudan and Egypt: Stories of the Struggle for Survival'. *LGBTQ Policy Journal*, 2015. https://lgbtq.hkspublications.org/2015/01/23/homosexuality-in-sudan-and-egypt-stories-of-the-struggle-for-survival/.

Bernard-Maugiron, Nathalie. 'La Constitution égyptienne de 2014 est-elle révolutionnaire ?' *La Revue des droits de l'homme. Revue du Centre de recherches et d'études sur les droits fondamentaux*, no. 6 (2014). https://revdh.revues.org/978.

———. 'La place du religieux dans le processus constitutionnel en Égypte après 2011'. *Archives de sciences sociales des religions*, no. 181 (2018): 47–68.

Bernard-Maugiron, Nathalie, and Baudouin Dupret. '"Les principes de la sharia sont la source principale de la législation". La Haute Cour constitutionnelle et la référence à la Loi islamique'. *Egypte/monde arabe*, no. 2 (1999): 107–26.

Bhala, Raj. *Understanding Islamic Law*. New Providence: LexisNexis, 2011.

Bousbih, Elyès, and Abderrahmen Yaalaoui. 'The Interplay of Politics and Religion in the New Tunisian Constitution: A Legal Analysis'. In *The Tunisian Constitutional Process: Main Actors and Key Issues*, edited by Mathieu Rousselin and Christopher Smith, 16–23. Duisburg: Centre for Global Cooperation Research, 2015.

Boyle, Kevin, and Juliet Sheen. *Freedom of Religion and Belief: A World Report*. London; New York: Routledge, 1997.

Bras, Jean-Philippe. 'Un État "civil" peut-il être religieux ? Débats tunisiens'. *Pouvoirs*, no. 156 (2016): 55–70.

Brems, Eva. *Human Rights: Universality and Diversity*. The Hague: Martinus Nijhoff Publishers, 2001.

Brown, Nathan J. 'Debating the Islamic Shariᶜa in 21st-Century Egypt'. *The Review of Faith & International Affairs* 10, no. 4 (2012): 9–17.

Brown, Nathan J., and Clark Benner Lombardi. 'Contesting Islamic Constitutionalism after the Arab Spring: Islam in Egypt's Post-Mubārak Constitution'. In *Constitutionalism, Human Rights, and Islam after the Arab Spring*, edited by Rainer Grote and Tilmann J. Röder, 245–60. Oxford; New York: Oxford University Press, 2016.

Campanini, Massimo. *Islam e politica*. Bologna: Il Mulino, 2003.

Cassese, Antonio, and P. Gaeta. *Diritto internazionale*. Bologna: Il Mulino, 2013.

Castro, Francesco. 'Diritto Musulmano'. In *Digesto delle discipline privatistiche: sezione civile*, VI:284–314. Torino: Utet, 1990.

Ceccherini, Eleonora. 'La questione dell'eguaglianza uomo-donna'. In *Tunisia: la primavera della Costituzione*, edited by Tania Groppi and Irene Spigno, 117–28. Roma: Carocci, 2015.

Charrad, Mounira M., and Amina Zarrugh. 'Equal or Complementary? Women in the New Tunisian Constitution after the Arab Spring'. *The Journal of North African Studies* 19, no. 2 (15 March 2014): 230–43.

Chynoweth, Paul. 'Legal Research'. In *Advanced Research Methods in the Built Environment*, edited by Andrew Knight and Leslie Ruddock, 28–38. Chichester, U.K.; Ames, Iowa: Wiley-Blackwell, 2008.

Colaianni, Nicola. 'Diritto di satira e libertà di religione'. *Rivista Italiana di Diritto e Procedura Penale* 52, no. 2 (2009): 594–620.

Colombo, Valentina, ed. *Basta!: Musulmani contro l'estremismo islamico*. Milano: Oscar Mondadori, 2007.

———. *Tunisia: A Nascent Democracy under Siege*. Brussels: European Foundation for Democracy, 2015. http://europeandemocracy.eu/wp-content/uploads/2015/09/Tunisia-a-nascent-democracy-under-siege.pdf.

Commins, David. 'Hasan Al-Banna (1906–1949)'. In *Pioneers of Islamic Revival*, edited by Ali Rahnema, 125–53. London; New York; Kuala Lumpur; Beirut: Zed Books; SIRD; WBP, 2005.

Dailler, Patrick, Quoc dinh Nguyen, and Alain Pellet. *Droit international public*. Paris: Lgdj, 2009.

Dalacoura, Katerina. 'Homosexuality as Cultural Battleground in the Middle East: Culture and Postcolonial International Theory'. *Third World Quarterly* 35, no. 7 (2014): 1290–1306.

Dellavalle, Sergio. 'Constitutionalism Beyond the Constitution: The Treaty of Lisbon in the Light of Post-National Public Law'. The Jean Monnet Center, March 2009. http://www.jeanmonnetprogram.org/paper/constitutionalism-beyond-the-constitution-the-treaty-of-lisbon-in-the-light-of-post-national-public-law/.

Dupret, Baudouin. *Adjudication in Action: An Ethnomethodology of Law, Morality and Justice*. Farnham: Ashgate Publishing, Ltd., 2011.

———. 'The Relationship between Constitutions, Politics and Islam: A Comparative Analysis of the North African Countries'. In *Constitutionalism, Human Rights, and Islam after the Arab Spring*, edited by Rainer Grote and Tilmann J. Röder, 233–44. Oxford; New York: Oxford University Press, 2016.

Dupret, Baudouin, and M. S. Berger, trans. 'Jurisprudence Abû Zayd'. *Égypte/Monde arabe*, no. 34 (1998): 169–201.

Dupret, Baudouin, and Jean-Noel Ferrié. 'Morale ou nature: Négocier la qualification de la faute dans une affaire égyptienne d'homosexualité'. *Négociations* 2, no. 2 (2004): 41–57.

El Fadl, Khaled Abou. 'The Centrality of Sharīʿah to Government and Constitutionalism in Islam'. In *Constitutionalism in Islamic Countries: Between Upheaval and Continuity*, edited by Rainer Grote and Tilmann J. Röder, 35–61. Oxford; New York: Oxford University Press, 2012.

El Fegiery, Moataz. *Islamic Law and Human Rights: The Muslim Brotherhood in Egypt*. Newcastle upon Tyne: Cambridge Scholars Publishing, 2016.

El Fegiery, Moataz Ahmed. 'Islamic Law and Freedom of Religion: The Case of Apostasy and Its Legal Implications in Egypt'. *Muslim World Journal of Human Rights* 10, no. 1 (2013): 1–26.

El-Daghili, Salwa. 'Al-Dawlah al-Madanīyah: A Concept to Reconcile Islam and Modern Statehood?' In *Constitutionalism, Human Rights, and Islam after the Arab Spring*,

edited by Rainer Grote and Tilmann J. Röder, 189–97. Oxford; New York: Oxford University Press, 2016.
El-Haj, Ali M. 'The Relationship between International Law and National Law in New and Amended Arab Constitutions'. In *Constitutionalism, Human Rights, and Islam after the Arab Spring*, edited by Rainer Grote and Tilmann J. Röder, 763–94. Oxford; New York: Oxford University Press, 2016.
Faraj, Omar. 'Religious Minorities under Pressure: The Situation in Egypt, Iraq and Syria'. In *Constitutionalism, Human Rights, and Islam after the Arab Spring*, edited by Rainer Grote and Tilmann J. Röder, 639–51. Oxford; New York: Oxford University Press, 2016.
Ferchichi, Wahid. 'Law and Homosexuality: Survey and Analysis of Legislation across the Arab World'. In *Middle East and North Africa Consultation of the Global Commission on HIV and the Law*. Cairo, 2011. http://bibliobase.sermais.pt:8008/BiblioNET/upload/PDF/0576.pdf.
———. 'L'homosexualité en droit tunisien ou de l'homophobie de la règle juridique'. In *Être Homosexuel au Maghreb*, edited by Monia Lachheb, 171–95. Paris; Tunis: Karthala, 2016.
Ferjani, Mohamed-Chérif. *Islamisme, laïcité, et droits de l'homme: Un siècle de débat sans cesse reporté au sein de la pensée arabe contemporaine*. Comprendre Le Moyen-Orient. Paris: Editions L'Harmattan, 2000.
Fiorita, Nicola. *L'Islam spiegato ai miei studenti. Undici lezioni sul diritto islamico*. Firenze: Firenze University Press, 2010.
Gaddes, Chawki. 'Il processo costituente (2011–14): fasi e protagonisti'. In *Tunisia: la primavera della Costituzione*, edited by Tania Groppi and Irene Spigno, 50–65. Roma: Carocci, 2015.
Gallala-Arndt, Imen. 'Tunisia after the Arab Spring: Women's Rights at Risk?' In *Constitutionalism, Human Rights, and Islam after the Arab Spring*, edited by Rainer Grote and Tilmann J. Röder, 599–614. Oxford; New York: Oxford University Press, 2016.
Gordon, Scott. *Controlling the State: Constitutionalism from Ancient Athens to Today*. Cambridge: Harvard University Press, 2002.
Gouda, Moamen. 'Islamic Constitutionalism and Rule of Law: A Constitutional Economics Perspective'. *Constitutional Political Economy* 24, no. 1 (March 2013): 57–85.
———. 'The 1978 Al-Azhar's Project for an Islamic Constitution'. *SSRN Electronic Journal*, 1 January 2011. https://doi.org/10.2139/ssrn.2437590.
Groppi, Tania. 'L'identità costituzionale tunisina nella Costituzione del 2014'. In *Tunisia: la primavera della Costituzione*, edited by Tania Groppi and Irene Spigno, 19–35. Roma: Carocci, 2015.
Grote, Rainer, and Tilmann J. Röder. 'Introduction'. In *Constitutionalism in Islamic Countries: Between Upheaval and Continuity*, edited by Rainer Grote and Tilmann J. Röder, 3–15. Oxford; New York: Oxford University Press, 2012.
Habib, Samar. 'LGBT Activism in the Middle East'. In *The Wiley Blackwell Encyclopedia of Gender and Sexuality Studies*, edited by Angela Wong, Maithree Wickramasinghe, Renee Hoogland, and Nancy A Naples, 1–6. Singapore: John Wiley & Sons, Ltd, 2016.
Hallaq, Wael B. *Sharīʿa: Theory, Practice, Transformations*. Cambridge, UK; New York: Cambridge University Press, 2009.
Halm, Heinz. *L'Islam*. Roma: Laterza, 2003.
Halmai, Gábor. 'Religion and Constitutionalism'. SSRN Scholarly Paper. Rochester, NY: Social Science Research Network, 21 May 2015. https://papers.ssrn.com/abstract=2609104.

Hamoudi, Haider Ala. 'Repugnancy in the Arab World'. *Willamette Law Review* 48 (2012): 427–50.

Hamzić, Vanja. 'A History in the Making: Muslim Sexual and Gender Diversity between International Human Rights Law and Islamic Law'. King's College London, 2012. https://ethos.bl.uk/OrderDetails.do?uin=uk.bl.ethos.628347.

Hayek, Friedrich A. Von. *The Constitution of Liberty: The Definitive Edition*. Chicago: University of Chicago Press, 2011.

Hédia, Baraket, and Olfa Belhassine. *Ces nouveaux mots qui font la Tunisie*. Tunis: Cérès éditions, 2016.

Hefny, Assem. 'Religious Authorities and Constitutional Reform. The Case of Al-Azhar in Egypt'. In *Constitutionalism, Human Rights, and Islam after the Arab Spring*, edited by Rainer Grote and Tilmann J. Röder, 89–121. Oxford; New York: Oxford University Press, 2016.

Her-Soon Tay, Alice. 'I valori asiatici e il Rule of Law'. In *Lo stato di diritto: storia, teoria, critica*, edited by Pietro Costa and Danilo Zolo, 683–707. Milano: Feltrinelli Editore, 2002.

Hirschl, Ran. *Constitutional Theocracy*. Cambridge: Harvard University Press, 2010.

Horchani, Ferhat. 'Islam and the Constitutional State. Are They in Contradiction?' In *Constitutionalism, Human Rights, and Islam after the Arab Spring*, edited by Rainer Grote and Tilmann J. Röder, 199–206. Oxford; New York: Oxford University Press, 2016.

Ingelse, Chris. *United Nations Committee Against Torture: An Assessment*. The Hague; London; Boston: Martinus Nijhoff Publishers, 2001.

Jackson, Vicki C. 'Comparative Constitutional Law: Methodologies'. In *The Oxford Handbook of Comparative Constitutional Law*, edited by Michel Rosenfeld and András Sajó, 54–74. Oxford; New York: Oxford University Press, 2012.

Jaspal, Rusi. 'Islam and Homosexuality'. In *The Wiley Blackwell Encyclopedia of Gender and Sexuality Studies*, edited by Angela Wong, Maithree Wickramasinghe, Renee Hoogland, and Nancy A Naples, 1–7. Singapore: John Wiley & Sons, Ltd, 2016.

Kamali, Mohammad Hashim. 'Constitutionalism in Islamic Countries: A Contemporary Perspective of Islamic Law'. In *Constitutionalism in Islamic Countries: Between Upheaval and Continuity*, edited by Rainer Grote and Tilmann J. Röder, 19–33. Oxford; New York: Oxford University Press, 2012.

———. *Freedom of Expression in Islam*. Cambridge: Islamic Texts Society, 1997.

———. *Principles of Islamic Jurisprudence*. Cambridge: Islamic Texts Society, 2005.

Khomeini, Ruhollah. *Islam and Revolution: Writings and Declarations of Imam Khomeini*. Edited by Hamid Algar. Berkeley: Mizan Press, 1981.

Kugle, Scott Siraj al-Haqq. *Homosexuality in Islam: Critical Reflection on Gay, Lesbian, and Transgender Muslims*. Oxford: Oneworld Publications, 2010.

Kugle, Scott, and Stephen Hunt. 'Masculinity, Homosexuality and the Defence of Islam: A Case Study of Yusuf al-Qaradawi's Media Fatwa'. *Religion and Gender* 2, no. 2 (2012): 254–79.

Kumar, Ranjit. *Research Methodology: A Step-by-Step Guide for Beginners*. Los Angeles: SAGE Publications Ltd, 2010.

Le Roy, Thierry. 'Constitutionalism in the Maghreb: Between French Heritage and Islamic Concepts'. In *Constitutionalism in Islamic Countries: Between Upheaval and Continuity*, edited by Rainer Grote and Tilmann J. Röder, 109–19. Oxford; New York: Oxford University Press, 2012.

Leo, Leonard A., Felice D. Gaer, and Elizabeth K. Cassidy. 'Protecting Religions from "Defamation": A Threat to Universal Human Rights Standards'. *Harvard Journal of Law & Public Policy* 34, no. 2 (2011): 769–84.
Lewis, Bernard. *From Babel to Dragomans: Interpreting the Middle East*. New York: Oxford University Press, 2004.
———. *The Crisis of Islam: Holy War and Unholy Terror*. New York: Random House Trade Paperbacks, 2004.
———. *The Political Language of Islam*. Chicago: University of Chicago Press, 1988.
———. *The Shaping of the Modern Middle East*. Reprint edition. New York: Oxford University Press, 1994.
———. *What Went Wrong?: Western Impact and Middle Eastern Response*. Oxford; New York: Oxford University Press, 2002.
Lombardi, Clark Benner. *State Law as Islamic Law in Modern Egypt*. Leiden; Boston: Brill Academic Publishers, 2006.
Longo, Pietro. 'L'islam nella nuova Costituzione: dallo Stato neutrale allo Stato "protettore"'. In *Tunisia: la primavera della Costituzione*, edited by Tania Groppi and Irene Spigno, 102–16. Roma: Carocci, 2015.
Mahmoudi, Said. 'International Human Rights Law as a Framework for Emerging Constitutions in Arab Countries'. In *Constitutionalism, Human Rights, and Islam after the Arab Spring*, edited by Rainer Grote and Tilmann J. Röder, 535–44. Oxford; New York: Oxford University Press, 2016.
Mansour, Khaled. 'Freedom of Expression in Egypt: How Long Hair, Pink Shirts, Novels, Amateur Videos and Facebook Threaten Public Order and Morality!' *International Journal of Applied Psychoanalytic Studies* 13, no. 3 (2016): 233–41.
Maudoudi, Abul A'la. *Comprendre l'Islam*. International Islamic Federation of Student Organizations, 1973.
Mayer, Ann Elizabeth. *Islam and Human Rights: Tradition and Politics*. Boulder, Colo.: Westview Press, 2013.
———. 'The Respective Roles of Human Rights and Islam: An Unresolved Conundrum for Middle Eastern Constitutions'. In *Constitutional Politics in the Middle East: With Special Reference to Turkey, Iraq, Iran and Afghanistan*, edited by Said Amir Arjomand, 77–97. Oxford; Portland: Hart Publishing, 2008.
McCarthy, Rory. 'Protecting the Sacred: Tunisia's Islamist Movement Ennahdha and the Challenge of Free Speech'. *British Journal of Middle Eastern Studies* 42, no. 4 (2015): 447–64.
Merad, Ali. 'Riflessioni sulla Dichiarazione islamica universale dei diritti dell'uomo'. In *L'Islam e il dibattito sui diritti dell'uomo*, edited by Andrea Pacini, 121–36. Torino: Fondazione Giovanni Agnelli, 1998.
Modood, Tariq, Randall Hansen, Erik Bleich, Brendan O'Leary, and Joseph Carens. 'The Danish Cartoon Affair: Free Speech, Racism, Islamism, and Integration'. *International Migration* 44 (2006): 3–62.
Moussa, Fadel. 'Dalle tre paure… alle tre grazie. Testimonianza di un costituente-costituzionalista'. In *Tunisia: la primavera della Costituzione*, edited by Tania Groppi and Irene Spigno, 75–88. Roma: Carocci, 2015.
Moustafa, Tamir. 'The Islamist Trend in Egyptian Law'. *Politics and Religion* 3, no. 03 (2010): 610–30.
M'rad, Hatem. 'The Process of Institutional Transformation in Tunisia after the Revolution'. In *Constitutionalism, Human Rights, and Islam after the Arab Spring*, edited

by Rainer Grote and Tilmann J. Röder, 71–87. Oxford; New York: Oxford University Press, 2016.

Muir-Watt, Horatia. 'La fonction subversive du droit comparé'. *Revue internationale de droit comparé* 52, no. 3 (2000): 503–27.

O'Flaherty, M., and J. Fisher. 'Sexual Orientation, Gender Identity and International Human Rights Law: Contextualising the Yogyakarta Principles'. *Human Rights Law Review* 8, no. 2 (2008): 207–48.

O'Sullivan, Declan. 'Egyptian Cases of Blasphemy and Apostasy against Islam: Takfir al-Muslim'. *The International Journal of Human Rights* 7, no. 2 (2003): 97–137.

Otto, Jan Michiel. 'Introduction: Investigating the Role of Sharia in National Law'. In *Sharia Incorporated: A Comparative Overview of the Legal Systems of Twelve Muslim Countries in Past and Present*, edited by Jan Michiel Otto, 17–49. Law, Governance, and Development. Leiden: Leiden University Press, 2010.

Otto, Jan Michiel. 'Towards Comparative Conclusions on the Role of Sharia in National Law'. In *Sharia Incorporated: A Comparative Overview of the Legal Systems of Twelve Muslim Countries in Past and Present*, edited by Jan Michiel Otto, 613–54. Law, Governance, and Development. Leiden: Leiden University Press, 2010.

Pacini, Andrea. 'Introduzione. L'Islam e il dibattito sui diritti dell'uomo'. In *L'Islam e il dibattito sui diritti dell'uomo*, edited by Andrea Pacini, 1–31. Torino: Fondazione Giovanni Agnelli, 1998.

Pacini, Andrea. *L'Islam e il dibattito sui diritti dell'uomo*. Torino: Fondazione Giovanni Agnelli, 1998.

Parolin, Gianluca P. '(Re)Arrangement of State/Islam Relations in Egypt's Constitutional Transition'. *NYU School of Law, Public Law Research Paper*, no. 13/15 (2013). https://ssrn.com/abstract=2251346.

Picotti, Lorenzo. 'Istigazione e propaganda della discriminazione razziale fra offesa dei diritti fondamentali della persona e libertà di manifestazione del pensiero'. In *Discriminazione razziale, xenofobia, odio religioso: diritti fondamentali e tutela penale: atti del seminario di studio, Università degli studi di Padova, 24 marzo 2006*, edited by Silvio Riondato. Padova: CEDAM, 2006.

Pillay, Nirmala. 'The Rule of Law and the New Egyptian Constitution'. *Liverpool Law Review* 35, no. 2 (August 2014): 135–55.

Pizzorusso, Alessandro. *Sistemi giuridici comparati*. Milano: Giuffrè, 1998.

Predieri, Alberto. *Sharīʿa e Costituzione*. Roma: GLF editori Laterza, 2006.

Qaradawi, Yusuf al-. *State in Islam*. Cairo: Al-Falah Foundation, 2004.

Quraishi, Asifa. 'The Separation of Powers in the Tradition of Muslim Governments'. In *Constitutionalism in Islamic Countries: Between Upheaval and Continuity*, edited by Rainer Grote and Tilmann J. Röder, 63–73. Oxford; New York: Oxford University Press, 2012.

Qutb, Sayyid. 'Il governo islamico: la giustizia sociale nell'Islam'. In *I Fratelli Musulmani e il dibattito sull'islam politico*, edited by Andrea Pacini, 25–34. Torino: Ed. della Fondazione Giovanni Agnelli, 1996.

———. 'L'islam e l'organizzazione della città'. In *I Fratelli Musulmani e il dibattito sull'islam politico*, edited by Andrea Pacini, 35–39. Torino: Ed. della Fondazione Giovanni Agnelli, 1996.

Rahnema, Ali. 'Islamic Jurisprudence and Public Policy'. In *Islam and Public Policy*, edited by Sohrab Behdad, 103–22. International Review of Comparative Public Policy 9. Greenwich, Conn.: JAI Press, 1997.

Redding, Jeffrey A. 'Human Rights and Homo-Sectuals: The International Politics of Sexuality, Religion, and Law'. *Northwestern Journal of International Human Rights* 4 (2006): 436–92.

Rehman, Javaid, and Eleni Polymenopoulou. 'Is Green a Part of the Rainbow? Sharia, Homosexuality and LGBT Rights in the Muslim World'. *Fordham International Law Journal* 37, no. 1 (2013): 1–52.

Rishmawi, Merat. 'The Arab Charter on Human Rights and the League of Arab States: An Update'. *Human Rights Law Review* 10, no. 1 (2010): 169–78.

Röder, Tilmann J. 'The Separation of Powers in Muslim Countries: Historical and Comparative Perspectives'. In *Constitutionalism in Islamic Countries: Between Upheaval and Continuity*, edited by Rainer Grote and Tilmann J. Röder, 321–72. Oxford; New York: Oxford University Press, 2012.

Sbailò, Ciro. 'I Costituzionalisti europei e il califfato nero'. *Federalismi*, no. 9 (2015).

Shaw, Malcolm N. *International Law*. Cambridge; New York: Cambridge University Press, 2008.

Sherif, Adel Omar. 'The Relationship between the Constitution and the Sharīʿah in Egypt'. In *Constitutionalism in Islamic Countries: Between Upheaval and Continuity*, edited by Rainer Grote and Tilmann J. Röder, 121–33. Oxford; New York: Oxford University Press, 2012.

Spigno, Irene. 'Diritti e doveri, tra universalismo e particolarismo'. In *Tunisia: la primavera della Costituzione*, edited by Tania Groppi and Irene Spigno, 91–101. Roma: Carocci, 2015.

Stahnke, Tad, and Robert C. Blitt. 'The Religion-State Relationship and the Right to Freedom of Religion or Belief: A Comparative Textual Analysis of the Constitutions of Predominantly Muslim Countries'. *Georgetown Journal of International Law* 36 (2005).

Thielmann, Jörn. 'La jurisprudence égyptienne sur la requête en hisba'. *Égypte/Monde arabe*, no. 34 (1998): 81–98.

Thornhill, Chris. 'The Sociology of Constitutions'. *Annual Review of Law and Social Science* 13, no. 1 (13 October 2017): 493–513.

Vidino, Lorenzo. *The New Muslim Brotherhood in the West*. New York: Columbia University Press, 2010.

Virgili, Tommaso. 'Apostasy from Islam under Sharia Law'. *Sant'Anna Legal Studies – STALS*, January 2015. http://www.stals.sssup.it/files/Apostasy%20in%20sharia%20law,%20STALS,%20def.pdf.

———. 'Libertà e democrazia nell'Islam: un nodo di Gordio?' *Federalismi*, no. 2 (2016).

———. 'Lifting the Integration Veil: Outcasts from Islam in Western Europe'. Brussels: Wilfried Martens Centre for European Studies, 2020. https://www.martenscentre.eu/wp-content/uploads/2020/06/paper_lifting_the_integration_veil-v2-web_1-1.pdf.

———. 'The "Arab Spring" and the EU's "Democracy Promotion" in Egypt: A Missed Appointment?' *Perspectives on Federalism* 6 (2014).

Wahba, Tawfiq ʿAli. 'Progetto di codice di pene coraniche in Egitto'. In *Dibattito sull'applicazione della Shariʿa*, edited by Andrea Pacini, 29–37. Torino: Edizioni della Fondazione Giovanni Agnelli, 1995.

Whitaker, Brian. *Arabs Without God*. North Charleston, S.C.: CreateSpace Independent Publishing Platform, 2014.

———. *Unspeakable Love: Gay and Lesbian Life in the Middle East*. London: Saqi Books, 2011.

Wolfrum, Rüdiger Abou. 'Constitutionalism in Islamic Countries: A Survey from the Perspective of International Law'. In *Constitutionalism in Islamic Countries: Between Upheaval and Continuity*, edited by Rainer Grote and Tilmann J. Röder, 77–88. Oxford; New York: Oxford University Press, 2012.

Zeghal, Malika. 'Competing Ways of Life: Islamism, Secularism, and Public Order in the Tunisian Transition'. *Constellations* 20, no. 2 (2013). http://nrs.harvard.edu/urn-3:HUL.InstRepos:12724047.

Zollner, Barbara. 'Mithliyyun or Lutiyyun? Neo-Orthodoxy and the Debate on the Unlawfulness of Same-Sex Relations in Islam'. In *Islam and Homosexuality*, edited by Samar Habib, I: 193–221. Santa Barbara: Praeger, 2010.

Reports, media and other sources

Abdel Hamid, Dalia. 'The Trap. Punishing Sexual Difference in Egypt'. Cairo: Egyptian Initiative for Personal Rights, 2017.

Abdella, Ibrahim. 'From Mubarak to Sisi: LGBT in Egypt, a Timeline of Repression'. Solidarity with LGBT Egypt, Lesbian and Gay Federation in Germany, 2015. http://www.lsvd-blog.de/wp-content/uploads/2015/08/Vortrag-%C3%84gypten.pdf.

Abu-Sahlieh, Sami A. Aldeeb. 'Full Transcript of Rached Ghannouchi's Lecture on Secularism – March, 2, 2012'. Savoir ou se faire avoir, 9 March 2012. http://www.blog.sami-aldeeb.com/2012/03/09/full-transcript-of-rached-ghannouchis-lecture-on-secularism-march-2-2012/.

AFP. 'Tunisia Bans Forced Anal Exams for Homosexuality'. News24, 22 September 2017. https://www.news24.com/news24/Africa/News/tunisia-bans-forced-anal-exams-for-homosexuality-20170922.

———. 'Tunisie – L'homosexualité coûte son poste au ministre de la Justice'. *24 heures*, 22 October 2015. https://www.24heures.ch/monde/afrique/homosexualite-coute-poste-ministre-justice/story/12536286.

AFP and Le Figaro. 'Tunisie: le candidat défendant les droits des LGBTQ exclu de la présidentielle'. *Le Figaro*, 14 August 2019. https://www.lefigaro.fr/flash-actu/presidentielle-en-tunisie-26-candidatures-validees-sur-une-centaine-20190814.

'Ahmed Naji'. PEN America. Accessed 26 January 2021. https://pen.org/advocacy-case/ahmed-naji/.

Al-Ali, Zaid. 'The New Egyptian Constitution: An Initial Assessment of Its Merits and Flaws'. openDemocracy, 26 December 2012. http://www.opendemocracy.net/zaid-al-ali/new-egyptian-constitution-initial-assessment-of-its-merits-and-flaws.

Amnesty International. 'Annual Report: Saudi Arabia 2010', 19 March 2011. https://www.amnestyusa.org/reports/annual-report-saudi-arabia-2010/.

———. 'Egypt 2019'. Accessed 22 January 2021. https://www.amnesty.org/en/countries/middle-east-and-north-africa/egypt/report-egypt/.

Arbour, Louise. 'The Arab Charter on Human Rights Is Incompatible with International Standards'. Humanists International, 11 March 2008. https://humanists.international/2008/03/arab-charter-human-rights-incompatible-international-standards-louise-arbour/.

'Atheist Egyptian Blogger Jailed for Videos Expressing His Views', Inside Arabia. 2 November 2019. https://insidearabia.com/atheist-egyptian-blogger-jailed-for-expressing-his-views/.

'Attaque du Cinéma Africart par des Islamistes: La Vie Culturelle Tunisienne Est-Elle en Danger?', Les Observateurs de France 24. 28 June 2011. http://observers.france24.com/fr/20110628-attaque-cinema-africart-islamistes-vie-culturelle-tunisienne-est-elle-danger.

Azuri, L. 'Dispute over Granting of State Award to Egyptian Liberal Sayyed Al-Qimni'. MEMRI, 6 October 2009. https://www.memri.org/reports/dispute-over-granting-state-award-egyptian-liberal-sayyed-al-qimni.

Banna, Hasan al-. 'Towards the Light'. Ikhwanweb, 1947. http://www.ikhwanweb.com/article.php?id=802.

Beek, Marije van. 'Wordt de Arabische Wereld Minder Religieus?' Trouw, 29 June 2019. https://www.trouw.nl/gs-b939ef48e.

'Beginning of End for Forced Anal Exams', Human Rights Watch. 26 September 2017. https://www.hrw.org/news/2017/09/26/beginning-end-forced-anal-exams.

Begum, Rothna. 'How Egypt Can Turn the Tide on Sexual Assault'. Human Rights Watch, 15 June 2014. https://www.hrw.org/news/2014/06/15/how-egypt-can-turn-tide-sexual-assault.

Ben Achour, Souhayma, and Mohammed Amine Jelassi. 'Analytical Reading for the Adoption of the Code of Rights and Individual Freedoms – Executive Report'. Fédération Internationale des Droits Humains (FIDH); Association de Défense des Libertés Individuelles (ADLI); Ligue Tunisienne des Droits de l'Homme (LTDH); Association Tunisienne des Femmes Démocrates (ATFD); Heinrich Böll Stiftung Tunisie, 2020. https://www.fidh.org/IMG/pdf/etude_resume_fr_ang_ar_web.pdf.

———. 'Lecture Analytique Pour l'adoption du Code des Droits et des Libertés Individuelles (CODLI)'. Fédération Internationale des Droits Humains (FIDH); Association de Défense des Libertés Individuelles (ADLI); Ligue Tunisienne des Droits de l'Homme (LTDH); Association Tunisienne des Femmes Démocrates (ATFD); Heinrich Böll Stiftung Tunisie, 2020. https://www.fidh.org/IMG/pdf/etude_juridique_web.pdf.

Ben Achour, Yadh. 'La force du droit ou la naissance d'une constitution en temps de révolution. (Pour Farouk Mechri)'. *Le blog de Yadh Ben Achour* (blog), 25 January 2015. http://yadhba.blogspot.com/2015/01/la-force-du-droit-ou-la-naissance-dune_25.html.

Berger, Miriam. 'She Raised the Pride Flag in Egypt. The Price Was Torture, Exile and Her Life.' *Washington Post*. Accessed 28 October 2020. https://www.washingtonpost.com/world/2020/06/16/sarah-hegazi-egypt-pride-flag-suicide/.

Bernard-Maugiron, Nathalie. 'Which Egypt in the New Constitution.' Interview by Michele Brignone. Oasis Center, 19 December 2012. http://www.oasiscenter.eu/articles/arab-revolutions/2012/12/19/which-egypt-in-the-new-constitution.

Bhira, Emma. 'Code des libertés individuelles en Tunisie: Pourquoi ça a tourné au fiasco ?' Gnet news, 30 January 2020. https://news.gnet.tn/28602-2/.

Boukhayatia, Rihab. 'Affaire Emna Chergui, Nième Duel Entre Liberté de Conscience et Atteinte au Sacré'. Nawaat, 15 July 2020. https://nawaat.org/2020/07/15/affaire-emna-chergui-nieme-duel-entre-liberte-de-conscience-et-atteinte-au-sacre/.

Carroll, Aengus. 'State Sponsored Homophobia 2016: A World Survey of Sexual Orientation Laws: Criminalisation, Protection and Recognition'. Geneva: International Lesbian, Gay, Bisexual, Trans and Intersex Association (ILGA), 2016. https://ilga.org/downloads/02_ILGA_State_Sponsored_Homophobia_2016_ENG_WEB_150516.pdf.

Carroll, Aengus, and Lucas Paoli Itaborahy. 'State Sponsored Homophobia 2015: A World Survey of Laws: Criminalisation, Protection and Recognition of Same-Sex Love'.

Geneva: International Lesbian, Gay, Bisexual, Trans and Intersex Association (ILGA), 2015. https://ilga.org/downloads/ILGA_State_Sponsored_Homophobia_2015.pdf.

Cavalliès, Thibaut. 'La Ligue de Protection de La Révolution: Le Bras Armé d'Ennahdha?' France Inter, 12 November 2012. https://www.franceinter.fr/emissions/ailleurs/ailleurs-12-novembre-2012.

Cook, Steven A. 'Tunisia: First Impressions'. Council on Foreign Relations, 12 November 2014. https://www.cfr.org/blog-post/tunisia-first-impressions.

Darrag, Amr. Interview with Dr. Amr Darrag on the new Egyptian Constitution. Interview by Diana Serodio. Arab West Report, 18 April 2013. http://www.arabwestreport.info/year-2013/week-16/20-interview-dr-amr-darrag-new-egyptian-constitution.

'Democracy'. Council of Europe. Accessed 28 October 2020. https://www.coe.int/en/web/compass/democracy.

Diab, Khaled. 'Confessions of an Egyptian Infidel'. *Daily News Egypt*, 15 August 2013. https://dailynewsegypt.com/2013/08/15/confessions-of-an-egyptian-infidel/.

'Dispute at Al-Azhar's "International Conference on the Renewal of Islamic Thought" Reflects Institution's Long-Standing Rejection of Religious Reforms in Egypt', MEMRI. 20 March 2020. https://www.memri.org/reports/dispute-al-azhars-international-conference-renewal-islamic-thought-reflects-institutions.

'Economic Misdemeanour Appeals Court Upholds Verdict against Blogger, with 3 Years Imprisonment and a 300,000 EGP Fine for Managing the "Egyptian Atheists" Facebook Page', Egyptian Initiative for Personal Rights. 23 June 2020. https://eipr.org/en/press/2020/06/economic-misdemeanour-appeals-court-upholds-verdict-against-blogger-3-years.

Eddhif, Ahlem. 'Le Code pénal à la lumière du Décret-loi 2011-115'. Reporters Sans Frontières, June 2014. https://www.reporter-ohne-grenzen.de/fileadmin/Redaktion/Downloads/Berichte/2014/140700_Le_Code_penal_a_la_lumiere_du_Decret-loi_2011-115_-_RSF-Gesetzesanalyse.pdf.

'Egypt: Epidemic of Sexual Violence', Human Rights Watch. 3 July 2013. https://www.hrw.org/news/2013/07/03/egypt-epidemic-sexual-violence.

'Egypt: Security Forces Abuse, Torture LGBT People', Human Rights Watch. 1 October 2020. https://www.hrw.org/news/2020/10/01/egypt-security-forces-abuse-torture-lgbt-people.

Egyptian Initiative for Personal Rights. 'Universal Periodic Review of Egypt 34th Session', 14 November 2019. https://eipr.org/en/press/2019/11/universal-periodic-review-egypt-34th-session.

'Egyptian Minister of Religious Endowment Gomaa: Zionism Sponsors Homosexuality and Atheism in Egypt', MEMRI. 21 September 2014. https://www.memri.org/tv/egyptian-minister-religious-endowment-gomaa-zionism-sponsors-homosexuality-and-atheism-egypt.

'EIPR Demands the Immediate Release of Detainees and Warns against Violations in Detention EIPR Calls on the Media to Halt Its Hate Speech and Incitement against LGBTQI Individuals', Egyptian Initiative for Personal Rights. 4 October 2017. https://eipr.org/en/press/2017/10/egyptian-state-wages-unprecedented-arrest-campaign-against-individuals-based-their.

Eltahawy, Mona. 'Egypt's War on Atheism'. *The New York Times*, 27 January 2015. https://www.nytimes.com/2015/01/28/opinion/mona-eltahawy-egypts-war-on-atheism.html.

EuroMed Rights. 'Tunisie: Recommandations du "Collectif pour les Libertés Individuelles"', 19 January 2016. https://www.facebook.com/notes/

euromed-rights-emhrn/tunisie-recommandations-du-collectif-pour-les-libert%C3%A9s-individuelles/169179610116331.

Ferchichi, Wahid. Article 230 du Code pénal: La criminalisation anticonstitutionnelle. Interview by Sana Sbouai, 26 May 2015. https://inkyfada.com/2015/05/article-230-code-penal-criminalisation-anticonstitutionnelle-homosexualite-tunisie/.

———. 'Tunisian Court Defends Advocacy of Homosexual Rights'. The Legal Agenda, 22 August 2019. https://www.legal-agenda.com/en/article.php?id=5831.

Foroudi, Layli. 'Blogger Flees Tunisia after Arrest: After Telling a Joke, One Tunisian Blogger Had to Flee Her Country to Avoid Prison'. *Index on Censorship* 49, no. 3 (2020): 42–43.

Fouad, Ahmed. 'Al-Azhar Refuses to Consider the Islamic State an Apostate'. Al-Monitor, 12 February 2015. https://www.al-monitor.com/pulse/originals/2015/02/azhar-egypt-radicals-islamic-state-apostates.html.

Freedom House. 'Egypt'. Freedom in the World 2020, 2020. https://freedomhouse.org/country/egypt/freedom-world/2020.

Gabra, Maher. 'The Ideological Extremism of Al-Azhar'. The Washington Institute for Near East Policy, 3 March 2016. https://www.washingtoninstitute.org/policy-analysis/ideological-extremism-al-azhar.

Gaetani, Giovanni. 'Do You Remember Mohamed, the Egyptian Atheist Kicked out from TV?' Humanists International, 27 September 2019. https://humanists.international/blog/do-you-remember-mohamed-the-egyptian-atheist-kicked-off-a-tv-interview/.

Gasparrini, Sabrina. 'Il Medio Oriente visto dal Cairo'. Radio Radicale, 5 December 2012. http://www.radioradicale.it/scheda/367573/il-medio-oriente-visto-dal-cairo.

Ghoshal, Neela. 'Dignity Debased: Forced Anal Examinations in Homosexuality Prosecutions'. Human Rights Watch, 2016. https://www.hrw.org/sites/default/files/report_pdf/globallgbtanalexams0716web.pdf.

Guellali, Anna. 'The Problem with Tunisia's New Constitution'. Human Rights Watch, 3 February 2014. https://www.hrw.org/news/2014/02/03/problem-tunisias-new-constitution.

Haddad, Gérard. 'Ghannouchi: "Le Modèle pour La Tunisie ? Les Pays Scandinaves"'. L'Obs, 25 December 2013. http://tempsreel.nouvelobs.com/rue89/rue89-monde/20131225.RUE0981/ghannouchi-le-modele-pour-la-tunisie-les-pays-scandinaves.html.

Human Rights First. 'Blasphemy, Freedom of Expression, and Tunisia's Transition to Democracy', May 2013. https://www.humanrightsfirst.org/resource/blasphemy-freedom-expression-and-tunisia%E2%80%99s-transition-democracy.

Human Rights Watch. 'Egypt: Events of 2020'. World Report 2021, 2020. https://www.hrw.org/world-report/2021/country-chapters/egypt#.

———. 'In a Time of Torture: The Assault on Justice in Egypt's Crackdown on Homosexual Conduct'. Human Rights Watch, 2004. https://www.hrw.org/reports/2004/egypt0304/.

Ibrahim, Ishak. 'Besieging Freedom of Thought: Defamation of Religion Cases in Two Years of the Revolution'. Cairo: Egyptian Initiative for Personal Rights, 2014. https://eipr.org/sites/default/files/reports/pdf/besieging_freedom_of_thought_0.pdf.

'IHEU Raises Concerns for Egyptian Atheist Sherif Gaber', Humanists International. 4 May 2018. https://humanists.international/2018/05/iheu-raises-concerns-egyptian-atheist-sherif-gaber/.

International Commission of Jurists. 'The Process of "Modernising" the Arab Charter on Human Rights: A Disquieting Regression', 20 December 2003. https://www.icj.

org/the-process-of-modernising-the-arab-charter-on-human-rights-a-disquieting-regression/.

International Council on Human Rights Policy. 'Sexuality and Human Rights'. Versoix: International Council on Human Rights Policy, 2009. http://www.ichrp.org/files/reports/47/137_web.pdf.

ISPI. *Med 2016 –What Role for Islam?*, 2016. https://www.youtube.com/watch?v=-YtAyBlOYkE.

Kasanwidjojo, Eline. 'Opposition to the Draft Constitution; Interview with George Massīḥa, One of the Members of the Constituent Assembly Who Has Withdrawn in Protest'. Arab West Report, 2 January 2013. http://www.arabwestreport.info/ar/opposition-draft-constitution-interview-george-massiha-one-members-constituent-assembly-who-has.

Le Collectif Civil pour les Libertés Individuelles (CCLI). 'État des Libertés Individuelles 2018: Bas Les Masques !', 2019. https://www.fidh.org/IMG/pdf/3._rapport_libertes_individuelles_2019_vs_fr_en-1.pdf.

———. 'Les Libertés Individuelles en 2019: Le Danger des Populistes!', 2020. https://tn.boell.org/fr/2020/07/07/etat-des-libertes-individuelles-en-2019.

Lewis, Bernard. 'Freedom and Justice in the Modern Middle East'. *Foreign Affairs*, 1 May 2005. https://www.foreignaffairs.com/articles/middle-east/2005-05-01/freedom-and-justice-modern-middle-east.

Littauer, Dan. 'Tunisia Rejects UNHRC Recommendation to Decriminalise Gay Sex'. Pink News. Accessed 29 June 2017. http://www.pinknews.co.uk/2012/06/06/tunisia-rejects-unhrc-recommendation-to-decriminalise-gay-sex/.

Lombardi, Clark Benner, and Nathan J. Brown. 'Islam in Egypt's New Constitution'. Foreign Policy, 13 December 2012. http://mideast.foreignpolicy.com/posts/2012/12/13/islam_in_egypts_new_constitution.

Long, Scott. 'Entrapped! How to Use a Phone App to Destroy a Life'. *A Paper Bird* (blog), 20 September 2015. https://paper-bird.net/2015/09/19/entrapped-how-to-use-a-phone-app-to-destroy-a-life/.

McCormick-Cavanagh, Conor. 'Is Homophobia at All-Time High in Tunisia?' Al-Monitor, 4 May 2016. http://www.al-monitor.com/pulse/originals/2016/05/tunisia-lgbt-homophobic-attacks.html.

'Minority Rights'. Ayn Rand Lexicon. Accessed 12 January 2021. http://aynrandlexicon.com/lexicon/minority_rights.html.

Mohamed, M. S. 'Sexuality, Development and Non-Conforming Desire in the Arab World: The Case of Lebanon and Egypt'. Institute of Development Studies, 2015. https://opendocs.ids.ac.uk/opendocs/bitstream/handle/20.500.12413/7115/ERB158_AccompanyingBrief.pdf?sequence=2&isAllowed=y.

Monceau, Valentine. 'En Tunisie: Un imam de Sfax réclame l'application de la peine de mort pour les homosexuels'. Stop Homophobie, 1 May 2016. https://www.stophomophobie.com/en-tunisie-un-imam-de-sfax-reclame-lapplication-de-la-peine-de-mort-pour-les-homosexuels-video/.

Office of the United Nations High Commissioner for Human Rights (OHCHR). 'Born Free and Equal: Sexual Orientation and Gender Identity in International Human Rights Law'. United Nations, 2012. https://www.ohchr.org/Documents/Publications/BornFreeAndEqualLowRes.pdf.

———. 'Born Free and Equal: Sexual Orientation, Gender Identity and Sex Characteristics in International Human Rights Law (Second Edition)'. United Nations, 2019. https://www.ohchr.org/Documents/Publications/Born_Free_and_Equal_WEB.pdf.

'OHCHR | Human Rights Committee'. Accessed 1 December 2020. https://www.ohchr.org/en/hrbodies/ccpr/pages/ccprindex.aspx.

'Open Letter to Dr. Ibrahim Awwad Al-Badri, Alias "Abu Bakr Al-Baghdadi", and to the Fighters and Followers of the Self-Declared "Islamic State"', 2014. http://www.lettertobaghdadi.com/.

Othman, Farhat. 'Appel à l'abolition de l'homophobie en Tunisie à l'occasion de La Journée Mondiale du 17 Mai'. Al Huffington Post Maghreb-Tunisie, 25 April 2016. http://www.huffpostmaghreb.com/farhat-othman/post_11418_b_9765218.html.

Ramadan, Adel. 'Asbab ᶜAdam Dusturiyyat Maddat Izdiraᵓ al-Adyan. Mudhakkira Shariḥa Li-Asbab ᶜAdam Dusturiyyat al-Madda (98w) Min Qanun al-ᶜUqubat al-Misriyy [Reasons for the unconstitutionality of the article on contempt of religions. A memorandum explaining the reasons for the unconstitutionality of Article 98 (f) of the Egyptian Penal Code]'. Cairo: Egyptian Initiative for Personal Rights, 2016. https://eipr.org/publications/%D8%B9%D8%AF%D9%85-%D8%AF%D8%B3%D8%AA%D9%88%D8%B1%D9%8A%D8%A9-%D8%A7%D9%84%D9%85%D8%A7%D8%AF%D8%A9-%D9%A9%D9%A8-%D9%88-%D9%85%D9%86-%D9%82%D8%A7%D9%86%D9%88%D9%86-%D8%A7%D9%84%D8%B9%D9%82%D9%88%D8%A8%D8%A7%D8%AA-%D8%A7%D9%84%D9%85%D8%B5%D8%B1%D9%8A-%D9%85%D8%A7%D8%AF%D8%A9-%D8%A7%D8%B2%D8%AF%D8%B1%D8%A7%D8%A1-%D8%A7%D9%84%D8%A3%D8%AF%D9%8A%D8%A7%D9%86.

Ramón Mendos, Lucas. 'State-Sponsored Homophobia 2019'. Geneva: International Lesbian, Gay, Bisexual, Trans and Intersex Association (ILGA), 2019. https://ilga.org/downloads/ILGA_World_State_Sponsored_Homophobia_report_global_legislation_overview_update_December_2019.pdf.

———. 'State-Sponsored Homophobia 2019: Global Legislation Overview Update'. Geneva: International Lesbian, Gay, Bisexual, Trans and Intersex Association (ILGA), 2019. https://ilga.org/downloads/ILGA_World_State_Sponsored_Homophobia_report_global_legislation_overview_update_December_2019.pdf.

———. 'State-Sponsored Homophobia 2020: Global Legislation Overview Update'. Geneva: International Lesbian, Gay, Bisexual, Trans and Intersex Association (ILGA), 2020. https://ilga.org/downloads/ILGA_World_State_Sponsored_Homophobia_report_global_legislation_overview_update_December_2020.pdf.

Reidy, Eric. 'Report Designates Tunisia First "free" Arab Country in Decades'. Al-Monitor, 8 February 2015. http://www.al-monitor.com/pulse/originals/2015/02/tunisia-free-arab-judiciary-political-challenges.html.

Riahi, Olfa. '"Affaire Mahdia": L'Enquête – "Athéisme, Délit de Pensée, Atteinte au Sacré ?"'. *To Be Good Again* (blog), 5 April 2012. https://tobegoodagain.wordpress.com/2012/04/05/affaire-mahdia-lenquete-atheisme-delit-de-pensee-atteinte-au-sacre/.

Roberts, Christopher. 'The State of the Right to Freedom of Expression in Egypt, Morocco and Tunisia, from 2011 to 2015'. Brussels: Avocats Sans Frontières, 2016. https://www.asf.be/blog/publications/the-state-of-the-right-to-freedom-of-expression-in-egypt-morocco-and-tunisia-from-2011-to-2015/.

Ross, Chuck. 'Islamic Georgetown Prof Offers Tortured Defense of Slavery and Non-Consensual Sex under Islam'. The Daily Caller, 11 February 2017. http://dailycaller.com/2017/02/11/islamic-georgetown-prof-offers-tortured-defense-of-slavery-and-non-consensual-sex-under-islam-video/.

Saber, Alber. 'Report: Inquisitions in Egypt 2014'. *Alber Saber* رباص ريبلأ (blog), 11 May 2014. http://www.albersaber.com/2014/11/report-inquisitions-in-egypt-2014-en.html.

Sabry, Bassem. '22 Key Points in Egypt's New Draft Constitution'. Al-Monitor, 23 August 2013. http://www.al-monitor.com/pulse/originals/2013/08/egypt-draft-constitution-guide.html.

Saker, Taha. 'Why Does Egypt's Largest Muslim Beacon, Al-Azhar, Refuse to Declare IS "Apostate"?' Egypt Independent, 14 April 2017. https://egyptindependent.com/why-does-egypt-s-largest-muslim-beacon-al-azhar-refuse-declare-apostate/.

Salem, Mahmoud. 'Why the Salafis Agreed to the Constitution'. Atlantic Council, 3 December 2012. http://www.atlanticcouncil.org/blogs/menasource/why-the-salafis-agreed-to-the-constitution.

Samti, Farah. 'On Human Rights Day, a Tunisian Court Sent Six Men to Prison for Being Gay'. Foreign Policy, 17 December 2015. https://foreignpolicy.com/2015/12/17/on-human-rights-day-a-tunisian-court-sent-six-men-to-prison-for-being-gay/.

Shams. 'Projet de loi présenté par l'association Shams au Parlement visant l'abrogation de l'article 230 du Code Pénal', 28 January 2016. https://www.facebook.com/lgbtrightstunisia/posts/450392075144444.

'Sheik Yousuf Al-Qaradhawi: Homosexuals Should Be Punished Like Fornicators But Their Harm Is Less When Not Done in Public', MEMRI. 5 June 2006. https://www.memri.org/tv/sheik-yousuf-al-qaradhawi-homosexuals-should-be-punished-fornicators-their-harm-less-when-not.

'Six Tunisian Students Freed from "sodomy" Prison Sentence', Amnesty International. 5 June 2018. https://www.amnesty.org.uk/six-tunisian-students-sodomy-gay-prison-lgbt-crime.

Soliman, Patrick. 'Two Years after Egypt's "Rainbow Flag Arrests", LGBTIQ People Face an Ongoing Security Crackdown'. openDemocracy, 22 September 2019. https://www.opendemocracy.net/en/5050/two-years-after-egypts-rainbow-flag-arrests-lgbtiq-people-face-an-ongoing-security-crackdown/.

Stewart, Colin. 'How "Debauchery" Law Set up Egypt's Gay Crackdown'. *76 CRIMES* (blog), 6 June 2014. https://76crimes.com/2014/06/06/how-debauchery-law-set-up-egypts-gay-crackdown/.

'Straight but Narrow'. *The Economist*, 4 February 2012. http://www.economist.com/node/21546002.

Suleiman, Mustafa. 'Egyptians Protest Award to Controversial Writer'. Al Arabiya, 13 July 2009. http://www.alarabiya.net/articles/2009/07/13/78580.html.

Tais, Amine. 'The Qur'an and Homosexuality'. Citizen of the World, 16 June 2016. http://aminetais.com/the-Qurᵓan-and-homosexuality/.

'Teens Convicted of Blasphemy for Video Mocking ISIS', NBC News. 16 February 2015. https://www.nbcnews.com/news/world/egypt-should-quash-blasphemy-convictions-christian-teens-who-mocked-isis-n537781.

'The Global Divide on Homosexuality'. Pew Research Center, 4 June 2013. http://www.pewglobal.org/2013/06/04/the-global-divide-on-homosexuality/.

'The Right to Apostasy in the World'. Humanists International. Accessed 2 January 2021. https://humanists.international/get-involved/resources/the-right-to-apostasy-in-the-world/.

'Tunisia: Halt Prosecution of Prominent Activist', Human Rights Watch. 29 January 2020. https://www.hrw.org/news/2020/01/29/tunisia-halt-prosecution-prominent-activist.

'Tunisia: Landmark Action on Women's Rights', Human Rights Watch. 30 April 2014. https://www.hrw.org/news/2014/04/30/tunisia-landmark-action-womens-rights.

'Tunisia: Men Prosecuted for Homosexuality', Human Rights Watch. 29 March 2016. https://www.hrw.org/news/2016/03/29/tunisia-men-prosecuted-homosexuality.

'Tunisian Professor Amel Grami: Homosexuality Emerged from Our Heritage', MEMRI. 20 December 2015. https://www.memri.org/tv/tunisian-professor-amel-grami-homosexuality-emerged-our-heritage.

'Tunisie: Achever les réformes en matière de droits humains', 28 February 2020. Human Rights Watch. https://www.hrw.org/fr/news/2020/02/28/tunisie-achever-les-reformes-en-matiere-de-droits-humains.

https://www.hrw.org/fr/news/2020/01/29/tunisie-mettre-fin-aux-poursuites-contre-un-defenseur-des-droits-humains.

'Unofficial Translation of Statement by Egypt's Supreme Council for Media Regulation', Human Rights Watch. 6 October 2017. https://www.hrw.org/news/2017/10/06/unofficial-translation-statement-egypts-supreme-council-media-regulation.

'Uphold Human Rights: Abolish Laws against Blasphemy and Apostasy Globally, IHEU Tells UN', Humanists International. 21 March 2017. https://humanists.international/2017/03/uphold-human-rights-abolish-laws-against-blasphemy-and-apostasy-globally-iheu-tells-un/.

Vinchon, Timothée. 'L'enfer du "test anal" en Tunisie'. VICE, 17 May 2017. https://www.vice.com/fr/article/vb7794/lenfer-du-test-anal-en-tunisie.

Virgili, Tommaso. '"Arab Spring" Yesterday and Today: The Tunisian Template'. Gatestone Institute, 2 August 2018. https://www.gatestoneinstitute.org/12793/arab-spring-yesterday-and-today-the-tunisian.

'Vote sur un Amendement de l'article 6: Supprimer "Liberté de Conscience" et "Libre Exercice du Culte"', Marsad. 4 January 2014. http://majles.marsad.tn/fr/vote/52caea0112bdaa7f9b90f457.

Yaacoub, Ramy. '219: A Detailed Cultural Translation of Egypt's Draft Constitution's Most Controversial Article'. Atlantic Council, 14 December 2012. http://www.atlanticcouncil.org/blogs/menasource/219-a-detailed-cultural-translation-of-egypt-s-draft-constitution-s-most-controversial-article.

Y.N. 'Tunis: Poursuivi pour homosexualité malgré un test anal négatif'. Kapitalis, 29 December 2018. http://kapitalis.com/tunisie/2018/12/29/tunis-poursuivi-pour-homosexualite-malgre-un-test-anal-negatif/.

Zeghidi, Mourad. 'Tunisie: La Liberté Inch'Allah !' JeuneAfrique.com, 10 August 2011. http://www.jeuneafrique.com/190476/politique/tunisie-la-libert-inch-allah/.

Legislation, case law and official documents

Baatour, Mounir. 'Appeal to the Court of Cassation, Case 6693/2015 [in Arabic]', 9 May 2016.

Ben Achour, Yadh, Salsabil Klibi, Hafidha Chekir, Mohamed Salah Ben Aïssa, Slim Laghmani, Amin Mafoudh, Chafik Sarsar, Mustapha Beltaif, and Ghazi Ghrairi. 'Muqtarahat Hawla Mashru^c Al-Dustur [Proposals on the Constitutional Project]', 1 June 2013.

Brandenburg v. Ohio, No. 395 U.S. 444 (U.S. Supreme Court 1969).

Case 1614/2013 (East Cairo Court of Appeal 26 January 2013).

Case 1757/2016 (Tribunal of Sfax 19 March 2016).

Case 4292/2018 (Tribunal of Sousse 27 April 2018).
Case 6693/2016 (Court of Appeal of Sousse 3 March 2016).
Case 6782/2015 (Tribunal of Kairouan 12 December 2015).
Case 33570/2017 (Tribunal of Tunis 23 November 2017).
Code de déontologie médicale [Tunisian Code of Medical Deontology], Pub. L. No. Decree 93-1155 (2018). http://www.legislation.tn/sites/default/files/codes/deontologiemedicale.pdf.
Code Pénal [Tunisian Criminal Code], Pub. L. No. Decree 9 July 1913 (2015). http://www.legislation.tn/sites/default/files/codes/Penal.pdf.
Code de Procédure Pénale [Tunisian Code of Criminal Procedure], Pub. L. No. Law 68-23 24 July 1968 (2018). http://www.legislation.tn/sites/default/files/codes/Procedurepenale.pdf.
Code des Télécommunications et ses textes d'application [Tunisian Telecommunications Code], Pub. L. No. Law 1/2001 (2016). http://www.legislation.tn/sites/default/files/codes/telecommunication.pdf.
Conseil National de l'Ordre des Médecins de Tunisie. 'Communiqué', 28 September 2015. https://www.facebook.com/OrdreMedTun/posts/430298250496205.
———. 'Communiqué: Le Consentement dans le Cadre de l'expertise Médicale', 3 April 2017. https://www.facebook.com/OrdreMedTun/photos/a.446870662172297.1073741828.411516739041023/641096052749756/?type=3&permPage=1.
Council of Europe. 'European Convention on Human Rights', 4 November 1950. No. 5. Council of Europe Treaty Series.
Criminal Code of Egypt, Pub. L. No. 58/1937. Accessed 30 June 2017. http://hrlibrary.umn.edu/research/Egypt/criminal-code.pdf.
'Déclaration des Droits de l'Homme et du Citoyen', 1789. https://www.legifrance.gouv.fr/contenu/menu/droit-national-en-vigueur/constitution/declaration-des-droits-de-l-homme-et-du-citoyen-de-1789.
'Declaration of Independence of the United States of America', 1776. https://www.archives.gov/founding-docs/declaration-transcript.
'Dossier Juridique'. Jabeurghazifree. Accessed 15 October 2020. http://jabeurghazifree.blogspot.com/p/dossier-juridique.html.
Dustur Jumhuriyyat Misr al-ᶜArabiyya [Constitution of the Arab Republic of Egypt] (2012). http://www.sccourt.gov.eg/SCC/?SCCPORTAL12C-JSESSIONID=w85J8wR6cdxWMEYrLkoyr90kjf9gLpwLcyKExQ3yEYMFawGNm6QT!-859048638.
Dustur Jumhuriyyat Misr al-ᶜArabiyya [Constitution of the Arab Republic of Egypt] (2014). http://www.sccourt.gov.eg/SCC/?SCCPORTAL12C-JSESSIONID=w85J8wR6cdxWMEYrLkoyr90kjf9gLpwLcyKExQ3yEYMFawGNm6QT!-859048638.
Dustur al-Jumhuriyya al-Tunisiyya [Constitution of the Tunisian Republic] (2014). http://www.legislation.tn/sites/default/files/constitution/constitution.pdf.
'Egypt's Constitution of 2012'. Translated by International IDEA. Accessed 3 November 2020. https://www.constituteproject.org/constitution/Egypt_2012.pdf?lang=en.
'Egypt's Constitution of 2014'. Translated by International IDEA. Accessed 11 November 2020. https://www.constituteproject.org/constitution/Egypt_2014.pdf.
'Egypt: Law No. 10/1961, on the Combating of Prostitution'. Accessed 18 November 2020. https://www.refworld.org/docid/5492d8784.html.
'English Translation of Magna Carta'. The British Library. Accessed 21 June 2017. https://www.bl.uk/magna-carta/articles/magna-carta-english-translation.

'Ennahdha's Constitutional Project [in Arabic]'. Accessed 30 June 2017. http://www.chawki.gaddes.org/resources/ennahdha.pdf.

'International Covenant on Civil and Political Rights: Declarations and Reservations'. United Nations Treaty Collection. Accessed 27 June 2017. https://treaties.un.org/pages/ViewDetails.aspx?src=TREATY&mtdsg_no=IV-4&chapter=4&clang=_en#EndDec.

Islamic Council of Europe. 'Al-Bayan al-ᶜAlami ᶜan Huquq al-Insan fi al-Islam [Universal Islamic Declaration of Human Rights]', 1981. http://hrlibrary.umn.edu/arab/UIDHR.html.

Islamic Council of Europe. 'Universal Islamic Declaration of Human Rights', 1981. http://www.alhewar.com/ISLAMDECL.html.

League of Arab States. 'Arab Charter on Human Rights', 2004. http://hrlibrary.umn.edu/instree/loas2005.html?msource=UNWDEC19001&tr=y&auid=3337655.

Lebanese Medical Association for Sexual Health. 'Anal Tests in Lebanon'. *Lebanese Medical Association for Sexual Health*, 7 July 2014. https://lebmash.wordpress.com/2014/07/07/anal-tests/.

Al-Majalla al-jazaᵓiyya [Tunisian Criminal Code], Pub. L. No. Decree 9 July 1913 (2018). http://www.legislation.tn/sites/default/files/codes/PenalArabe.pdf.

Office of the Public Prosecutor of Tunis. 'Legal Complaint against Nadia El Fani, Doc. n. 7032915/2011 [in Arabic]', 7 July 2011.

Order of medical examination [in Arabic], No. Document 1027, Case 2032/2016 (Court of Appeal of Sfax 25 May 2016).

Organisation of the Islamic Conference. 'Cairo Declaration on Human Rights in Islam', 1990. http://hrlibrary.umn.edu/instree/cairodeclaration.html.

Prosecutor's Office at the Counterterrorism Section of the Court of First Instance of Tunis. Case 3860/31 against Mounir Baatour [in Arabic] (6 November 2019).

Qanun al-ᶜUqubat [Egyptian Criminal Code], Pub. L. No. 58/1937 (2020). https://man*shūrā*t.org/node/14677.

Refah Partisi and Others v. Turkey, No. Application Nos. 41340/98, 41342/98, 41343/98 and 41344/98 (European Court of Human Rights, Grand Chamber 13 February 2003).

'The Constitution of the Arab Republic of Egypt, 1971'. Accessed 5 January 2020. https://constitutionnet.org/sites/default/files/Egypt%20Constitution.pdf.

'The Constitution of Tunisia, 1959'. Accessed 8 February 2021. https://wipolex.wipo.int/en/text/188948.

'The Yogyakarta Principles: The Application of International Human Rights Law in Relation to Sexual Orientation and Gender Identity'. Accessed 27 June 2017. http://www.yogyakartaprinciples.org/.

'Tunisia's Constitution of 2014'. Translated by UNDP and reviewed by International IDEA. Accessed 11 November 2020. https://www.constituteproject.org/constitution/Tunisia_2014.pdf.

U.N. Committee Against Torture. 'Concluding Observations on the Third Periodic Report of Tunisia', 2016. CAT/C/TUN/CO/3.

———. 'Conclusions and Recommendations of the Committee against Torture: Egypt', 2002. CAT/C/CR/29/4.

U.N. Committee on the Elimination of Discrimination Against Women. 'General Recommendation No. 28 on the Core Obligations of States Parties under Article 2 of the Convention on the Elimination of All Forms of Discrimination against Women', 2010. CEDAW/C/GC/28.

U.N. Committee on the Rights of the Child. 'General Comment No. 4: Adolescent Health and Development in the Con-Text of the Convention on the Rights of the Child', 2003. CRC/GC/2003/4.

U.N. General Assembly. 'International Covenant on Civil and Political Rights', 16 December 1966. Vol. 999, p. 171. United Nations Treaty Series.

———. 'International Covenant on Economic, Social and Cultural Rights', 16 December 1966. Vol. 993, p. 3. United Nations Treaty Series.

———. 'Universal Declaration of Human Rights', 10 December 1948. G.A. Res. 217 A (III).

U.N. Human Rights Committee. 'Communication No. 488/1992: Toonen v. Australia', 1994. CCPR/C/50/D/488/1992.

———. 'Concluding Observations on the Initial Report of Indonesia', 2013. CCPR/C/IDN/CO/1.

———. 'General Comment 22, Art. 18: The Right to Freedom of Thought, Conscience and Religion', 1994. HRI/GEN/1/Rev.1.

———. 'General Comment 27: Article 12 (Freedom of Movement)', 1999. CCPR/C/21/Rev.1/Add.9.

———. 'General Comment 34, Art. 19: Freedoms of Opinion and Expression', 2011. CCPR/C/GC/34.

U.N. Human Rights Council. 'Discriminatory Laws and Practices and Acts of Violence against Individuals Based on Their Sexual Orientation and Gender Identity. Report of the United Nations High Commissioner for Human Rights', 2011. A/HRC/19/41.

U.N. Working Group on Arbitrary Detention. 'Opinion No. 22/2006, François Ayissi et al. v. Cameroon', 2006. A/HRC/4/40/Add.1.

———. 'Yasser Mohamed Salah et al. v. Egypt'. U.N. Doc. E/CN.4/2003/8/Add.1, 2002.

Venice Commission. 'Opinion on the Final Draft Constitution of the Republic of Tunisia', 17 October 2013. https://www.venice.coe.int/webforms/documents/default.aspx?pdffile=CDL-AD(2013)032.

'Vienna Convention on the Law of Treaties', 27 January 1980. Vol. 1155, p. 331. United Nations, Treaty Series.

Encyclopaedia and dictionary entries

'Al-Azhar University'. In *Encyclopedia Britannica*. Accessed 23 June 2017. https://www.britannica.com/topic/al-Azhar-University.

'Apostasy'. In *Merriam-Webster*, n.d. https://www.merriam-webster.com/dictionary/apostasy.

'Atheism'. In *Merriam-Webster*, n.d. www.merriam-webster.com/dictionary/atheism.

'Blasphemy'. In *Merriam-Webster*, n.d. https://www.merriam-webster.com/dictionary/blasphemy.

Bosworth, Clifford Edmund, Bernard Lewis, Charles Pellat, and Emeri van Donzel, eds. 'Liwāṭ'. In *The Encyclopaedia of Islam*, V:776–79. Leiden: Brill, 1986.

Esposito, John L., ed. 'Human Rights'. In *The Oxford Dictionary of Islam*. Oxford Islamic Studies Online. New York: Oxford University Press, 2003.

———, ed. 'Hurr'. In *The Oxford Dictionary of Islam*. New York: Oxford University Press, 2003.

———, ed. 'Islamic Council of Europe'. In *The Oxford Dictionary of Islam*. Oxford Islamic Studies Online. New York: Oxford University Press, 2003.

———, ed. 'Ummah'. In *The Oxford Dictionary of Islam*. Oxford Islamic Studies Online. New York: Oxford University Press, 2003.

Gardet, L. 'Fitna'. In *The Encyclopaedia of Islam*, edited by Bernard Lewis, Charles Pellat, and Joseph Schacht, II:930–31. Leiden: Brill, 1991.

'Heresy'. In *Merriam-Webster*, n.d. https://www.merriam-webster.com/dictionary/heresy.

'Heterodox'. In *Merriam-Webster*, n.d. https://www.merriam-webster.com/dictionary/heterodox.

'Homosexuality'. In *Merriam-Webster*, n.d. https://www.merriam-webster.com/dictionary/homosexuality.

Lewis, Bernard, Charles Pellat, and Joseph Schacht, eds. 'Dustūr'. In *The Encyclopaedia of Islam*, II:638–77. Leiden: Brill, 1991.

Moseley, Alexander. 'John Locke: Political Philosophy'. Internet Encyclopedia of Philosophy. Accessed 21 June 2017. http://www.iep.utm.edu/locke-po/.

Murphy, Emma. 'Habib Bourguiba'. *Encyclopedia Britannica*. Accessed 25 June 2017. https://www.britannica.com/biography/Habib-Bourguiba.

Rosenthal, F., and Bernard Lewis. 'Ḥurriyya'. In *The Encyclopaedia of Islam*, edited by Bernard Lewis, Victor L. Ménage, Charles Pellat, and Joseph Schacht, III:589–94. Leiden: Brill, 1986.

Wehr, Hans. 'رعى'. In *A Dictionary of Modern Written Arabic*, edited by Cowan J. Milton. New York: Spoken Language Services, Inc., 1976.

———. 'اسلام'. In *A Dictionary of Modern Written Arabic*, edited by Cowan J. Milton. New York: Spoken Language Services, Inc., 1976.

———. 'مساحقة'. In *A Dictionary of Modern Written Arabic*, edited by Cowan J. Milton. New York: Spoken Language Services, Inc., 1976.

———. 'فجور'. In *A Dictionary of Modern Written Arabic*, edited by Cowan J. Milton. New York: Spoken Language Services, Inc., 1976.

———. 'فسد'. In *A Dictionary of Modern Written Arabic*, edited by Cowan J. Milton. New York: Spoken Language Services, Inc., 1976.

———. 'قدس'. In *A Dictionary of Modern Written Arabic*, edited by Cowan J. Milton. New York: Spoken Language Services, Inc., 1976.

———. 'مقدس'. In *A Dictionary of Modern Written Arabic*, edited by Cowan J. Milton. New York: Spoken Language Services, Inc., 1976.

———. 'لواط'. In *A Dictionary of Modern Written Arabic*, edited by Cowan J. Milton. New York: Spoken Language Services, Inc., 1976.

Index

For Product Safety Concerns and Information please contact our EU
representative GPSR@taylorandfrancis.com
Taylor & Francis Verlag GmbH, Kaufingerstraße 24, 80331 München, Germany

www.ingramcontent.com/pod-product-compliance
Ingram Content Group UK Ltd.
Pitfield, Milton Keynes, MK11 3LW, UK
UKHW022128190926
475702UK00013B/1688
9781032051260